Praise for *Unbound*

"Ben Mattlin writes with grace and humor about a lifetime of being disabled. These essays form an autobiography of sorts which is by turns instructive and inspiring. Although he may be a reluctant advocate, he is a powerful and eloquent one."

—JAY MCINERNEY

"Ben Mattlin's book does that rare thing: makes you think, makes you wonder, makes you hope, makes you angry, and makes you want to take action in both personal and collective ways. A beautiful and potent contribution to the stories about extraordinary bodies in ordinary time."

—EMILY RAPP BLACK, *New York Times* best-selling author of *Frida Kahlo and My Left Leg*

"Ben Mattlin is one of our most clear-thinking and insightful writers on the subjects of disability and society's flawed approach to difference. In this wise and irreverent collection, which spans from memories of high school as a child who didn't entirely fit in, to thoughts about the promise of the Americans with Disabilities Act, to reflections on the dark side of Jerry Lewis's Muscular Dystrophy Labor Day Telethon, he is at his absolute best."

—ADAM COHEN, author of *Supreme Inequality: The Supreme Court's Fifty-Year Battle for a More Unjust America*

UNBOUND

Unbound

NOTES FROM A RELUCTANT DISABILITY ACTIVIST

Ben Mattlin

— BLAIR —

Printed in the United States

Blair is an imprint of Carolina Wren Press.

The mission of Blair/Carolina Wren Press is to seek out, nurture, and promote literary work by new and underrepresented writers.

We gratefully acknowledge the ongoing support of general operations by the Durham Arts Council's United Arts Fund and the North Carolina Arts Council.

Portions of this book previously appeared in *The New York Times*, *The Washington Post*, *TIME*, *Newsweek*, *Los Angeles Times*, *Chicago Tribune*, New York *Daily News*, CNN, *The Daily Beast*, *USA Today*, *Self*, Vox Media, *The Harvard Independent*, *The Write Place at the Write Time*, *Tryst*, and blog posts for Facing Disability and Aging with Dignity. They are reprinted with permission. Other portions are edited transcripts of radio commentaries for NPR and interviews for Brockton Public Library, *Disability After Dark*, *Disability Matters*, *Living Beyond Challenges*, and the Meltzer Center for Diversity, Inclusion, and Belonging. They are used with permission.

Library of Congress Control Number: 2025932758
ISBN: 978-1-958888-52-0

For my wife.

"Grow old along with me!

The best is yet to be . . ."

"Inclusion without power or leadership is tokenism."
—LEAH LAKSHMI PIEPZNA-SAMARASINHA, *Care Work: Dreaming Disability Justice*

"We are not a fully realized movement until we are a fully inclusive movement."
—KEITH JONES, president of SoulTouchin' Experiences

"'You're high maintenance,' " he said. He was right. I take a village."
—GEORGE HODGMAN, *Bettyville: A Memoir*

CONTENTS

MIXED-UP MEDIA

STIGMA AND REPUTATION

ONGOING ISSUES AND IRRITATIONS

INVISIBLE BUT PRESENT

Introduction

THIS IS NOT A MEMOIR

Memoirs, by definition, are based on memories. This book isn't like that. Instead, it consists of interviews and essays from the actual times when I was developing my thoughts about and awareness of disability issues. Altogether, it forms a portrait of the evolution of a quiet rebel and reluctant activist—and perhaps a bit more about me as a complicated, flawed human being.

It begins with a reflection on my high school experiences. At that time, I was about the furthest thing from an activist. But I was beginning to become more cognizant of my disability, which sounds funny since I'd had it since birth. My muscle weakness—spinal muscular atrophy, to be specific—meant I never walked. I graduated from a baby stroller to a manual wheelchair. In college, I upgraded to a full-time motorized wheelchair. But still, even then, I thought if I was clever enough and smart enough and, well, "normal" (read: *nondisabled*) enough, maybe nobody would notice my impairments.

At least I knew for sure that they would not hold me back. Or so I thought.

Yes, I honestly believed I could do practically anything and be like everybody else. My emaciated limbs, curlicue spine, and physical restrictions did not matter. The blissful ignorance of youth!

But the real world hits everybody sooner or later. It's inevitable, inescapable. For me, that meant realizing the full extent of my limitations and, more importantly, the stigmas that came with them. Romantic rejections. Professional rejections. Disappointments that could perhaps be attributed to a number of factors. After all, everybody gets spurned and dumped sometimes. Don't they? But I could not rule out discrimination. What's now called ableism (I always called it "crip-ism"). It may not have been intentional. The attitude that people held about me may even have been well-meaning. No one wanted to be hurtful exactly. I just somehow didn't fit their expectations or desires.

Nevertheless, with the generous help of family and friends, I found ways to survive. Did I mention that I am incredibly fortunate and privileged? I don't think I ever felt truly threatened by these financial or attitudinal barriers. I always knew that I would survive. I just wasn't ever sure exactly how.

As a rule, disabled people are inventive. We have to be. As the late disability justice crusader Stacey Park Milbern told the Disability Visibility Project, "People with disabilities are used to the world not being accessible and having to make things work out of nothing. You know, the world literally isn't made to house us, it feels like sometimes. So we get to be really creative solvers and, I think, aren't constrained to boxes, can kinda see pictures that others can't see."

The pieces in this collection are divided into four broad sections, grouped by theme. They are not in chronological order, though the first section does concern my early years. It begins with two essays about how I learned to channel my innate creativity, which was further nurtured in me in childhood, particularly in high school. The first piece was actually first published in my high school alum magazine. Thirty years had passed since graduation. Already middle-aged, I pondered crucial turning points in my development as a human being and as a lover of words. And how, in time, I'd found I could tap into this wellspring of experiences to formulate my own sense of self—an identity separate from the one that society seemed to foist upon me.

The second essay is one I wrote decades earlier, while still in high school. It provides a different interpretation of my creative and rebellious spirit.

Neither one is more true than the other. They just reflect disparate aspects of my early years.

Then comes a piece I wrote in college. Because of my disability, I had caused something of a sensation on campus. I milked that attention and controversy for all they were worth. This reflection was also my way of introducing myself to my thousand-plus new classmates, presenting myself as I wanted to be seen but probably not as I was actually being seen by them.

In truth, people seem to find a lot of things about me hard to believe, as became increasingly clear in the years following college. I found that my disability—or rather the mismatch between my disability and the world around me—was a rich vein of literary inspiration. I became an observer of my own alienation. Through my writing, I tried to point out our society's foibles vis-à-vis its disabled citizenry.

This segues into a section about difficult conversations. My entrée into activism inevitably led to several in-depth opinion essays about complex disability-related issues. For instance, why does the idea of a cure for my neuromuscular weakness feel like a betrayal of my sense of disability pride? What are the implications of the right-to-die movement and other burning issues of our time for disabled people like me?

The third section concerns social aspects of disability—how media reflects and promotes unfair stereotypes, along with some ways we should combat these societal ills.

The final chunk is both a reflection on what I've learned from these diverse experiences and a few thoughts about ongoing advocacy and where the movement and we as a society may be heading. Now that I'm in my sixth decade, I've become less self-centered, less concerned about my dreams and desires and my place in the world and more attuned to the fate of the disability community as a whole. As a group, disabled people are much better off than we used to be, yet there are still so many left behind. Why is that, and what can be done about it?

The journey these pages are about to take you on is primarily one of the mind, but it's also one of the body. An active mind in an inactive body, perhaps? No, I don't think that's quite right. Or fair. Being disabled doesn't deprive you of physicality. Many of the indignities I've faced concerned my body, or my bodily autonomy. Though I've never run or jumped, my physical being is always alive and humming, and sometimes under threat. It feels and senses and reacts, and is maddeningly vulnerable to all manner of upsets and dangers. Many disability studies scholars today refer to the "bodymind" as a single entity rather than a duality. It's indeed difficult to separate one from the other. Certainly I am always aware of my flesh-and-blood form. Given my inherent muscular weaknesses, the very acts of breathing, swallowing, balancing, and other functions that most people would deem involuntary often take a presence of mind for me to accomplish.

"I am not my body," says a disabled character in Tom Stoppard's 2006 play *Rock 'n' Roll*. "My body is nothing without me." That feels true, or it rings true to me, to my sense of my being. I am not my body. I am not my disability. But I am also not my mind. I am both, and more. As are we all.

Portrait of the Cripple as a Young Man

The Long and Winding Road

ONE ALUM'S JOURNEY

Here are reflections from my high school alum magazine, written (some might say overwritten) when I was squarely middle-aged. The institution I'm referring to is a small private school in New York City named after the Austrian philosopher and social reformer Rudolf Steiner (1861–1925).

The sound pouring from my computer headset was a revelation! A rich, complex concoction of snappy, singable lyrics melded seamlessly with a spectrum of cross-genre instrumentation. The overall effect suffused me with energizing digital clarity. I felt shaken, as if an old truth I'd never realized had suddenly become gloriously obvious.

Which, in fact, is about what it was. This musical miracle was the Beatles' *Sgt. Pepper's Lonely Hearts Club Band*, the forty-three-year-old classic newly reremastered on CD (its second reissue). The songs were as familiar as my own skin. What *was* new, however, was in the details—distinct, subtle quirks, such as the Irish lilt of the distraught, self-centered mother in "She's Leaving Home," or how the guttural sounds of lovemaking (I guess) that end "Lovely Rita" crash into the jarring opening chords of "Good Morning Good Morning."

But enough Beatles geek talk!

My point is, some things reverberate throughout a lifetime, yet somehow only come into focus after many years. My Steiner education was a lot like that.

Those who knew me in the Rudolf Steiner High School class of 1980 might not be surprised at my Beatles enthusiasm or my geek talk. When others were rocking out to Led Zeppelin and Pink Floyd, I was hawking the superiority of that old-time rock 'n' roll and, later, ever the nonconformist, new-wave bands such as the Clash or Elvis Costello and the Attractions.

Oh my God! He's writing about rock music in a Steiner publication!

Hold on. There *is* a purpose to this. To wit: one never forgets the music of one's high school years. Whether it's the Frank Sinatra of my father's generation or—who?—Lil' Kim today, it remains stamped on your psyche like an aural tattoo. Even when you've moved on, hear it as an adult and you're invariably pulled back into the mists of memory.

[Fade to mist.]

I came to Steiner after eight years at a now-defunct Upper West Side progressive school where teachers were called by their first names and report cards were filled with comments, no letter or number grades. It was hard to find a high school willing to admit a thusly undocumented student—especially one in a wheelchair.

My backstory: I have always used a wheelchair and was quite accustomed to it. The schools were not.

Steiner was an exception—a courageous savior, a godsend.

Not that I wasn't nervous, landing smack-dab among a group of kids most of whom had known each other since kindergarten. *Eurhythmy?* [An artistic sort of athletic class that was taught there, and the butt of many jokes.] One of many mysteries.

Yet somehow I felt welcome. Now, from the vantage point of age forty-seven—complete with mortgage, marriage, two teenage kids, a gastroenterologist, and so forth—I miss those carefree days. But I don't miss my adolescent insecurities or embarrassing, self-righteous opinions... not to mention the freakish formfitting fashions and bushy hairstyles. The ghosts that mock from faded photos.

Something more lasting, however, was born and nurtured in me at Steiner. Something hard to define. Call it a creative spirit. The sense of looking inward to look outward.

However you define it, it's had me by the throat and heart ever since. For me it's emerged as a love of writing. And yes, I learned it in those musty old rooms of 15 East Seventy-eighth Street.

My parents worked in publishing. From them I was already familiar with the rules of writing. Yet I wasn't actually inspired to do it until Steiner. Steiner planted in me a sense of joy in giving voice to creativity. I did not come to it easily as, say, a devoted reader. I wish I had been one of those children who read books voraciously, but in fact I was scared of literature. Books were basically preludes to tests. They were required for education or status. They were not for enjoyment.

I won't name names. A variety of Steiner teachers in countless ways led me to think of the written word from the other side, the creative side—as a demonstration of the writers' craft, the building blocks of a kind of art. I began to appreciate literature from the writer's point of view, or my perception of it, rather than an academic's or critic's. I began to wonder, and notice, how sentences got fashioned the way they did. I delighted in conjuring how one got from the blank page to the finished, polished project. And I yearned to decode the process.

Steiner supplied the necessary gametes for engendering within me a rapacious demiurgic spunkiness. (How's that for sounding literary?) I'll simply thank the Academy for that—the academy of anthroposophical pedagogy, or whatever. You know who you are, or were.

After high school, I was committed to an institution. That institution was called Harvard University.

In the months before moving to Cambridge, I dreaded what I might find inside its ivied walls. I imagined unbearable preppiness and a conservative, overly cerebral milieu. And indeed, it took me practically till my senior year there to feel acclimated, but I'll save that saga for another alum magazine.

As my college graduation neared—1983–84—it seemed the thing to do with the rest of my life was become a lawyer. This would be practical, and profitable! It was either that or business school. Ah, the Reagan years!

Only problem, I didn't really want to do either. I had another calling buried deep within me, partially hidden. The excavation began when I submitted a short story to a selective fiction-writing class . . . and was accepted!

From there on I chose electives that interested me, not just those I felt I *should* take. A history of cinema. An introduction to English Romantic poetry. I took classes that addressed and inspired my need for artistry, that echoed what Steiner had helped develop in me but had sadly fallen into disrepair from lack of use.

Most of my final year was spent writing a 125-page "honors essay." I'll spare you the brilliant topic of my lengthy devotion. In the end, my three-professor panel of readers found it lacking in intellectual rigor but praised my writing style. I graduated cum laude.

Afterward, I decided on a new five-year plan. I'd pursue a writing career. If I couldn't get anywhere in that time, I'd take the LSAT.

Five years was all I asked. But I didn't have to wait that long.

Within a few months I landed my first paid article on the front page of the weekly *Los Angeles Business Journal*. I got the gig through my alumni career office, and because the editor liked my student writing samples. More assignments followed, but he didn't hire me for the staff position for which I originally interviewed. That was a pattern that became all too common. One freelance assignment led to another, but never a full-time job offer. So much for the easy career path of an Ivy League grad.

It was a tight job market, to be sure, but gradually I had to accept another painful reality. It would've been foolish to deny that my disability may have been playing a role. I never accepted that as an excuse for failure, but considering how I kept getting turned down for work—often from the very same publishers who gave me freelance assignments—what other conclusion could I draw?

Once, at a job interview with a trade magazine publisher for whom I'd already written several articles, the editor asked me point-blank, "How would you manage daily tasks such as making photocopies?"

I smiled and tried to reassure her. I'd had a summer job in internal communications at IBM, I explained, and never had a problem. She pressed further, so I said if I ever got stuck it was easy to ask someone to push the copy button for me.

She locked me in a tight stare. "Yes," she said abruptly, "but if we hire you, you'd be here to help *us*, not for us to help *you*."

Needless to say, I didn't get the job. That one or any other.

Still, I kept getting occasional freelance assignments, gaining experience and trying to accept that people who wanted my work didn't want to have me around to deal with in person.

Then, one summer afternoon, I ran into Mr. Piening in Central Park. I know I said I wouldn't name names, but my late class teacher is worth the exception. He invited me to contribute a piece to a Steiner alum magazine not unlike this one. And a flame was rekindled.

Maybe I didn't need an assignment to get me writing! I could write for fun, for practice, for a sense of accomplishment. Maybe it would even lead to something, I reasoned. After all, how else could anyone know what I was capable of?

I started trying to write a novel. After a few years it was done. It was about trying to secure a place in the adult world from the perspective of a young man in a wheelchair. I even secured an agent, but sadly, the manuscript remains on a dusty shelf with the two others I wrote after that one. As with my senior-year honors essay, publishers were encouraged by the style but not the substance.

Still, I kept writing. What else could I do? My inner Steiner told me that maintaining creative output was crucial to my development and sense of self.

Around this time, I became enamored of a cause, my first flirtation with political activism. Best of all, my side won. We were victorious! In 1990 the Americans with Disabilities Act was signed into law. It didn't actually help me get a job, but it validated my sense of unfairness and discrimination.

An even greater boon was the pace of technology. Writing longhand and typing on a keyboard were becoming impossible as my meager muscles deteriorated further. To the rescue came voice-recognition software. With the power of dictation, I could interface (as we used to say) with the computer faster and better than ever. Soon, email enabled me to gather sources and conduct virtual interviews without ever rolling away from my desk—not to mention being able to file stories without messengers or FedEx. And the internet made research a breeze, especially valuable for someone with limited mobility.

This was particularly good because my freelance career was about to get turbocharged. After my first daughter was born, I found a fresh, rich vein of freelance work in—of all things!—financial journalism. Which to my surprise I loved. I learned about myriad industries and companies and the people behind entrepreneurial innovations. The dot-com boom was hot, and I became very busy. I found I could charge more and more for my services. I even got listed on the mastheads of several magazines as a contributing editor!

Then the capital markets skidded to a halt. Many of my clients folded. Yet now I had a marketable portfolio of published clips.

I started submitting article ideas to new clients. Besides financial pitches, I kept composing personal essays about my experiences as a disabled American. Though I was used to seeing my name in print, I got a special charge out of appearing in new magazines and websites and, especially, on newspaper op-ed pages and, later, in radio commentaries. These weren't assignments. These pieces were my own original ideas. They were from the heart. I was proud of my journalistic achievements, but as the movie ads say, this time it was personal!

In time, the reactions to my essays blew me away. Phone calls and emails from around the world! I was reaching people in a way my bread-and-butter work never could. And I did it by first looking within, as I'd been taught many years ago. Not to overstate it, but it almost felt like the fulfillment of a mission first whispered into my ears at Steiner.

A few years ago, when I passed forty, I was seized with a new idea. What if I put all this together into a kind of memoir? Not just my personal experiences but the incredible changes I've lived through and benefited from. The advancements in technology, medicine, and disability rights. I'd come of age during the disability revolution!

In fairness, this wasn't entirely my idea. For many years people told me to write my life story. Perhaps I was finally ready—had sufficient perspective and platform, as media types say—to tell it right.

Yes, I realize everybody is writing a memoir. Nonetheless, I continue to believe I have something unique and important to communicate. Something that will reach a lot of people's hearts and minds.

But, of course, it isn't that easy. No matter how compelling my topic, getting a book published is a crapshoot at best.

I now have an agent (a new one!), and I'm not surrendering. Call me stubborn. Indeed, with my aforementioned kids and mortgage and other responsibilities, why on earth would I pursue this speculative endeavor? Why have I kept at this hopelessly haphazard game of writing all these years anyway? I must be dense, or masochistic. How many rejection letters can one person take?

Maybe I'm addicted. I'm hungry for my next fix of creative satisfaction.

For me, though, a more critical factor is that expressing myself in words is simply a part of who I am. It may have started at Steiner, but now it's in my identity. It's become a life's pursuit that's encoded in my being.

Like those Beatles classics, writing is something I know I can depend on, will inevitably return to, and can always draw energy from. I'm hooked.

Sure, on bad days I could be forgiven for cursing the creative spark that my Steiner education lit within me. But I don't, because I'm never sorry for the path I've chosen. (Or has it chosen me?)

And if Steiner provided the map, then I am forever in its debt.

Superheroes and Me

I wrote the following short, admittedly cringe-worthy essay while still in high school. It's a window onto some of my earliest realizations about being disabled. Plus, it explains my creativity and rebellious nature from a completely different—juvenile but nonetheless true—perspective.

Like most of the pieces in this collection, it's been edited for clarity, to avoid repetition, and to update some of the most offensive language. (I don't personally find the word handicap *offensive when used in a historical context, since it's what I grew up with, but I apologize in advance to readers who take exception to this outdated and inappropriate term.)*

I am told that the first sign of my handicap was my inability to sit up by myself at seven months. In time, I was diagnosed as being intellectually disabled, which my parents found absurd. After years of examinations by a horde of doctors, I had a muscle biopsy and was reported to have a rare, inherited, neuromuscular disease that, in my case, is stable rather than progressive. (Or so we thought.) Little is known of it, and nothing as yet can be done to cure it.

I attended a nursery school and kindergarten for "normal" children. I have a sense that I was very serious and aloofly observant of the others, though this probably is not true. More likely, this was an image of what I wanted to be. I admired the serious, the uninvolved, the nonconformist. This might have been a subconscious defense against any social discomforts I had. If I was insecure about being physically different—and feeling at all inferior—what better way to reassure myself than to disassociate myself from the majority on the basis of spiritual or mental superiority?

I tend to deny this and say that I was inclined to be serious because my idols—television characters like Captain Kirk and Mr. Spock, the rough-and-ready Cartwright family, and Chief Robert T. Ironside—were serious and rather gruff.

Of all of my idols, Ironside is the most significant. Not only was he tough, serious, and wise; he, too, used a wheelchair. I felt that I, like Ironside, could defend myself if necessary. When my friends saw a James Bond movie, they might imagine themselves able to fight off physical threats. Well, I, too, had such fantasies. I could not kick, jump, or punch, and I accepted that, but I was confident that I could pay back any other child who "assaulted" me—by thinking. My unusual circumstance had honed my mental preparedness. Logic, rather than brawn, would be the wellspring for my retaliation.

This is not to say that my childhood was a succession of fights. With my bent for dramatic tension, I may have preferred it that way, but reality had something else in mind. Something gentler.

After kindergarten, I attended the Walden School, the only nonspecialized private school that was willing to accept a student in a wheelchair. I soon made many friends who helped me reach things and pushed me wherever I wished—even around the bases at top speed in our Wiffle ball games.

I left Walden after eighth grade because I felt I wanted to go to a more rigorous, more academic school. Walden's philosophy of education dealt more with developing students' personalities than exercising their brains, I felt certain. I say this scoffingly not because I do not believe in social education but rather because that often becomes a guise for a lack of intellectual education.

I transferred to the Rudolf Steiner School. Although it had steps at the entrance and was equipped with only a tiny, one-(standing)-person-at-a-time elevator, it agreed to take on my disability. For the school, it was a new frontier; for me, it was old hat.

Then adolescence set in, and I'll never forgive it. Not only was I a stranger in a new school; I became a stranger to myself. My admiration of the aloof developed into acute sarcasm and antisociability. I found that these qualities were not appreciated at Steiner. (They had not been popular at Walden, either, but Walden was bigger, and I was part of a group of antisocialites.) I had difficulty relating to my classmates at Steiner—and they had difficulty relating to me, and my handicap. I soon found it hard to distinguish between who really liked me and who sympathized with me. I became insecure. I was unsure of every movement I made and rarely spoke out in class. I felt doomed to inadequacy. If anyone ever offers me the opportunity to relive my early teens, I will refuse immediately.

I had another problem in ninth grade: I was due to have a back operation in the summer and didn't expect to return to school until November. I told no one in school for fear of eliciting more pity.

Over the summer, lying in my hospital bed for four months, I decided it was time for a change. The solution to the problem of cloying solicitousness was in me, in my attitude. If I accepted my condition (and I always had before), my classmates could do no less! Phase one of the program would be candor about my surgery. From bed, I wrote an article for the school newsmagazine explaining my absence with candor and, I hope, a good dose of humor.

Next, I had to be more friendly. When I returned to school, I joined every extracurricular group I could. Getting to know as many people as possible became my all-important goal. Pretty soon I found that I enjoyed school, or rather the people in school, tremendously. My antisociality faded! Tenth grade was replete with achievements: a broader circle of friends, closer friendships, and a starring role in the class production of Kaufman and Hart's *You Can't Take It with You.* (Okay, I had to be Grandpa Vanderhof, but it *is* a leading roll.) I attended nearly every school dance and even a dance at another school, went out with friends, and attended the annual farewell-seniors party. The year's achievements were epitomized by a yearbook full of flattering messages!

My growth did not stop there. I gained more confidence and established closer friendships in eleventh grade. The older I grew, the more confident and relaxed I became. Social amenities came more naturally.

I am glad I learned what I did about self-confidence and sociability, for I believe that to be an important key to happiness. One cannot wait for friends and blessings to come simply on their own. And I am happy, too, in other aspects of my life. Even the divorce of my parents has not proved entirely detrimental: it has left me free of many of the restrictions of family that plague so many of my peers.

As for senior year: despite the increased workload, I am fully enjoying it, devoted to the idea of instilling more confidence in my younger peers than I had—without losing my senior image, of course.

Life on Wheels—An Equal Chance

After high school, I was off to college two hundred miles away. To live on campus. In dorms. Without my parents or familiar hired helpers to bathe and dress me and otherwise tend to all my basic custodial needs. I felt lucky to have the opportunity, but I had no idea how I would manage.

I wasn't the first wheelchair user ever to go to my so-called prestigious school, but I was the only one at that time and may have been the first admitted; the only other chair user I knew about had become disabled while already a student, thanks to a spinal cord injury.

But I was in luck! It was the first year that federally funded institutions, including private colleges that received federal tuition grants, had to become accessible for disabled students. I was a beneficiary of the activists who had come before me, but I was also a pioneer. Or, more accurately, a test case. A guinea pig.

In retrospect, it was another scary time in my life, one I met with characteristic false bravado. My dad and I arranged for a series of paid attendants and occasional volunteers to see to my personal care and other needs. The nearly four-centuries-old campus wasn't quite up to the demands of accessibility regulations, but it was beginning to try, with mixed results, as will become clear from the next essay, which was written at that difficult time. This was early in my freshman year—the honeymoon period, you might say. This piece was part of my application (or "comp," for competition) to join the staff of the student-run weekly newsmagazine. As in the previous example, there is outdated terminology—"handicapped," "wheelchair-bound," and so forth. I didn't know any better then. Maybe this language reflects my own internalized ableism, but more likely it simply reflects the terms most widely used at that time. Anyway, I made the cut and got on staff but never had time to submit more articles than this one. I did, however, also contribute one cartoon. I loved drawing comics in those days, something I no longer have sufficient physical strength to do, alas.

In the midst of the academic year and the deadlines that go with it, Harvard students—especially freshmen, who are faced with some new "core" regulations—may feel frustrated, picked on, or even downright small. But the university has some new requirements to meet, too. As of September 1980, all school programs must have been made accessible to those of us who were then referred to as "handicapped." With a campus as old as Harvard's, this is certainly a challenging task, if not an outright impossibility. But a "wheelchair-bound" student can negotiate Harvard more easily than you might imagine. I know—I'm one, and I've been getting along fine.

My story begins before I even applied to Harvard. I was interested in what various colleges had done to improve access to facilities. As might be expected, some campuses were well set-up; others were not at all. (One institution, whose name I shall omit because I'm not sure how to spell it, admitted they'd find it "damn difficult" to meet my needs.)

When I first visited the campus, Ruth K———, then head of the student group ABLE (Advocating a Better Learning Environment), introduced me to Quincy House, its ramps and elevators, a university-sponsored van for the transportation of disabled persons, and other aids in the offing. People seemed interested and enthusiastic about having a student like me. The place was willing, but the works remained practically untried.

A word about myself: I have always attended "normal" school where I was the only disabled student. I am not afraid of a school designed for the ambulatory. But I was planning to live on campus; frankly, I was anxious about how a college, especially Harvard, could effectively accommodate me. Let's face it: this place is old. It's full of cracks and bumps and stairs. (New York, where I grew up, also has cracks, bumps, and stairs, but, I think, not quite so many.)

In due course, I was accepted, and after considering all factors, I decided to go ahead with my Harvard career.

That brings us to last June. The university was busy planning for my arrival. I was phoned by the freshman dean's office (FDO) for the dimensions of my widest and heaviest wheelchair. As the summer progressed, I found myself engaged more than once in conversations with the FDO, particularly with Will M———, a senior adviser. We discussed every aspect of my life (and I mean *every*).

I was forced to consider questions I couldn't begin to answer. Daily activities I had never thought twice about before were suddenly objects of scrutiny. How big should a bathroom be? Did I really need a tub or would the shower do? Could I open the front door to my suite by myself? The future was nebulous; all I could do was guess at the answers.

I visited Cambridge twice more, to ensure that all systems were go. By the time I arrived in September, everything was arranged. I was to live on the ground floor of Canaday, a modern, spacious complex built with me (that is, my sort of "problem") in mind. The building and grounds people promised to widen a few doorways and smooth a few bumps for me, and so the forecast began to look less gloomy. As for academics, I was asked to peruse last year's course catalogue over the summer to get an idea of what I might take. Courses I picked would be in accessible rooms.

All that remained was to test the system out. One of the first places I ventured when I arrived in September was Mem Hall, for registration. "Mem Hall," you might be thinking, "that old place with the steps in front of it." That's what I'd thought. But then I strolled around back—there were two ramps. The haze of uncertainty was clearing.

Another place I came across early on was the Freshman Union. Again I saw stairs. And again I saw just how well Mother Harvard was looking out for me. Behind the side door (which is at street level) is an elevator. Furthermore, the matrons of the Union are only too happy to assist those in need by carrying trays and such. I was running out of things to worry about.

And so it went. In time I discovered the ramped side door and the automatic lift, which render the ground floor of Emerson Hall completely accessible. (The upstairs, however, is a different story—if you'll pardon the pun.) Robinson has ramps to the ground floor. Lamont, Widener, and the Science Center all have ramps and elevators. If there are any I've forgotten (or haven't discovered yet), I hope they'll forgive me.

When did all this come about? According to Sandra M———, a senior who assisted a "wheelchair-bound" student her freshman year, very few of these support systems were around four years ago. Emerson and Robinson halls were a hassle, and the Union was nearly impossible. The work done is recent, and according to official sources more may be on the way.

Why, I wondered, has Harvard been so receptive to the needs of "the handicapped"? I could find no evidence of a rich, disabled alumnus behind these goings-on. Is the administration simply obeying the law, as Ray W———, the present head of ABLE, believes? In fact, he wishes the university were doing more.

I think the school is doing more than meeting the law. When I mentioned to Will M——— that the gate nearest and most accessible to both the Union and my dorm was locked each night before dinner, I didn't expect a change in security policy. But, to my surprise, that gate now remains open until 8 p.m., cutting my transportation time to and from dinner in half. And, while I'm not sure if it's Harvard's doing, many curbs in and around the square have been cut so that a wheelchair may roll across the street more easily—unattended if need be.

My roommate/attendant's needs were met also. A fellow undergraduate student here [who was taking a year off], he asked for and received a "special" ID, allowing him use of the libraries and interhouse privileges.

Most recently, Moral Reasoning 13 was moved from the second floor of Harvard Hall, a monument to stairdom, to the first floor of Emerson (upsetting several classes, I regret to say) so I could attend more effortlessly. Not completely effortlessly, but that's the nature of Prof. M———'s courses.

In addition, word has it, my pathway will be among the first cleared of snow. (I asked them to stop the snow altogether, but that, they said, couldn't be done.)

How much is the university legally required to give me? I asked Dean Thomas C———, the faculty's coordinator for the "handicapped," just what the law entails. He told me that all educational institutions receiving federal aid must offer disabled people the same programs they offer anyone else.

This starts with nondiscrimination in admissions and financial aid and goes right through to housing, transportation, and, of course, classrooms and lecture halls—within reason. Dean C——— explained to me that every square inch of campus space does not have to be on level ground or accessible by wheelchair. Sever Hall, for example, is not accessible and cannot be made so without major construction. But any course must be made available to a disabled person wishing to take it. Either the class will be moved or the administration will arrange to have that person carried past the barrier, as was done last year with a senior who couldn't walk.

The university has vigorously and efficiently worked toward eliminating all barriers. Keep your eyes open, peer down side paths, and you'll see all the ramps and elevators about. For all those Stanford and UC Berkeley students who warned me about hardships among the time-worn buildings of the East, I invite you to come and eat your hearts out. I have no regrets.

September's Legacy

TAKING ON HARVARD IN A WHEELCHAIR

Several years later, CNN commissioned the following blog post about my college experiences, which I've edited to avoid repetition. You'll note my change in attitude, upon reflection, about Harvard's accessibility efforts. But otherwise, this piece pretty much picks up the thread.

For many, back-to-school is a season of anticipation, nostalgia, and shopping. For me, it evokes memories of an unsung historical event: the integration of Harvard.

No, I'm not talking about racial integration; I'm talking about the full inclusion of students with disabilities.

When I entered the college as a freshman in 1980, it happened to coincide with a new requirement to become accessible [for disabled folks], under Section 504 of the Rehabilitation Act of 1973.

I was a seventeen-year-old lifelong wheelchair user. . . . But, as my parents often said, there was nothing wrong with my head.

I had little awareness of the historical precedent I was setting. At seventeen, I was too self-centered for that. I was preoccupied with how I'd cope my first time living away from my parents, depending on full-time, live-in, personal-care attendants. Yet I had an Ivy League freshman's cockiness, too. Somehow I'd manage. I'd always managed before, hadn't I?

To be sure, the school had had students with disabilities before me. But those students had to make do, beating or circumventing access barriers without complaint. After all, it was a centuries-old campus. How much could one expect?

I, on the other hand, had rights—and expectations. I challenged the university in a whole new way.

I was an inadvertent pioneer. I mean, it wasn't my fault. I hadn't fought for my rights. They fell into my lap.

I remember meeting with university officials the summer before my freshman year got under way. We discussed every detail of my life and needs. Boxers or briefs? (Just kidding.) I also had to prepick classes so the administration could ensure mine would be held in accessible classrooms, of which there were too few. If I changed my mind, I could be out of luck.

Not that pioneering was an unfamiliar role for me. My parents had insisted on my attending "regular" schools at a time when that was unheard of. In the 1960s, according to government statistics, only one in five disabled kids was educated in a public school—usually a separate (dare I say *segregated*?) special-ed school. The majority stayed home or got sent off to underregulated residential institutions.

More than a million disabled kids had no access to the school system at all. Many states even had statutes specifically excluding the Deaf, blind, or intellectually disabled from public schooling!

I vaguely recall how the schools my older, nondisabled brother attended refused to accept me, how my parents had to argue and beg on my behalf. They knew separate wasn't equal, but they had no legal recourse. My parents were private school kind of people, and I ended up at the only private schools willing to take a kid in a wheelchair. It's no exaggeration to say that for many years I assumed I was simply too dumb for my parents' first-choice schools.

Today, of course, it's completely different. After countless pieces of legislation, reauthorizations, government commissions and legal rulings, wheelchair ramps and lifts, Braille and recorded books, sign-language interpreters, "shadow teachers," and other accommodations are commonplace in schools as they are elsewhere.

Parents of so-called special-needs kids still have to fight sometimes to ensure fairness, but they have rights and a grievance process on their side. Integration is the standard that must be met.

Ultimately, my college experience had its ups and downs, as might be expected of what was a revolutionary new concept. Sadly, it wasn't just the ancient brick buildings and cobblestone paths that posed inexorable barriers; sometimes hidebound traditions can be equally obdurate.

Nevertheless, how the demographics of education have changed became especially clear to me recently when my kids' school held a "diversity day." (My kids don't have [physical] disabilities, but some of their classmates do.)

I boldly volunteered to lead a discussion about people with disabilities. To my surprise, I wasn't the only one.

Romance—and Its Discontents

How Thirty Blocks Became Thirty Years

Not long after my college graduation, ML and I moved to Los Angeles. She and I had shared an apartment during my senior year, partly because I'd grown sick of the isolating, lonely, half-baked accessibility measures of Harvard housing and partly because we were in love.

What follows are several pieces about our relationship—and why it has now lasted more than thirty years.

The first is from the popular New York Times *"Modern Love" column. I had been trying to get this published for several years. The version that was finally accepted was drawn from my second book,* In Sickness and In Health: Love, Disability, and a Quest to Understand the Perils and Pleasures of Interabled Romance *(2018, Beacon Press).*

When ML and I started our relationship on that humid night in Stamford, Connecticut, we may not have expected it to last. After all, I was unable to scratch my own nose, let alone walk. And she was three years older than me and far more independent.

I asked if I could kiss her. I had to ask because I couldn't lean in on my own; my body doesn't work that way.

So she leaned in and kissed me as I had never been kissed before.

"You were just a kid," she told me recently.

I was nineteen. She wore her straight auburn hair in a short boy-cut then. More than thirty years later, she still does, though the color has faded. I wasn't only attracted to her iconoclastic spirit, alluring eyes, and figure; I was on a mission to lose my virginity.

I was born with an incurable neuromuscular condition, but my lifelong disability has never prevented me from doing anything I set my mind to. My disability certainly wasn't going to keep me from having a girlfriend, getting married, or having a family.

I now write with a voice-recognition computer program. I no longer have the strength to hold or use a pencil. I drive my motorized wheelchair with a hypersensitive, lip-controlled mini joystick. Nevertheless, that first girlfriend and I have been married for nearly three decades.

It's a relationship that, in many ways, has only become more mysterious to me as the years have passed. Early on, I took for granted the fact that I would find love. I was cocky that way. But over time I have wondered why and how my marriage has worked out. So when I landed a contract several years ago to write about love between people with disabilities and people without, I figured I would start with my own marriage.

When I asked ML what she first saw in me—a wheelchair-using teenager whose condition was only going to worsen—she said, "You weren't aggressive. But you had a hunger that was sexy."

It felt strange to be interviewing her. She is, after all, my lifelong companion and the mother of our two kids, both now in college.

"I knew I was safe with you," she said. "It was only going to go as far and as fast as I wanted, which was something I needed at the time."

I had learned to live with my disability just as the world was learning to live with people with disabilities as a political force, a civil-rights movement. That no doubt helped my cause, which was simply to live a full and normal life.

She'd had no experience dealing with someone like me. But she learned to live with my limitations—those caused by my atrophied muscles, my respiratory distresses and myriad external obstacles and attitudes—through real-world, on-the-job training.

Rewinding the mental movie of our lives together, I see us on our first date a few weeks after that kiss, talking during a long evening stroll. We struggled to keep pace with each other as we moved by different means.

There was an Elvis Costello concert in Manhattan. I made her walk thirty blocks through the sweltering stench of Hell's Kitchen in her date shoes and slinky pink dress because in those days New York buses and taxis weren't wheelchair accessible, and I didn't yet have a van.

Along the way, strangers harassed us with rude remarks. We ignored them, but such comments would follow us for the rest of our lives. I believe a part of us grew stronger because of them. The novelty of our relationship became an asset, not a liability. We thought, in our innocence: Why shouldn't we throw in our lots together?

Toward the end of that night, emboldened by a couple of Black Russians downed at a bar on the walk back, I suggested she ride on my lap. "Your feet hurt," I said.

She resisted, but like many disabled people, I had learned not to take no for an answer. Although then, as before, everything relied on my powers of persuasion. And my charm. Or so I like to think.

"Really," I said. "Climb on. It won't hurt." Whether I meant it wouldn't hurt her or me, I no longer recall.

Was it the sheer force of my personality—my gentle boldness—that made her not only jump on my lap but also fall in love with me? It certainly wasn't the ease with which I move through life.

But there was another reason. A few years earlier, she had come to Stamford for the summer to look after my infant half brother. She was still in college and was at loose ends. So by that first date, we had already spent a lot of time living in the same house.

"I think that's how you flew under my radar," she said. "Because we were able to become friends first without any pressure."

This proximity also gave her time to get used to my disability, to see how my family handled it, to demystify it. Nevertheless, even if my disability made me seem harmless, she admitted she was nervous during our first sexual encounters in the weeks that followed that concert—afraid, primarily, about injuring me.

"You were so fragile looking," she said. "And I was worried about balancing in the tiny bed. And if there was a problem, would I have to go get your attendant? Or worse, your dad?"

I shudder to think. None of that had ever occurred to me.

"But you survived the first few encounters," she said. "And then came the miracle when I was able to lift you."

I remember it well. Several months later, on a desperate whim, she tried lifting me out of my wheelchair and discovered she could. I weighed about 120 pounds—not nothing—yet somehow she managed it. Which meant from then on we could go almost anywhere and do anything without an attendant tagging along.

Over time, she wanted to do more for me: shaving me, for instance, or clipping and cleaning my fingernails. At first I resisted, but she did these things better than any paid person could. She had a vested interest in my grooming.

For better or worse, disability tends to break down the barriers of privacy. When someone must assist you with dressing, bathing, and using the bathroom, you come to understand each other's most intimate processes and needs. (I still have paid help every day, but she fills the gaps.)

"We faced challenges as they arrived, survived them, even grew from them," she said. "But if I had foreseen them all at once, they would've been too terrifying."

Terrifying? I want to ask her more about that. But I suppose I shouldn't be surprised. You meet problems as they arise. Besides, the important question on my mind is: What happens when those challenges become too much?

"I think the same is true for many people," she said. Meaning we all face challenges we didn't anticipate. "Disability is part of it. But there are so many kinds of troubles families endure."

Early on, before we had children, I got deeply involved in disability rights (and pride), a movement that can sometimes view nondisabled people as the enemy, as oppressors. For a while this led me to feel more bonded with a disabled woman and fellow advocate than with my wife.

Then, ten years ago, I nearly died from complications of gastrointestinal surgery, a monthslong crisis that humbled us both.

I wanted to know: What would she do differently if she had it to do over again? What advice would she offer a young, nondisabled woman considering a relationship with a disabled young man?

"I think I was better off not knowing the challenges," she said. "Perhaps just the knowledge that we're still together and best friends all these years later. To know that in advance would sustain me in those times when it didn't seem possible."

True. Most couples face seemingly indomitable trials. What's different about us is we dealt with those tests sooner, not later. We began with few illusions or unrealistic expectations (unless you consider my wanting to have sex, get married, and start a family to be unrealistic).

And the truth is that once you have had your children straighten you in your wheelchair or drive it down the street when your hand gives out, your whole perception of propriety and family roles tends to get upended. Which is another way of saying that my disability has been, in a strange way, liberating, allowing us to live, and love, as we wish.

A Marriage with Special Circumstances

When NPR commissioned a commentary for Valentine's Day, I came up with a somewhat different reflection on my marriage.

I've always thought unlikely attractions—Romeo and Juliet, Cinderella and Prince Charming—were the romantic ideal. Some people say my wife and I are an unlikely match. She doesn't have a disability.

We had our first date in the summer of 1982. I asked her to an Elvis Costello concert. To me, she was irresistibly attractive—smart and easy to talk to. She thought I was gentle, funny, and good company. Before our date, I worked out a spiel—a good-natured, but frank explanation of what exactly I could and could not do. I tried to imagine the kinds of things that might be on her mind. I have weak muscles, that's all, I said. I have full sensation from head to toe, since I'm not technically paralyzed. And I'm not delicate, so don't worry about hurting me.

When news of our relationship broke, my family was pleased. Her mother, however, expressed concern. I felt hurt but not surprised. My mother-in-law and I are friends now, yet other people have a hard time accepting our couplehood. People say I must be rich, or my wife must be an incorrigible do-gooder. Strangers ask in disbelief if we're related. They assume we're brother and sister, or that she's my nurse. We get better reactions when she rides on my lap in my wheelchair.

At home, we keep our wedding portrait prominently displayed. That way, visitors don't assume I became disabled after the marriage, and she's only staying with me out of loyalty. When my wife was pregnant with our second daughter, one nurse saw me and abruptly pulled her aside. She wanted to know if the baby was really mine. I don't know which of us was more insulted.

This prejudice about disabled people is deeply ingrained in our society. So deeply ingrained that federal disability benefits programs have rules punishing, even disqualifying, recipients who get married. My wife and I have spent practically every moment together since we first shared an apartment. Perhaps facing obstacles like these have strengthened our resolve, our commitment to each other; and perhaps that is the most romantic ideal of all.

An Intimate Take on Love in an Interabled Relationship

I had hit on a theme that was picked up by an online program called Now This. *This time, my tone is more conversational. But it makes clear that, more and more, I was telling the story of my romance as a launching point for a larger political message.*

Our society is pretty accepting now of interracial, interfaith, same-gender couples—all kinds of situations. But somehow interabled romance seems like it's still a bit "out there" for people.

I was born with a congenital neuromuscular delight called spinal muscular atrophy, but I was fortunate that I grew up in a situation where I had a pretty normal life and normal expectations. So, when I was in college, like a lot of kids in college, I thought a lot about sex. The girlfriend that stuck around, now my wife, who is not disabled, had no experience with disabled people before me.

We never thought about that difference. It was just us, and we'd work things out. But early on, people would say, "Oh, he must be rich! Why else would she be with him?" Strangers assume that she's my nurse, my sister, my mother. People tell her she's a saint for being with me. They tell me, "You're so lucky to have anyone."

Everyone, every couple, sacrifices a little bit and puts up with things in the other person. But as soon as a wheelchair or other disability enters the equation, people assume it's a major deficit and the other party is heroic. Just look at celebrity interabled couples such as Michael J. Fox and Tracy Pollan or ex-Congresswoman Gabby Giffords and her husband, the astronaut (and now senator) Mark Kelly. The headlines talk about them as noble and unusual, possessing a "special kind of love," you know?

It does no good if disability is looked down on or looked up to and put on a pedestal. Either way, it's still separate and different.

It's especially hard, I think, for newly disabled people, if they have this sense that they're going to be locked out, going to be unwelcome in all that society has to offer. Equal access is not just about ramps and doorways. It's also access to social life, including love and sex and marriage.

I think maybe sometimes people fear disability the way they fear aging. Of course, there's more disability among the older population, naturally. And I think sometimes couples like my wife and myself and like other couples I've interviewed have already faced some of those things that people fear, things that most people age into. But we face them earlier. And those relationships that survive know that they can get past the things that people fear and, in a funny way, the experience can draw them closer. There's a shared intimacy that many interabled couples enjoy that other couples would really envy if they understood it. There are fewer pretenses. You know the other person's vulnerabilities early on. And once you learn not to be afraid of those vulnerabilities and to trust each other, you can actually emerge a stronger couple than you might have been without the disability.

Valentine's Is Coming. Rethink Your Assumptions About the Disabled and Romance

Sometimes loving the person you love is a political act in itself. Or so I argued in the pages of The Washington Post.

To you, it may be all about chocolates vs. flowers. But to me, Valentine's Day raises questions about our society's shared notions of the ideal romantic hookup.

Romeo and Juliet? Mr. Darcy and Elizabeth Bennet? More modern readers might offer Christian Grey and Anastasia Steele.

Worthy examples, all. Yet what do these fantasies tell us about our assumptions? Besides being white, cisgender, and heteronormative, every one of these fictional lovers is nondisabled.

I take exception to this stereotype. My disability has prevented me from being able to do many things—most recently, from using my hands. But it's never stopped me from thinking, feeling, having opinions, having sex, or marrying and raising a family.

For twenty-eight years, I've been married to a nondisabled woman. Together we have two college-aged kids. Does that surprise you? Why? Love, caring, and commitment often flourish regardless of superficial differences.

Perhaps ours is an unusual pairing, but we are far from the only interabled couple I know. Still, many outsiders treat us with a certain disbelief. In public, we frequently encounter oddly distressing reactions. At best, strangers assume we're not together—as in the helpful person who holds the elevator door for me and tells my wife to go on ahead. "Thank you, but we're together," one of us usually says. (Even then, some do-gooders feel moved to praise us as inspiring! Nice, I suppose, but is it really appropriate?)

At worst are those who assume she's my nurse—who ask her what my name is, or whether I need the bathroom. "Your husband?" they say in disbelief when my wife sets them straight. One time, some dolt went so far as to question whether I was really the father of our children.

Many folks, I concede, aren't used to seeing couples like us. We don't exactly fit the common image of conjugality. What I don't get, though, is why in this day and age—when our society has embraced interracial, same-sex, and other varieties of wedlock—is it so hard for people to understand our brand of love? Why do so many still resist the idea that ours is a normal relationship, not a superhuman phenomenon? Does interabled romance really represent a kind of final amatory frontier?

It shouldn't. It is not a new concept. What are *Beauty and the Beast*, *The Phantom of the Opera*, or *The Hunchback of Notre-Dame* but stories of longing between the physically disenfranchised and the physically fit?

Of course, most of those tales didn't end so well, from a disability perspective. Unrequited yearning was the narrative norm for romantically inclined people with disabilities. Even the Beast had to lose his beastliness before he and Beauty could live happily ever after—that is, he had to become cisgender, heterosexual, nondisabled, and good-looking.

Granted, there have been exceptions. For example, the 1946 film *The Best Years of Our Lives* upended the genre. In it, Harold Russell portrays a veteran who lost both of his hands during World War II. His nondisabled sweetheart convinces him that he doesn't have to live a life of lonely self-pity, and they live happily ever after. (Russell, who lost his hands in an accident while serving in the army, won an Academy Award for the role.)

But the underlying theme of emotional rescue still paints disability as a problem to solve, rather than a common trait or fact of life. We see the trope in such recent movies as *Me Before You* and the putatively true *Breathe*. This sort of cliche is so prevalent that author Kenny Fries has proposed the "Fries test" to assess disability portrayals in the media. Inspired by the Bechdel test, which first appeared in 1985 and evaluates cinematic depictions of women, the Fries test asks: Do the disabled characters have their own narrative purpose other than the education and profit of a nondisabled character? Is the character's disability not eradicated either by curing or killing?

The unfair characterizations are so pervasive that one recently engaged partner in an interabled relationship complained to me, "I've searched libraries and databases, and I can find no examples to help convince my parents that this is okay!"

People with disabilities and their intimate partners simply want to be accepted, not sanctified or pitied. Some will even tell you they enjoy a deeper degree of intimacy than you could ever imagine. If so, it likely comes from a kind of interdependency, a heightened sense of give-and-take.

So, on Valentine's Day—as at any other time—don't write us off. Reconsider your romantic assumptions. I'm sure that, by celebrating love in all its shapes and variations, you'll see there's more to it than you ever imagined.

"Opinion: Valentine's Is Coming. Rethink Your Assumptions About the Disabled and Romance" by Ben Mattlin was first published in The Washington Post on February 13, 2018.

An Activist Is Born

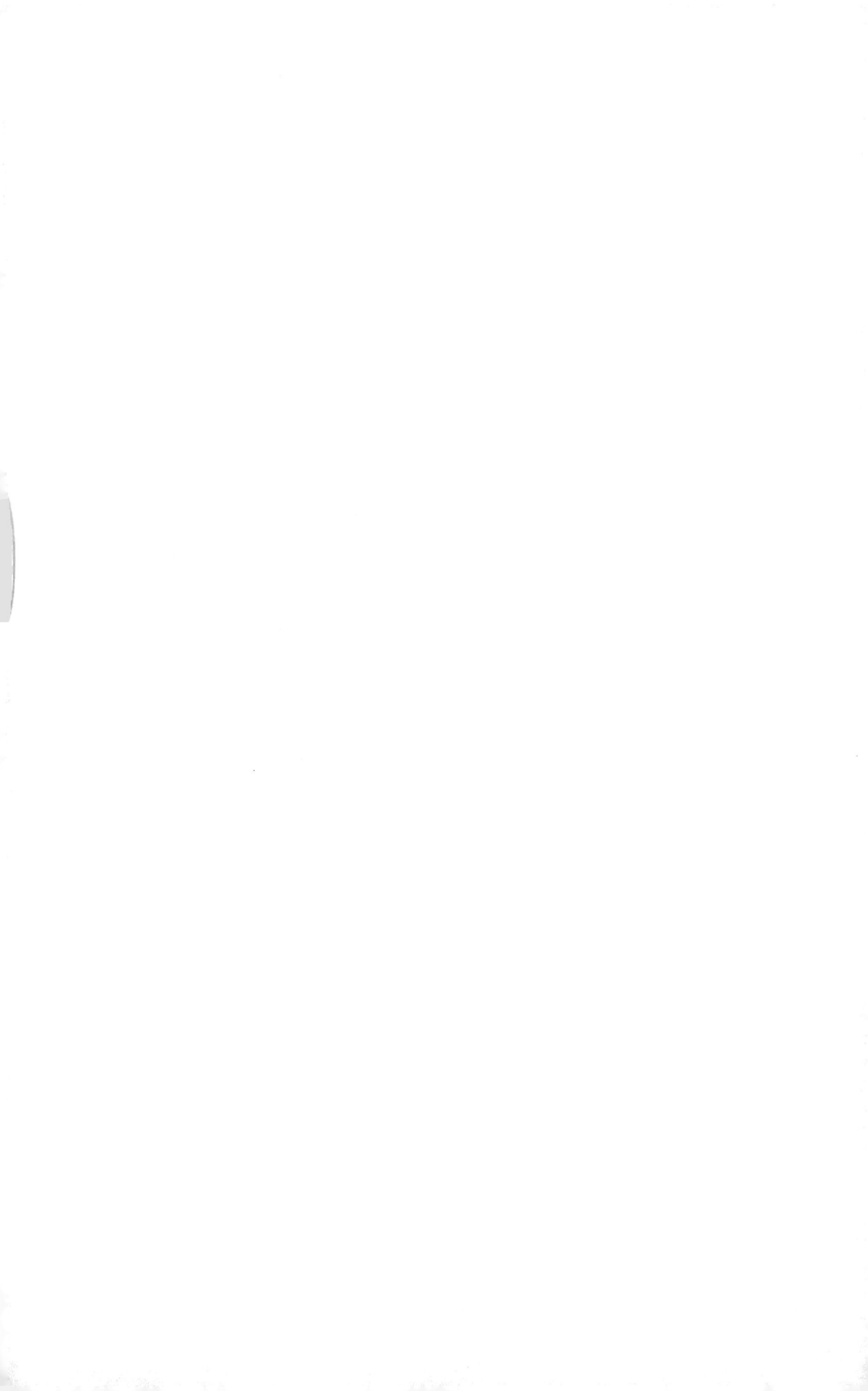

Disability Etiquette

HOW THE DISABLED WANT TO BE TREATED—WITH DIGNITY, WITHOUT GUILT

Before ML and I moved west, I had looked for work in New York, my hometown. I had decided to apply for jobs that could use my writing skills. But entry-level openings at newspapers, magazines, and book publishers didn't really call for much writing. I could read manuscripts and proofread, but I wasn't sure about the other, more hands-on clerical-type tasks that employers were looking for. I recall one magazine editor who told me to get experience elsewhere, outside of New York, before trying to ply my trade in the nation's publishing capital.

That was all the nudging I needed. ML's family lived outside L.A., and I was eager to move away from snowy climes anyway.

In L.A., I still didn't find steady work, but I did land a few freelance assignments for business-to-business magazines. Thus encouraged, I kept writing. But as mentioned before, I couldn't shake the feeling that I was being discriminated against by potential employers.

In retrospect, that's why I gradually became more involved in disability rights.

In the years after the Americans with Disabilities Act (ADA) passed, I read a survey that said most Americans still felt uncomfortable around disabled people. I proposed an article that essentially tried to explain how nondisabled people ought to behave around folks like me and my new friends in the movement. It was a simple, if not simplistic, approach for resolving differences. SELF *magazine bought the idea.*

I felt I had to keep it pretty upbeat and straightforward. But this essay shows my early awareness of some issues facing disabled people and society's misperceptions of us.

Say it's raining and you notice a blind woman at the corner who's struggling to balance her umbrella, briefcase, purse, and guide dog. Do you:

1. Ignore her, go on about your business, and allow her to preserve her independence?
2. Grab hold and steady her across the street?
3. Stare silently until she demands help or spills important documents all over the corner?
4. Ask her if she needs help?

The answer: 4. Even though current wisdom says that people with disabilities are supposed to ask for help when they need it, if you see *anyone* struggling, disabled or not, you should surely ask if they need help.

Forty-three million Americans have some kind of physical or mental disability, according to the U.S. Congress. That's one in six of the whole population. (Now the numbers are more like seventy million and one in four.) In 1990, to promote a more open, accessible society for all citizens, Congress passed the Americans with Disabilities Act. This legislation, for example, requires employers to accommodate the special needs of the disabled.

So we'll all be together, more than ever. Below are simple guidelines for handling this new world, from the authorities and from somebody who's used to covering a lot of ground in a wheelchair.

The guidelines reflect a fresh way of thinking about the disabled. Says Carol J. Gill, PhD, president of the Chicago Institute of Disability Research and herself a wheelchair user as a result of childhood polio, "Society is beginning to look at us as a bonus—an elaboration of the human landscape."

- Bear in mind that people with disabilities are not all that different from you. Disability is normal. It happens all the time—temporarily, as after a skiing accident, or permanently, from any number of causes, including old age.
- Treat us as individuals. When meeting new people, I would prefer them not to stereotype me or assume that because I am in a wheelchair I am somehow like other wheelchair users they may have known.
- Before you get into the subject of a person's disability, ask permission first. "Show that you're aware you're breaching a boundary," recommends Dr. Gill. Before asking, you might wait a few minutes until

you know each other better. It's not just a *wheelchair* across the aisle from you but a *person* who happens to use this personal vehicle to get around, much the way you use a car. More than two questions in a single conversation may seem invasive. Be prepared to hear, "Okay! Enough about my disability!"

- Use nonjudgmental language. It's fair-minded, not just "politically correct," to use words that are value neutral. We'd rather be called "people with disabilities" or "disabled people" than "the handicapped," which today carries some negative connotations. An acceptable alternative: "the disabled." I don't think of myself as "wheelchair bound"; I am a wheelchair user. Those who are blind, Deaf, or hard of hearing don't mind being referred to as such. And don't use a disability as an insult, such as calling somebody "blind" or "deaf" when you really mean oblivious or stubborn.
- Don't be overprotective or artificially kind. People with disabilities are not made of fine china. Allow us what disability activists call "the dignity of risk." The benefits of independence outweigh the hazards.
- Choose to help, or not to help, without guilt. If a disabled person asks you for assistance, don't feel you have to say yes. Our needs don't necessarily trump yours.
- Always ask before you help. Never just grab hold and pull—you may knock somebody off balance! A disabled person should not be touched any more or less than anyone else—and that includes not petting or distracting service dogs.
- Let the disabled person direct your efforts. A general "Need help?" is better than "Can I hold your purse?" When guiding a blind person, for example, let her rest a hand on you. "I can tell everything I need from that," says Cherrie Pomerantz, a project specialist with National Medical Enterprises in Santa Monica, California, who is blind and who recruits qualified people with disabilities for the company's Overcoming Challenges program. Pomerantz adds: "But don't get angry if I want to be independent!" Gill agrees. "Recognize us as capable authorities on our disabilities," she says.
- Include us. People with disabilities appreciate hugs, handshakes, and kisses as much as anyone. But often it's hard to initiate contact when you're in a wheelchair and everyone else is standing. Remember: We do not mean to seem aloof.

My wife, who is not disabled, is occasionally told (by people who don't know me) that she's a saint for marrying a man who's such a burden. Her response: "He's no more of a burden than any other husband! Maybe less. He always carries the groceries home on the back of his chair, sometimes carries me on his lap, and never leaves the toilet seat up!"

An Act That Enabled Acceptance

A few years later, shortly before the twenty-fifth anniversary of the ADA, I asked my new, occasional editor at The New York Times *if the paper of record was planning to run anything to commemorate the milestone. It wasn't. I saw an opportunity.*

No matter how much I may have preferred to focus on the humorous, interpersonal aspects of living with a disability in a nondisabled world, I ultimately could not avoid zeroing in on a number of profound and far-reaching disability rights issues. It was as if, by this point, I knew too much. I understood more clearly. Plus I was getting more and more angry about a certain lack of progress. I did, however, use the example of my love life to make my larger point. And I think my eternal optimism showed through, whether I meant it to or not. I guess it's true what they say: the personal is political.

You might notice, too, how the portrayal of my college experience seems much darker in this piece than in the earlier ones—another sign of my growing awareness of and irritation with injustices I'd faced.

Visit me and you'll see, prominently displayed in my living room, my wedding portrait. My wife looks radiant in a lacy white cloud, standing beside tuxedoed me in my motorized wheelchair. I'm not propped on a sofa or lounger; my wheelchair is deliberately not cropped out of the photo. It's literally part of the picture, as it's always been for us.

We were married almost exactly one year before passage of the Americans with Disabilities Act (ADA). But on our wedding day, my disability—and my concomitant lack of basic civil-rights protections—was far from our minds.

Of course, the ADA had nothing to do with marriage equality. What it did do, the government noted, was mandate equal access in employment, public accommodations, and government programs for anyone who "has a physical or mental impairment that substantially limits one or more major life activities" or "a history or record of such an impairment" or "is perceived by others as having such an impairment." This meant public spaces like stores, theaters, and restaurants had to install ramps or electric lifts; many doorways had to be widened; elevators revamped with Braille buttons; and public restrooms altered. Employers, too, had to make "reasonable accommodations" for disabled workers, such as allowing flex time or providing telephone headsets or appropriate computer software.

Before the ADA, only public schools and other institutions that received federal funding faced similar requirements. A few states—notably, California—had already established some accessibility standards, but nothing as broad-based as the ADA.

Back then, I was only marginally aware that I could be—or even had been—discriminated against. I tended to minimize my disability and its impact on others. My wife and I were probably more concerned about the fact that I was a New York urbanite and she a suburban Californian. We met on summer break from college, talking endlessly during long warm-evening strolls, trying to keep pace with each other though we moved by different means. Our many differences, I think now, were part of the attraction. To me, her West Coast free-spiritedness was exotic; to her, my determination must have seemed like a force of nature. Also, she told me later, seeing the no-nonsense way my family assisted me at home helped demystify my limitations and needs. The novelty of our relationship felt like an asset, not a liability.

Certainly, the longevity of our union also owes a great debt to honest communication and creative problem solving. The wedding photo is a good example. We put it up only after we grew tired of deliverymen and repairmen and housecleaners asking if she was my sister or my nurse. Some have praised her for staying with me. It makes us want to scream: "No! The disability didn't come as a tragic surprise. It was there from day one, a strand in the very fabric of our lives together."

The picture also comes in handy if my wife isn't home and some clueless visitor addresses my attendant instead of me, discounting my presence. I'll try to draw attention to the photo, as a way of saying, "Hey, I live here, and I have a life beyond these wheels."

When I was in grade school, my parents fought to get me "mainstreamed" into regular classrooms rather than segregated in special education. (Full inclusion, as it's now known, didn't become law until I was in eighth grade.) When I started college, despite new accessibility regulations, I painfully recall that one dean quashed my request for roommates instead of the isolation of separate dorm accommodations. He said he feared how my disability might affect *them*. Forget about how this sequestration affected *me*.

More shocking still is how easily I accepted his judgment. Accommodating the disabled did seem like an impossible imposition then. Indeed, when the ADA passed, one of the biggest fears was what it would cost businesses, even though the law plainly states that accommodations can't cause "undue hardship" for other patrons or employees or the employer's bottom line. (The Department of Labor found that modifications for workers with disabilities averaged only $500 each.) Moreover, businesses that make accessibility modifications can receive tax benefits—a deduction of up to $15,000 a year for removing barriers, as well as a tax credit of up to $5,000 annually for small businesses.

People with disabilities also represent a huge potential market. The United States Census counts nearly one in five Americans as disabled, and we spend $17.3 billion a year on travel alone, according to the Open Doors Organization, a Chicago-based nonprofit.

Looking back, perhaps the most unexpected achievement of the ADA isn't the wheelchair lifts on buses or the sign-language interpreters at political conventions. It's that it gave people like me a sense of entitlement, of belonging, of pride.

The ADA is about more than physical accessibility; it's about dispelling stereotypes, ensuring parity and fairness, creating opportunities, and opening up our society to the full spectrum of types and needs. It's about accepting, even welcoming, a huge and often marginalized segment of the population.

Our two teenage kids, both able-bodied, have grown up in a different world. Recently, one came home from their high school's Diversity Day incensed by a presentation about disabilities. "It was all about being kind to people who face difficulties, which is fine," she said, "but there was nothing about respect or empowerment or equality!"

Maybe I'll bring my wedding portrait to the next Diversity Day. Whether we knew it or not at the time, our brand of mixed marriage sends a powerful message.

Living Beyond Challenges

By this point, my writing was starting to attract some attention. The following podcast interview was with a journalist named Jim Harold, who had made a career covering unusual phenomena such as UFO sightings. I believe he invited me onto his program because he was looking for "inspiring" stories, not because he thought I was an extraterrestrial. I accepted because I was looking to build what publishers call my "platform."

In this conversation, I laid out my connection to the disability rights movement up to that point. The conversation has been condensed and edited for clarity.

Jim: How and when did you become first cognizant of and involved in the disability rights movement?

Ben: When I was in college, I read about the movement that was starting up in the early '80s. But it was really afterward that I found out more. I moved to Los Angeles, for a change of weather mostly, and I looked for jobs. I would get assignments to write articles for magazines, but nobody would hire me to actually work on staff. I began to realize there *is* prejudice out there. You like my work but don't want me around?

I read more and more about this disability rights movement and the effort to get the ADA passed. And I thought, *Wow, I'm not the only one*. There are a lot of folks out there like me who don't identify with the only public image I had of people with disabilities, which was sort of [from] the Jerry Lewis telethon. You know, the pitiful, maybe inspirational, Tiny Tim sort of thing. I knew that wasn't me. I didn't think of myself as a patient or a medical tragedy or a medical miracle or any of that stuff. I'm just a regular guy. And these disability rights activists, that's what they're saying. We're regular people, and we're facing these obstacles that are unfair and unnecessary.

So I got involved—writing letters and submitting op-eds to the newspapers and reading some of these people who were pretty amazing, some more severely disabled than I am and yet very strong and empowered and righteous. You know? They helped me sort out a lot of my feelings, my kind of mixed feelings. I mean, on the one hand, I was this pretty fortunate kid with high expectations for a career. On the other hand, I had this severe disability and faced these obstacles, and it seemed kinda hopeless at times. Which was it? The disability rights leaders showed me another way. I could be both. I *was* both. You know, they are not mutually exclusive. You can have a disability and still be smart and educated and live a regular life.

So that's why I say [the movement] saved my sanity. I mean, the ADA passed, which was miraculous, but it didn't get me a job. It didn't make me rich and successful. But it helped me realize that I was not alone. It gave me a framework for coping with what I'd been struggling with.

Jim: Many times when people talk about some of the movements of the past forty years, they talk about the Civil Rights Movement, the women's liberation movement, [and] currently there's a lot of talk about the gay rights movement. However, people seem to leave out the disability rights movement. I would argue it's just as important as any of those.

Ben: Yes, I agree. Absolutely. Obviously, it was inspired by the Civil Rights Movement. We've come a long way. But there's still a long way to go. And unlike other groups, it's the only minority that anybody can join at any time. You know, you have an accident and you—I mean, there are temporary disabilities. You can break a leg and you have crutches, and you're temporarily a member of our minority group. Or permanently. Disability is obviously more common among older folks. But there are all kinds—all ethnic backgrounds and everything else. We are an equal opportunity minority.

Jim: You're right—that is so poignant and so well said. It's equal opportunity. You never know when you're going to join that minority. I think that really puts a pretty strong point on it.

But I do want to ask about this, because you kind of mentioned it before. Sometimes in doing this show I have to look at my own thought process, and sometimes—as a currently nondisabled person—I have to think, am I guilty of these things, these prejudices, in some way? One of the things that would seem to be most annoying to me is this idea of the different, the *other*. That if you're disabled, you're different—other than the disability. You're different in some other way. What I get from what you're saying and from other people I talk to is, Look . . . I'm disabled, [and] I can be smart. I can be not so smart sometimes. I can be a nice guy. I can be a jerk. I can be brilliant. I can be whatever. Anything anybody else can be. I just happen to be disabled. Is that kind of the right direction?

Ben: I think that's right, sure. I mean, I've always thought a disability like mine—I'm in a wheelchair, a pretty high-tech motorized wheelchair. I have a bit of a spinal curvature. My arms are thin because I don't have muscles—people may see me on the street, and that's what they see. They see DISABILITY, in all caps. But that's just one aspect of who I am.

There are people with less visible and even invisible disabilities, who may have a different experience of it. But I guess for me it's always been important to make the point that it's only part of the package. Sometimes a more important part, and sometimes completely unimportant. You know? It informs who I am because I've always had this disability, and it's affected my experiences in life. So I don't mean to minimize it or say it's nothing. Because it *is* something, and I'm proud of it. In a way, it's certainly taught me things that are important to who I am. But it doesn't define me.

Jim: I know you were born in the early 1960s. Explain a little about what the prognosis was for you at that particular time.

Ben: When I was born, I'm not even sure the diagnosis existed. I had amyotonia, which meant "lack of muscle development." But the cause was not clear.

I was about three or four when I had a muscle biopsy and, by and by, I think I was about six when I finally got my diagnosis, which now is [better] understood. I mean, there are genetic markers, and there is an explanation which is more scientific than I can deal with about protein deficiencies and so forth. But it's a pretty broad, umbrella term, really. Some show signs at a very young age, and they don't live very long at all [though that's started to change, thanks to new treatments]. I was sort of on the cusp and, at the time, it was thought that I would not survive. There are also adult-onset forms and various others.

When I was a child, it was thought to be very rare. It was pretty much unknown. It is true, though, that it is the number one genetic cause of childhood mortality. About half the babies diagnosed with it die before age two. [Neither of these is true today.]

In my case, mine plateaued—as the doctors say—when I was about six. It basically slowed. I was able to crawl a bit as a baby and, after age six, well, it didn't stop exactly. I've had more weakness in the last ten or twenty years. But [the rate of progression, or muscle degradation,] slowed down considerably. And one never knows what to expect, frankly. I could still lose functioning from here, at a gradual pace. That's the story.

Jim: In terms of your parents, obviously they went out seeking an answer and eventually, as you said, found what was going on. How did they react? Was their reaction to try to empower you and try to maybe go a little further, an extra step, than other families at that time? How did they explain it as you grew older, [in terms of] how *you* should react to it?

Ben: It's obviously very difficult for parents facing this situation. And in those days, there were no support groups. There was no disability rights movement. There were no rights. So it was a particularly rough time.

I'm fortunate that my parents had the emotional and financial resources to cope pretty well. They felt—and I guess imbued in me the feeling—that I was entitled to everything life had to offer, that I shouldn't be denied any opportunity that, say, my older brother, who is not disabled, had.

Nevertheless, schools would not accept me. They didn't have to in those days. My parents fought and fought to get me into regular schools, as opposed to a separate, segregated special-ed institution, which was the norm in those days. So I didn't go to the same schools as my brother because [the schools] wouldn't take me. But [my parents] found schools that would take me. They wanted me to be socialized with other kids.

My parents were different. My dad was and still is at eighty-five years old more focused on solutions, I think, on trying to solve things. He would consult various experts of all sorts. There were some crazy ideas. There was one doctor somewhere in Europe—I forget where—who had some theory that a blood transfusion with animals would help cure me. We didn't go that route.

My mother was more, well, with her it was more of a psychological thing. I had to learn to speak up for myself, assert myself, take responsibility for my life, not feel sorry for myself. You know, not sit there and, as she would say, "Don't curse the darkness when you can light a candle."

Both were helpful to me, I think. There was an attitude component—you have to learn to cope and make the best of things. And there was a practical side, where you need to find solutions for things and not give up. I think this served me well in many ways.

On the other hand, as I got older, I found there were obstacles that were real, and I couldn't bring them down. Obstacles to employment, for instance. That's when I began to realize that society is not fair, and I became involved in disability rights.

Jim: I want to talk to you about the experience of going to school and particularly getting into and graduating from an Ivy League college, [which] is a major accomplishment for anyone, and you had—let's face it—an extra challenge dealing with your disability.

Ben: I prefer to say that it wasn't so much the challenges of my disability but the challenges of the school's unfairness toward my disability, if I can make that distinction. The administration was trying, which was one reason I went there.... Some schools I remember contacting were unsure about how they were going to comply with the law and were sort of discouraging. Others bent over backward to show that they were in compliance [with the new access laws]. Amherst College accepted me into the freshman class before I'd even applied. I guess it was affirmative action.

Jim: One thing that I would think would be particularly frustrating in your situation, and you're obviously a brilliant, brilliant man—

Ben: I don't know about that.

Jim: Well, I'll say it. You're obviously brilliant. And sometimes perhaps, I'm guessing this has happened, somebody sees you in a wheelchair and they don't address you. Maybe they address another person, your companion, if somebody is with you—

Ben: Absolutely. All the time.

Jim: Or maybe treating you as though you're their intellectual equal when in fact you could run intellectual circles around them. Some of those things, I'm guessing. I'm sure that's been a source of frustration from time to time.

Ben: Oh, it happens all the time! It's as simple as the waiter in the restaurant who turns to my wife and says, "What will he have?" Or not at all—to be completely ignored. Yeah, I've had that happen. They take my wife's order, my friend's order, whatever, and walk away. "Hey, you forgot about me!"

There are even doctors who won't look at me or listen to me. If I'm with my wife, she often has to say, "Ask *him*. Talk to *him*. Don't ask *me* what he wants or what he feels." I mean, that happens all the time. You get used to it, and in a way you don't. It's irritating. And [there are] people who can't believe that I, you know, have children or that I went to a good college. All that stuff.

Jim: I'll ask one more question on this, and then I want to go to the positive. Because there is so much that is positive about your story and what you've been able to do. Why do you think people have those prejudices? Is it fear? Is it just not understanding? Is it lack of exposure, although you would think that doctors would be exposed to people with disabilities on a regular basis?

Ben: Sometimes I think doctors are the worst. To them, someone like me represents a failure of the medical profession, in a way. They can't fix me. They can't cure me. And they know I'm complicated, and they don't want to deal with it. At least with some doctors I get that feeling.

But as you learn about disability history, some of these not-so-good images go way back in our culture. We don't realize it, till we think about it. Whether it's the monsters with deformities, the limping, creeping ghoul with the facial deformity or the hook hand—all these things that we associate with villainy. The deformed body equals the deformed soul, which later switched to a somewhat kinder "we shouldn't hate and fear these people. We should feel sorry for them. We should help them." The telethons. The pity approach. "Poor things. We need to be merciful and kind."

It's really only the disability rights movement that brought this idea of respect and equality. You know, if the person is on a pedestal, [seen] as a saint or an object of pity or an object of fear, that's not someone you're going to hire for a job or someone you're going to want to marry or have in the family. The disability rights movement was, and is, in my mind, about equality.

As I said, there has been progress. You can see it on TV. There are characters with disabilities in major roles or in movies. But, you know, it could go further. We could be—as we were saying before—appreciated as fuller beings, just like anybody else. Not just the kid in the wheelchair with a sarcastic attitude or whatever, but just a regular person. In the mix. In the mix of Black, white, yellow, green, gay, straight, whatever. Just part of the landscape.

Jim: One thing that I'm very interested about is where you feel there's been the most progress, and what gives you cause for hope going forward. Because, Lord knows, there are a lot of things that one could point out that are still unfair, and hopefully those will get better. But where have things improved over the last few decades in your experience? Where do you see the most progress?

Ben: There's so much. Partly, it's medical and technological, both of which have enabled people with disabilities to live longer and to get out in the world. To do more things. That helps. People see people in wheelchairs or [who are] blind, Deaf, or whatever in the shopping malls and movie theaters. That helps, I think. And certainly the attitude has changed. When I started writing about my disability experiences twenty years ago, people were not always ready to hear the message. I had a lot of explaining to do that I don't have to do now. It's sort of understood that there are people out there, that there is this movement and it's the right thing. There are still a lot of questions, and misperceptions, but the attitude is I think more open and accepting. There are better depictions in the media than there used to be. There are more prominent people with disabilities employed and working in public view. So yes, there is progress in all those ways. But I'm not sure I'm answering your question right.

Jim: No, you've answered. I think you've certainly answered it. . . . I want to talk a little about what you're doing today. Tell us a little about your work, what you're up to today, and what excites you about that work.

Ben: Mostly I've been a financial journalist lately, which I've come to enjoy, for a variety of magazines and websites. Which really has nothing to do with disability per se, although sometimes there's an overlap. There are, for instance, a lot of financial planning issues around long-term care, caring for the elderly, caring for children with disabilities.

People keep telling me, "You should write a book about your life." And I think, "Nah. Who am I? I'm just a regular guy." But as I've gotten older and kind of reflected back and gotten some perspective, [I've realized that] I have seen a lot of changes that directly benefited me. Things that have helped people with disabilities. So maybe there is a story to tell—partly about my personal development and things I've faced, but also about the broader landscape for Americans with disabilities. I like to think that people who read it will laugh and cry and be entertained and learn something at the same time.

That's kind of my message, the thing that gets me most excited: it's spreading this vision I have about disability equality, about life with disabilities being not just a bunch of complaints and medical or technological needs, or even not just political activism, but as an aspect of human life that's interesting in its own right, with its own history and roots. That's a message that may be worthwhile for everybody to read, because, as we said, anybody can become disabled. There are valuable lessons here that have universal appeal.

I Almost Couldn't Help Becoming an Advocate

By this point, it's pretty clear that I had become intrigued by, or infatuated with, the disability rights movement. But what it meant to me shifted over time.

I wrote a short essay about my ever-changing involvement for SMA News Today.

The disability rights movement in the U.S. is known for many achievements —the Individuals with Disabilities Education Act of 1975, blocking buses to demand accessible transit in 1978, the Rehabilitation Act of 1973 (which wasn't fully enacted until 1980), the Capitol Crawl [a March 1990 protest in Washington, D.C., where roughly sixty activists famously left their wheelchairs and crutches to climb the Capitol steps to demand Congress pass the Americans with Disabilities Act (ADA)].

But the crowning accomplishment to date is the Americans with Disabilities Act itself. Passed thirty-one years ago, the ADA outlawed discrimination against disabled people. In theory, at least.

But just because we have rights on the books doesn't mean they are always honored or enforced. It doesn't mean fairness is assured. It doesn't mean we have justice.

I was reluctant to come to the cause. Activists always seemed so angry, and I wanted nothing more than to get along with people. Yet as a lifelong wheelchair user, I kept coming up against obstacles and prejudices. If I wanted to go on living my life the way that felt right to me, I had a lot to combat. I almost couldn't help becoming an advocate. Besides, the rights community answered so many gnawing questions I'd been ignoring. For instance, why do some people treat me differently? Why do I have to make a special effort to get people to respect what I have to say? Why can't I get a job?

The movement gave me more than an agenda—it gave me a perspective. It taught me that the bulk of my most vexing problems came not from within but from without. In a fully accessible society, my limitations could practically be reduced to mere inconveniences.

An added benefit: Once I learned what the disability community had accomplished and continues to fight for every day, I began to feel better about myself. I felt proud to be disabled.

I want to keep moving our community to a better place. For many, enforcement of basic rights remains a dire necessity. Even life-and-death dire. I only hope I can be a good enough advocate.

Will more members of my SMA community join me? There is still so much to do. We may not always agree, but the movement needs all the voices and energies it can get.

Nothing Pitiful About It

An Open Letter to Jerry Lewis

THE DISABLED NEED DIGNITY, NOT PITY

One of the first disability causes that really resonated with me—as mentioned in the "Living Beyond Challenges" podcast—was the opposition to the pity-mongering approach of old medical-charity fundraisers. Well, one in particular.

To many activists, the Muscular Dystrophy Association's Labor Day Telethon starring Jerry Lewis was the worst offender. Every year, before a viewership that rivaled the Super Bowl's, this cavalcade of stars highlighted kids with neuromuscular disabilities like mine. They were described as "hopeless," "devastated," "diseased," and worse.

I knew this particular fundraiser well. As a child, I had taken part in the annual campaigns. For my parents, I think this charity represented their dearest hopes. It was also their only connection to other disabled kids and their families. But I never felt fully comfortable with it, and—as you'll see in the following essay, published in the Los Angeles Times *back in 1991—I quit being a poster child at the tender age of seven or eight.*

This familiarity with the enemy made me the perfect person to protest against the saccharine and omnipresent "Jerry's kids," or so my newfound activist pals insisted.

The essay I wrote at their urging became my first true act of disability advocacy. I was never one for attending protest marches, though I did demonstrate against the telethon in person once or twice in subsequent years. But if I could use my writing ability to help the cause, I was all in. I had found my niche.

The reactions to this bit of writing became further encouragement. I received phone calls of support from strangers, as well as a couple of freelance writing assignments. Not long after, however, I also received threatening notes from Muscular Dystrophy Association (MDA) supporters, who accused me of un-

dermining a worthy endeavor. I had to wrestle with my conscience a bit. Which ultimately only strengthened my resolve.

The telethon went on, and I kept writing against it—occasionally making the same arguments as in that first piece, rehashing my favorite zingers, but also trying to expand on them and answer some of the backlash I'd received and doubts I'd harbored. My second piece about it, sixteen years after the first, became my debut in The Washington Post.

I'm proud to say that my side won. Or so I thought. The Jerry Lewis Labor Day Telethon officially ended in 2015. But then, like a villain in a movie, it briefly rose up again in 2020, in a new guise. A new generation of activists asked me to respond. How could I refuse? This had become my personal cause, and no one knew it better than I did.

Dear Jerry Lewis:

I was born with a muscular-dystrophy-related disease, and your Labor Day telethons have always turned my stomach. I actually appeared on one in the late 1960s, as the Muscular Dystrophy Association poster child for the New York metropolitan area.

Now I am twenty-eight, a college graduate, a self-employed writer, married, still in a wheelchair. I can finally formulate what I felt as a child: Despite your undoubtedly honorable intentions, you are sadly misinformed about disabilities. Moreover, you are misleading the nondisabled population while offending the rest of us.

You and your organization have done much good, to be sure, and I myself have benefited from your financial resources. But people with disabilities do not need or want to be characterized as objects of pity. Last year's Americans with Disabilities Act mandates our equal participation in society, including employment. What we need is to stress competence—not outmoded notions of charity.

Speaking of "the dystrophic child's plight" or calling disability a "curse" reinforces the offensive stereotype that we are victims. Wheelchairs are not "steel imprisonment," nor are we who use them "confined" or "bound"; they are liberating aluminum and vinyl vehicles. Similarly, phrases like "dealt a bad hand" and "got in the wrong line" are unfair. Disability is not "bad" or "wrong."

Other examples abound: Being dressed or fed by others is a hassle, but not an "indignity." There is no shame in needing others, no loss of dignity. Our needs are more personal and continuing than other people's—nothing to be ashamed of.

Saying that they are is to say our lives are somehow inferior. Is this how you feel? You have said our lives are "half"—we must learn to "do things halfway," be good at being "half a person."

Perhaps more disturbing is your use of the archaic word *cripple*. While some of us have recently taken it on as a kind of hip slang among ourselves or for political purposes—much like the gay rights group Queer Nation—this does not mean you should.

Worse still may be your ubiquitous "Jerry's Kids"—never more absurd than when followed by "of all ages." Yes, a lot of MDA's clients (not necessarily "patients") are kids, but do you know how hard it is to become, and be treated as, a self-respecting disabled adult in this society? You may argue it is a term of affection, but you wouldn't refer to your late friend Sammy Davis Jr. as your "boy."

What's really surprising are your inaccuracies. Your tales of disabled kids being taunted by other kids, for example, do not ring true. Most nondisabled kids whom I knew growing up couldn't wait to push my chair. They would even compete to be "chief wheeler."

You further allege that wheelchairs don't fit under restaurant tables, when for years they have come with "desk armrests." And what's this about their not going through metal detectors at airports? Big deal—they're metal! They go around them and are searched separately.

At times, you seem to understand. You talk about our right to live with dignity. What that means is access to schools and jobs, equipment like computers and vans, attendants, and respect. The MDA can't be responsible for all this. But misleading people—potential employers, potential spouses, and even newly disabled people who don't know any better—only works against these goals.

I realize pity works—last year's telethon raised more money than ever before. And I know some folks think you're a saint. But I also know there were protests at last year's telethon—and will be more—asking why it has taken so long to find a cure and demanding a financial accounting.

Perhaps people would not be so upset if the association spoke less about finding a cure and did more to improve our lives as they are.

I know MDA does buy wheelchairs and such. But what does it do to make our world more accessible and to promote employment? How many people with disabilities are employed by the organization and its corporate sponsors?

Don't get me wrong. Muscular dystrophy can be a killer, and we mourn those who have died. Yet, despite the impression that one may get watching the telethon, we are not all terminal. And even if you whip MD, you will not end disability. It is here to stay; so are we.

Why not, this year, present active, well-adjusted disabled people—not superheroes but normal people—who nonetheless have used or could use financial assistance to achieve their goals of independent living?

The harm being done is considerable. A dynamic, young, educated, professional woman I know, who grew up with a disability similar to mine, says she cannot watch your telethon because it makes her want to kill herself. "Is that what people think of us?" she asks.

Your pity campaign is so dispiriting, so destructive, that no matter how many millions you raise, the ends do not justify the means. Why not wield your sizable influence to fight our real enemies? What truly handicaps us most are the obstacles—architectural, financial, and attitudinal—erected by others.

No Longer One of "Jerry's Kids"

When I was six years old, I appeared on the Jerry Lewis Labor Day Telethon for the Muscular Dystrophy Association. I don't have muscular dystrophy, but I was born with a similar progressive neuromuscular weakness.

On the broadcast, I was asked for my name and age. That's about all. Then I was dismissed.

I never met Jerry Lewis. I never became famous, as I'd dreamed. I was cute, though, with big blue eyes and unruly blond curls, and I was in several magazine and newspaper ads for MDA. For one of them, I was positioned standing in leg braces—which I'd used years earlier for physical therapy, before discovering the torture didn't actually do me any good—and I was told the caption over my head would be, "If I grow up, I want to be a fireman."

I didn't like this. *If?* My prognosis was a normal life expectancy. Besides, I didn't want to be a fireman! I wanted to be a scientist or a detective. So, in the photo, I'm crossing my fingers where no one can see. I decided not to do another ad.

Many years later, when I was an adult, I used this image to protest the telethon's simplistic treatment of "Jerry's Kids." I found that many others were mounting similar demonstrations. Now I find myself asking whether our message was heard. The TV hosts still ask us to "help Jerry's kids." But does the public understand that, even more than help, those of us with disabilities want respect?

Perhaps. MDA now pays lip service at least to the idea of disability rights. The telethon now shows some kids with disabilities doing active things. Yet fundamental problems remain.

Today's telethon, for example, will feature nondisabled celebrities onstage raising money for disabled kids, who are mostly offstage. I know the purpose of the telethon is to raise money, and that people won't tune in unless there are performers they want to see. Nevertheless, can you imagine an NAACP fundraiser hosted exclusively by white people?

If you are not disabled, you may think this is a relatively minor issue. But it matters. The other day my wife and I were at the theater with our two young children. During the intermission, an usher dutifully came over and asked my wife if I needed to use the restroom.

"How should I know?" she answered. "If you have a question for my husband, why don't you ask him yourself?"

The usher did not make that mistake again.

The larger issue is one of respect. And while I understand the sympathetic impulse (and marketing power) of a slogan like "Help Jerry's Kids," I don't think it helps us gain respect.

Of course, MDA may respect the disabled more than its fundraising tactics imply. If it wants to stand out as an advocate for disability rights, however, it should set a better example—and demand that its corporate contributors do as well.

When most people see those of us with severe, progressive neurological conditions, they want to help, and I am not ungrateful. The desire to cure is probably human nature. And MDA's main mission is to be a medical charity; it claims to spend seventy-seven cents of every dollar it raises on services, an admirable percentage, and finances hundreds of clinics and medical researchers.

Still, for the past thirty years, the message of the disability rights movement has been as consistent as it is simple: We're fine as we are. We don't need fixing. We need access. We need respect. We need jobs. In other words, we need the same things everybody else does.

So today, I won't be watching the telethon. My wife and I and our two kids have better things to do.

"Opinion: No Longer One of 'Jerry's Kids'" by Ben Mattlin was first published in The Washington Post *on September 3, 2007.*

Why the Return of the Muscular Dystrophy Association Telethon Is Unwelcome News

The Muscular Dystrophy Association recently announced its celebrity-studded telethon would be returning after a six-year hiatus. To many of us in the disability community, this was not welcome news.

The onetime Labor Day staple was notorious for pity-peddling and inspiration porn. The reboot, with Kevin Hart at the helm in place of the late Jerry Lewis, looks to be no better.

Granted, we can't judge the broadcast until it airs. Yet it's already clear the charity has learned nothing from its past errors. Hart, for starters, is no more appropriate a host than Lewis was. He might make a welcome ally; in fact, a portion of this year's intake will go to his Help from the Hart Charity for underserved communities. But he has never identified with the disability community, with disability rights or disability justice—other than from the charity model. He may understand disabled people as needy, which many of us are, but he hasn't established that he respects disabled people or understands that our issues are civil rights issues.

Representation matters. Of course, the show needs a big star, and there are none with the neuromuscular qualifications, at least not yet. But even the guest list is distinctly nondisabled (Eva Longoria, Michael B. Jordan, etc.). The sole exception, Jillian Mercado, the groundbreaking model and actor who has a form of muscular dystrophy, announced on Twitter that she has misgivings about participating. She wants to represent her community fairly and said, "If they have a problem with this . . . then [I'll] remove myself."

By comparison, the Cerebral Palsy Foundation always uses members of its community in fundraising. For years it held telethons emceed by Tom

Ritter (brother of the late TV star John Ritter), who has cerebral palsy, and this year's virtual event featured actor Micah Fowler, who has cerebral palsy.

Worrisome, too, is the name "MDA Kevin Hart Kids Telethon," which is blatantly reminiscent of the old "Jerry's kids" motto and smacks of the same patronizing connotations. (Speaking of offensive connotations, Hart, like Lewis, has come under fire for homophobic slurs.) "Jerry's kids" might sound cute, but infantilization of disabled people is a serious and widespread problem. It's not just waiters who ask our dinner companions, "What will he/she be having?" The attitude undercuts efforts to improve our perpetually high jobless rate, which remains at roughly twice that of those who are not disabled.

To be sure, many disabled folks need financial assistance. Living with a disability is expensive. A new motorized wheelchair can cost more than a car. Medicaid and private insurance don't fully cover personal-care help, breathing machines, or necessary medications. (Google "most expensive drug," and you'll see it's a treatment for spinal muscular atrophy, one of the neuromuscular disabilities the MDA purports to address.)

But does the MDA supply any of those things? According to its website, if you need a wheelchair it will provide "referrals to community resources." True, it subsidizes lab research and, as a possible result, people with muscular dystrophy are living longer. I myself might be an example. But maybe those scientific developments would have occurred anyway. In any case, I can't help feeling there is a better, more appropriate way to raise funds, a way without the stigmatizing humiliation.

I concede the MDA could still surprise us. It has, in recent years, largely stopped calling us "patients," instead using "clients" or "consumers," which sounds more empowering.

Nevertheless, its current ads—one says, "Kids with neuromuscular disease need your support more than ever"—are astonishingly similar to the smarmy hokum of the 1970s. That's when I quit being a poster child. I was tired of the lies; I didn't hate my disability, and I wasn't pining away for a cure. Later, I joined demonstrations against the "pity parade." The MDA's response was to criticize our efforts and try to demoralize us.

When the telethon was canceled in 2015, we thought we'd won. Evidently, we were wrong.

All we want the MDA to do is stop the condescension; stop portraying us as needy, sickly children. Stop undermining what we hope to achieve. If the

MDA truly wants to help improve our lives, it must listen to us and respect our views. Let members of our community guide its priorities and fund-raising efforts. Answer fundamental questions such as how many disabled people are on its payroll, and whether it holds corporate sponsors to any standard of accessibility.

In other words, it should put its money where its mouth is. And until that happens, until it welcomes our input and addresses our issues, we will continue protesting.

"Opinion: Why the Return of the Muscular Dystrophy Association Telethon Is Unwelcome News" by Ben Mattlin was first published in The Washington Post *on October 19, 2020.*

Publicly Disabled

Miracle Boy Grows Up

BEN MATTLIN SPEAKS TO JAY MCINERNEY

With these antitelethon essays, I began to build a new sense of myself as a disability writer. But there wasn't much money in that. Still, that first op-ed (and others that followed) encouraged me to write a book about my life, my perspective on growing up disabled, and my gradual exposure to the disability rights movement.

By the time I started my memoir, I had drafted three novels—none of which were published. The first was based on my life, but I felt I had to couch it in fiction. Since reactions to disability-related stories at that point were not exactly encouraging—one editor told me that the idea of someone living as I had and marrying a nondisabled woman, as I had, was just too unbelievable!—my next two attempts at novel writing had zero disability components. But they fell flat, too.

It felt like a bold and daring move to pen the true tale of my coming-of-age, without the gloss of fantasy.

I went through a number of partial drafts and submissions to agents. Years passed. I read popular memoirs to try to learn the craft, and I picked up tips here and there from agents and editors. Finally, in 2012, Miracle Boy Grows Up: How the Disability Rights Revolution Saved My Sanity *was published.*

It will always hold a special place in my heart.

After it came out, I promoted the hell out of it. The first interview here is from The Daily Beast. *The second is from the Disability Matters podcast, hosted by Joyce Bender, who is a disabled person herself. Both have been edited for clarity.*

Ben Mattlin grew up before laws protected people like him. He speaks to Jay McInerney about his new memoir.

Jay: I met Ben Mattlin when he attended a reading I was giving in New York some twenty-five years ago. I admit, he was easy to pick out of the crowd—occupying a wheelchair in the front row. We talked after the reading and stayed in touch. Over the years I saw Ben in New York and Los Angeles, where he currently resides, and gradually learned about his life. Ben isn't your typical guy in a wheelchair. He attended top New York City private schools and graduated from Harvard, and he is a contributor to *Institutional Investor*, the *Los Angeles Times*, and NPR. He's married and has two kids. But Ben wasn't supposed to be able to do any of these things.

Ben was born at a time before there were laws protecting his right to attend any school he wanted, or to be treated as an equal applicant for jobs, and he was fortunate to grow up during a time when the disability rights movement was gaining traction. Laws were changing all the time, ensuring equality for the disabled at work and school. Developments in voice-recognition software enabled Ben to make a living following his passion, writing. I have always hoped that Ben would write a memoir, and here it is, *Miracle Boy Grows Up*, a very honest and entertaining look at the realities of living with a serious disability.

I guess the obvious place to start is, what's your writing process? How do you write and how has that changed with technological advances?

Ben: To write this book, I started first thing every morning (well, after coffee) while I was still somewhat dreamy-headed. Parked my wheelchair in front of the laptop, which is on a table in a corner of my living room. Kids were at school, wife was at work, and my attendant kept mostly quiet. And I made myself keep writing, following my outline (I had never used an outline before!), in twenty-page chunks before going back to do revisions. It went surprisingly quickly.

The process itself involved lots of closing-of-the-eyes to focus the mind and conjure memories—as well as unexpected bouts of weeping. Some memories are more painful than others.

How do I write physically? I use voice-recognition software. I was one of the early adopters of this technology when it became feasible in the early 1990s. Before that, I slowly and painstakingly pecked out one letter at a time, sometimes using the eraser end of a pencil for leverage, and other times copying and pasting letter by letter. When I could write longhand, I did that sometimes and then paid a typist. But even in those bad old days of the 1980s—after I had begun looking for work, in vain—I knew I had to learn to "interface with a terminal with sufficient rapidity," as one would-be employer put it. So I kept up with technology. I remember going to an early demonstration of voice-recognition computing at the California State University in Northridge. The machine took up an entire room, you had to dictate extremely slowly—Word. By. Word.—and the equipment cost about $40,000. Still, I was thrilled by the possibility. I hoped but doubted I would live long enough to see voice recognition become something I could use.

To my amazed delight, in very few years there was a home version available for less than $5,000. I finagled the state vocational-rehabilitation department into splitting the cost with me. The technology was still slowish, and I had to dictate into DOS and subsequently convert documents into Windows. Yet I was ecstatic! I had been wanting to use a computer for so long! Three months later I had written a second novel, whereas my first novel—etched out manually, letter by letter—had taken five years to complete. Voice-recognition computing was simply the right tool for the job.

Now, of course, you can buy a version for about a hundred bucks. And it's faster and more accurate than ever.

Jay: What's the genesis of *Miracle Boy*? Didn't you first try an autobiographical fiction approach?

Ben: You're exactly right! I was afraid to tell my story directly, wanted to couch it in a fanciful (and imitative) yarn of sex and intrigue. That was doomed to failure for several reasons. First, I was in my twenties and didn't really have sufficient perspective on my life to tell it right. Second, it was the 1980s, and the world wasn't ready for the kind of disability story I had in mind. The Americans with Disabilities Act hadn't even passed yet. People like me just weren't on people's radar. We weren't recognized as a minority group, let alone an interesting, diverse minority group with something to say.

Also, I wasn't prepared to be honest then. Not until I was in my forties did I realize that I no longer worried if people thought I was cool. I didn't have to coat my story in a hip sheen. There was no need to pretend, to fashion myself as something other than what I was and am. I could write about and from my own perspective—write truthfully, authentically—and perhaps establish something new.

But still, I had a block. I just didn't believe my life was as interesting as people kept telling me.

It was only when I saw my life through someone else's eyes that I began to get the idea. I had hired a young man from UCLA as my part-time "PA," as we say. That's "personal assistant" or "personal-care attendant." He got me washed and dressed and in my wheelchair in the morning. To me he was a particularly impressive young man—from Africa, with a thirst to better himself and then better his nation. I was as inspired by him as he was by me.

I was no stranger to being called inspiring. Most disabled people are, and we grow tired of it. So I didn't take it personally. But what he actually said was, "How do you stay so positive?" Apparently, most men he knew were practically drowning in anger. Which got me thinking about my relationship with anger and more constructive emotions. I certainly have my moments of rage, but somehow—it was true, he was right—I invariably came around to feeling hopeful. Why?

So I began writing about where my sense of optimism came from. I wasn't at all familiar with the memoir form and had no idea what I was doing. But soon the idea filled me up. It practically grabbed me by the throat. I had to continue.

I sent out pages, got feedback. A few kindly agents gave me homework assignments—memoirs I had to read. Soon memoirs were all I read. Not celebrity memoirs, either. I wanted books that justified themselves by their literary merit. I began to gain a sense of what worked and what didn't, at least to me. I was still dead set on writing the unadorned truth, but I had to do it in a way that leveraged my strengths as a writer... and would appeal to readers.

Ultimately I had some sample chapters and an outline. But I couldn't complete the book until I had a contract. Just couldn't make that leap. It took five years to find a publisher. At that point, like a taut and twisted rubber band, I sprang into action and completed the book in about two months.

Jay: Were you inspired or influenced by other memoirs? Are you a fiction or nonfiction guy?

Ben: Well, I'm a real guy, but my taste has always run toward fiction—until I started working on this book. Then I became obsessed with memoirs, and pretty much read nothing else. At its best, a memoir blends the importance of history and the relevance of journalism with the readability—the sheer escapist enjoyment—of a good novel. (At worst, it's self-indulgent narcissistic score-settling, or just boring.)

For me, the archetype of the modern memoir has to be Frank McCourt's *Angela's Ashes*. From it I learned the importance of limning a particular setting, a sense of place. With humor and charm McCourt's masterpiece transports you, yet it also has an immediacy that I hoped to emulate as well. Only, without the brogue.

At the same time, I was moved by Mary Karr's voice, especially in *Lit*, which I think is her best. I should have had no interest in that book—what do I care about a divorced mother's battle with alcoholism and ultimate Catholic epiphany? Yet she drew me in and carried me along breathlessly. Not because of the events in her story. It was 100 percent because of her voice, her writing style. Magic! Also, it's a memoir about adults, not just childhood, which I wasn't sure was possible before reading this.

I liked the way Wilfrid Sheed's *In Love with Daylight* weaved his childhood experience with polio into a narrative about alcoholism and other challenges. It normalized the disability experience as one of the many facets of a complicated life—not the centerpiece, but not trivial either.

Jeannette Walls's *The Glass Castle* is maddening but irresistible. It contains such riveting graphic detail that you simply can't put it down. From it I think I learned that no matter how upbeat I may try to be, readers need a sense of danger, too—some feeling that things might not turn out all right after all.

Also I enjoyed Liz Murray's *Breaking Night*, which helped me learn the difference between writing everything you can remember about your past and focusing in on those events that are relevant to your theme—specifically, those events that are not the same as everybody else's, that make your particular story interesting, different, and worth publishing.

I could go on and on, but I don't want to leave out Harriet McBryde Johnson's *Too Late to Die Young*, Simi Linton's *My Body Politic*, Jean Stewart's *The Body's Memory*, and Anne Finger's *Elegy for a Disease*, among others related to disabilities. Each of these delves into the disability perspective from a savvy, self-aware viewpoint that taught me a great deal about the interchange between the political and personal.

Disability Matters

Joyce Bender: Ben, how about if we begin by telling our listeners a little bit about your experience living with a disability as a young child when your family was told that you were going to have a short life expectancy.

Ben: I was born in 1962 on Thanksgiving Day, as a matter of fact, and everything was great. But when I was about six months old, my mother noticed that I wasn't sitting myself up the way my older brother had when he was six months old. If they put me down in a sitting position, I tended to fall over. I couldn't stabilize myself.

So I was taken around to all kinds of doctors, and there were all sorts of diagnoses. Nobody really knew what was going on except that I was what they call a "floppy baby." That's still a scientific term, Floppy Baby Syndrome. It was probably five years later that I was properly diagnosed. It's now estimated something like one in every forty people is a carrier for my condition, but you have to have two carriers [to make a baby with my disability]—and even then there's a fifty-fifty shot of the child not having it. Anyway, it's rare, but not as rare as we once thought.

In about half the cases, babies who were diagnosed in infancy didn't make it past their second year. The odds are better now. Medical technology keeps improving. But in those days there was no telling how long I'd live.

My parents didn't know what to do. There wasn't really a disability rights movement. Well, it was starting off in pockets, but it wasn't well known. There wasn't much advocacy. There weren't support groups.

When I was about six, my muscle weakness kind of stabilized or slowed down dramatically, so the life expectancy was not quite as dire, I guess. But I could still catch a bad cold and not be able to cough or clear my lungs, and that could become pneumonia and that would be it. So I've lived all these years with a sense of vulnerability, which I didn't acknowledge when I was young. I thought I was Superman or something, just because I had a vivid fantasy life. Now that I'm more mature and self-aware—or try to be—I realize it's kind of amazing that I've lived to this age.

I think I'm talking too much.

Joyce: No, you're not. You're not. But tell me [more about your experiences growing up, in school]. What were some of your biggest obstacles?

Ben: We had to move across town to be near a school that was willing to take me. My first-grade teacher was working on her dissertation on this new concept called "mainstreaming handicapped kids." I have a copy of her dissertation to remind me about the things she did to make it easier for me in the classroom. For instance, one day early on she had the kids come up and touch my wheelchair so they would be less afraid of it.

Joyce: The teacher told them to do that?

Ben: Yes. One by one, each child would come up to me just to make contact and not be so afraid.

There was one child who threatened me, though, who said he was going to push my chair down the stairs. This was a different year—fifth grade, maybe. [Here's where my vivid fantasy life served me well.] My heroes were Captain Kirk and Chief Ironside, so I tried to be a tough guy. I tried not to show him I was scared. Maybe I'm not remembering accurately, but I think I said, "You're not going to push me down the stairs, because you'll get in big trouble. I can't stop you if you want to do it, but you're just trying to scare me, because you'd be stupid to do that."

Eventually he gave up, walked away, and someone came along and rescued me and got me to my next class. So there were occasional dangers, but I always tried to have a circle of friends, a "club," as we used to call it, and I was sort of in charge of it. Yes, I was bossy. My club was mostly the kids who were best at pushing my wheelchair, because I really couldn't move myself in those days. I did not have an electric-powered wheelchair like I do now.

Joyce: Ben, you know how frustrating it is for people with disabilities to gain employment, and I maintain that part of that is due to pity. That's why we say we need paychecks, not pity. Which leads me to my next question, which is the Muscular Dystrophy Association Jerry Lewis telethons. I saw that old poster of yours: "When I grow up, I want to be a fireman." So, Ben, what was that like working with the Jerry Lewis Telethon?

Ben: Forgive me, but I have to correct you. It wasn't "when I grow up," it was "*if* I grow up."

Joyce: Oh, my God. That is even worse!

Ben: Yeah, that was the kicker. That was a real pull-your-heartstrings. You've seen the poster. I was awfully cute. I was six or seven, and at first I was thrilled! I'm going to be famous! I'm going to be a star! Well, it didn't work out that way. [It was] a full-page magazine ad, just me. No Santa Claus, no other kids [as there had been in my previous poster-child appearances for MDA]. Just me. They made me stand in leg braces, which I had used for physical therapy. I hated them. I don't use them anymore, but they were supposed to be good for me. And with these leg braces, I could sort of balance. I could stand, but I wasn't really standing. I was kind of just balancing in these leg braces.

At that point my understanding was that my life expectancy was not that dire anymore. Maybe they were just kidding me because I was a kid, but in any case, my parents certainly felt it was a terrible thing to tell a child, "You're going to die soon." It was a very bad message, which I didn't believe was true, plus I didn't want to be a fireman. I mean, that was ridiculous! I knew I couldn't climb ladders and jump into burning buildings. I wanted to be like my heroes on TV. I wanted to be a policeman or a detective or a superhero or something.

No, I knew I would have to have a desk job, an intellectual job, not a physical job like a fireman. But I could not convince them to change the caption. So in the photograph, you can't tell because it's kind of behind me, in the shadows, but I am crossing my fingers.

I didn't like that they were lying about me. Afterward I told my parents, "I don't want to do this anymore," and they said, "Okay," and that was my last ad for the telethon.

Years later, I found out that I wasn't the only one that felt a bit alienated by the images that the charity used for raising money, and still uses. I joined protests and I published essays about why they've got to change. And they were unreceptive at first. I mean, I got some nasty mail about my protest activities. But on the other hand, it *has* changed. I mean, Jerry Lewis is gone, the telethon is gone, and a lot of their communications are better. They've got a long way to go still, I know, but I do think it's a lot better than it used to be.

[A small discussion ensues about pity and self-pity, which leads to questions about suicide.]

Joyce: Do you believe that people with significant disabilities face more discouragement than others?

Ben: This is a complex issue. If you've lived with a disability and you've ever been in any kind of medical setting, or maybe anywhere else for that matter, you know how people can often discount, trivialize, or minimize your life, your quality of life. The assumption that maybe you're better off dead is pretty widespread—sometimes, most shockingly, within the medical establishment. It's certainly happened to me.

I was hospitalized seven years ago with a pretty serious infection. They tell me I was near death. Fortunately, my wife was there. So when they asked her, "Is he worth saving? Should we do everything we can?" she said, "Yes." What's the term they use? "Full code," or something. She told them to take every means possible to save my life.

The only reason they asked was because of my disability. That's why they weren't sure. I mean, they didn't mean any harm, but I do think there is the sense that people, particularly medical people, presume that we're not happy with our lives and would maybe be not quite as worth saving as others.

This gets even more complicated when you get into the finances of it. Look, it's cheaper to [remove life support or] give somebody a prescription for poison than to treat them.

Joyce: You know, I've heard this from so many people that have significant disabilities—they hear, "Wow! It's amazing you're alive."

Ben: Yeah.

Joyce: That whole thought, especially when it comes from a medical professional, is terrible. It has the undertones of, "Are you sure you want to be here?"

Ben: Yes. The worst thing to me is, as people with disabilities get marginalized, not employed, it's dangerous and depressing. And, yes, you may say, you know, "Let me kill myself. It'll make things easier for myself and everybody around me." That's what scares me. Sometimes we have to be saved from ourselves, too.

I would rather we work first on making things better for people with disabilities [so we] can be a part of society, feel welcome and valued as we are, before we start talking about suicide as a solution.

Joyce: It almost reminds me of eugenics, you know?

Ben: Yes. Exactly.

Joyce: I'm going to move from all that horrible stuff to something very positive. How did the disability rights revolution save your sanity, and what made you write this book?

Ben: At first I didn't want to. I mean, I'm just a disabled person like any other. I've gotten by because what choice did I have? You have to do the best you can with what you've got, and you live your life and go on. But in my early forties I thought, looking back, maybe there's something to my story. I've seen tremendous changes for people with disabilities, medically, technologically, and, of course, in terms of disability rights. That story should be told. People don't realize (a) what it's like, and (b) how much it's changed. I tried to interweave with my biography a bit of a history of the modern disability rights movement, of which I gradually became aware. I kind of grew up with the movement. I didn't always know it was happening, but my upbringing paralleled the movement.

But after a while, I had a few issues with the movement. Basically, I wanted to get on with my life. I got married, we were talking about having children, which we now have—two—and I just had other things going on for me.

[Still, the movement was a] total change in the way people with disabilities were perceived. It didn't save my life per se, but it certainly saved my sanity. It helped me figure out where I stood—no, that's not the right word—where I was positioned, my status in society, and how to cope with the challenges that were making me very depressed, like lack of employment and inadequate access to many other things. It taught me how to cope with all these awkward, uncomfortable, and unfair situations. The disability rights movement gave me and all of us clues on how to cope, as well as a sense of pride in the history of people with disabilities. That's why I say it saved my sanity. It helped me to feel better about myself and know how to cope in the world. . . . I'm grateful for the [disability activists who came before me]. I really am.

Joyce: I know this one is going to be hard to answer. But what are you the proudest of? What would you say is your greatest accomplishment?

Ben: Surviving? The great Harriet McBryde Johnson, another role model for me, I don't have the quote in front of me, but she said something like, "I'm in the first generation to survive to such decrepitude." It's true. Someone like me probably wouldn't be alive at this age in a previous generation. I'm proud of my family, my kids, my wife, heck, my parents. I mean, I wouldn't be here without them, without their understanding and support. So I can't take all the credit.

Joyce: Ben, what message would you like to leave with our listeners today?

Ben: A diagnosis is not all we are. We have to try to remember the humanity in all of us, have empathy, understand the other person's point of view. We all have prejudices of one kind or another. I don't mean just racial hatred. I mean we observe things about people based on superficial assumptions, and as long as we're aware of that and admit that, it should become easier to be open and inclusive and respectful of the great variety and diversity of humankind. Gosh, it sounds like I'm giving a sermon or something. I am not running for president, just spouting my personal philosophy.

Are There No Wheelchairs in Heaven?

(FORMERLY, VALUING LIFE, WHETHER DISABLED OR NOT)

From the campaign against pity, it wasn't much of a stretch to argue against the idea of "better dead than disabled."

Nobody actually said that to me, as far as I recall. But there was a widely accepted sentiment that some disabled people found relief or release in death. I confronted this head-on at a memorial service for a disabled friend and colleague. It became my first accepted commentary for NPR's Morning Edition. (Content warning: This section concerns death and suicide.)

A few years ago a friend of mine died unexpectedly at thirty-nine. We both used motorized wheelchairs and needed assistance with tasks such as washing, dressing, and eating, but his disability came from a motorcycle accident fourteen years earlier. Mine is from birth. So I'm used to being quadriplegic. He wasn't. He would sometimes ask, with startling frankness, "How do you do it? How do you manage?" I never knew how to answer.

One morning, my friend's attendant found him dead. With a smile on his face, we were told at the packed memorial service. A young minister explained that he'd been, "A free spirit, trapped in an unresponsive body. Now that spirit is truly free." We were told he'd gone to a place where he could walk again. His dad added, "Walk? He's probably playing basketball in the nude."

The words stung. Mourners need to believe their loved one has gone to a better place. Yet what was the message here? Death sets you free and cures disability? Was he better off dead than disabled? I realize I'm biased. I have never ridden a motorcycle or done half the other physical things my friend used to love, but I do know one can live a pretty full life with a disability.

Indeed, some people find life after disability more intense, more deeply appreciated than it was before. My lifelong experience with disability has made me a creative problem solver and, ironically, perhaps, a diehard optimist, if only because I've had to be. It's taught me a great deal about patience, tolerance, and flexibility.

My disability is part of who I am. Why couldn't my friend's family value the disabled man he'd become? How limited is this vision of life, and of the afterlife? Are there no wheelchairs in heaven?

I'm not buying it. For me, if there is a heaven, it's not a place where I'll be able to walk. It's a place where it doesn't matter if you can't.

Developing Self-Worth

(Content warning: The next two chapters contain discussions of death.)

Spinal Muscular Atrophy Doesn't Define Me

Many disabled folks feel intimately familiar with death. Even if we have a normal life expectancy, which some disabled people don't, we're often acutely susceptible to mishaps and illnesses. Or we might be survivors of perilous accidents, horrific violence, or dangerous diseases.

About two years after my NPR commentary that asked whether there are wheelchairs in heaven, I had a bad turn. I was hospitalized for three months, all of it in the intensive care unit. It started with a C. diff infection in my colon, which my doctor misperceived as a colitis flare-up. By the time I got to the emergency room, the infection had eaten away most of my large intestine. I was given a colostomy pouch—a literal sack of shit that's stuck on my belly. I was released home just in time to spend Christmas with the kids.

But that night—Christmas Eve—I had terrible stomach pains. My new abdominal appendage filled up not with poop but with blood. At 4 a.m. my wife, ML, called 911.

It turned out that the surgeon had left a small internal incision when he was removing my colon. I was bleeding inside. The internal injury became infected. And as it spread, it became a kind of blood poisoning known as septicemia.

I can barely remember what happened next. I fell into a coma. I awoke to see my father and older brother hunched over my bed. ML had called them with an urgent message. Namely, I was not expected to survive.

But I did survive. In those three months in the ICU, I had a series of minicomas, pneumonias, blood clots, and other scares. When I was finally released, it was under the condition that we rent a hospital bed for home, a ventilator, feeding apparatus for a nasogastric tube (I was not allowed to eat regular food), and other paraphernalia, as well as hire daytime nurses. Otherwise, I would've had to go to a convalescent center, which ML and I both felt would be a horrible fate. We had visited relatives in these sorts of institutions, and they were not pleasant places. What's more, the closest one to our home was a good hour away.

So for the next nine months, I was at home with an ever-changing army of nurses and a lot of equipment. Many of the nurses, I'm sorry to say, were pretty useless. Kind but clueless. It may sound corny, but ML truly "nursed" me back to good health. She learned how to change my colostomy bags (which she still does) and how to suction my new tracheostomy (which she still does occasionally, whenever needed). She became a master at loading the feeding apparatus with the pablum nutritional supplement (which is no longer needed, thank heaven!).

I lost about a year of my life during this ordeal. But afterward, I had a new sense of purpose and energy. One of the first expressions of that renewed vigor was another commentary for NPR's Morning Edition. This one set the stage for increasingly bold assertions about my self-esteem, my abhorrence to medicalizing my existence, and my objections to pity.

These became themes I would develop further in future writings.

SMA, which stands for Spinal Muscular Atrophy, occurs in one of every six thousand births. Commentator Ben Mattlin has SMA and is paraplegic.... Many people with disabilities dream of the day a cure becomes available. Ben is not one of them.

I get a lot of recommendations to join Facebook groups with names like Fight SMA. I never respond.

Fighting it is a noble cause, and I feel for parents who've lost their babies [to SMA and other conditions], but it's not my cause. I can never support a group that aims to cure me. My disability is part of who I am. It's all I've ever known. Who would I be without it? It doesn't define me, but it has informed every aspect of my life. Even as a child, I never dreamed of walking. Flying, yes. I wanted to be a superhero, but I never wanted to be just like everyone else.

My big brother, who doesn't have SMA, once asked me what I'd do if there were an operation that could fix my muscles but risked leaving me worse off or dead. "No thanks," I said. Even then, it was the thought of losing my trademark wheels that terrified me, not death.

I can see that being able to do more physically would be helpful. I'd like to be a little less dependent on other people and machinery. But when I try to picture myself stripped of my disability, it leaves me feeling cold and lost. My Facebook friends might not agree. Many people with SMA do feel more physically vulnerable than I do.

Yes, I know I wouldn't be here without scientific progress. Yet I can't help having a mental block against medicalizing disability. It just doesn't square with my particular form of disability pride. After all, if you dream of a cure, aren't you saying we're not okay as we are? And if we focus on medical fixes, don't we risk misdirecting our energies away from the external inequities that we can and must end? The barriers of architecture, attitudes, and economics that truly handicap us.

Disability is a fact of life. It's here to stay, so why not celebrate it as another part of human diversity? Call me crazy, but I sort of like myself just the way I am.

"Cure" Me? No, Thanks

Reclaiming your right to exist as you are, despite an often unwelcoming and unaccommodating world, can be a powerful political statement. You have to address your feelings about yourself and, in a sense, what value you bring to the world. You have to wrestle with deep-seated insecurities—to face head-on the self-hatred that activists today call internalized ableism.

Or at least I did, and still must do every now and then.

How do you rescue your sense of self-worth when just about everything around you seems to say you don't belong or you're lucky to be tolerated and accommodated? Such quandaries led me to several more essays, such as this New York Times *submission, which expands upon some of the ideas expressed in the previous NPR commentary.*

Near the end of last year, the Food and Drug Administration approved the first drug for the treatment of spinal muscular atrophy (SMA). A number of my Facebook friends rejoiced. "A Christmas miracle!" one of them declared. But I am not so sure.

Yes, SMA is the number one genetic cause of infant death. And the new drug, Spinraza, sold by Biogen and developed with Ionis Pharmaceuticals, will be a godsend for many. Without it, babies born with this condition, which causes debilitating muscle weakness, have only slightly better than a 50–50 chance of surviving past age two.

According to clinical studies of more than 170 patients who took the drug, 23 percent of infants died and 40 percent achieved an otherwise unlikely or impossible degree of motor function, such as the ability to sit up unassisted and even, in some cases, to stand and walk.

Spinraza is supposed to be beneficial for those with a later onset, too, because it works by increasing the body's production of the SMN protein, which is what's lacking in those of us with SMA. But the long-term effects are unclear. The FDA approved the drug in less than three months under "priority review."

As someone born with SMA fifty-four years ago . . . I fear for those like me who may never look at their lives the same way again. I fear that Spinraza, while giving hope, and perhaps a stronger and longer life to some, may also release a torrent of self-doubt, of pent-up insecurity about our inexorable dependence and emaciated bodies. In some ways, it could make it harder for many of us to live with this type of disability.

Like many disabled adults, I've long since become accustomed to my physical limitations and all they entail. Call me set in my ways, but I can't fathom *not* tooling around on wheels or no longer needing assistance with all manner of physical tasks, such as brushing my teeth and driving my lift-equipped minivan. I'm comforted to be always in the company of helpful people and devices, to truly understand the notion that no man is an island. This is the only way I've ever known.

Even as a child I felt this way. My mother, a firm believer in the power of modern medicine, would tell me about Jonas Salk and his polio vaccine, to shore up her hope of an SMA cure. I recall responding that I didn't want to give up everything I'd grown used to, everything that made me *me*. My disability experience had already informed my perspective on the world, and I had no interest in risking any alteration.

I know now that it's not all about me. My disability takes a toll on my family. It's a drain on my wife's energy and time, not to mention the wherewithal of our children. It's a financial burden on my father and stepmother, who help with the bills (my personal-care attendants alone cost $40,000 a year).

Yet none of them are urging me to take the leap. It's not as if Spinraza is truly a cure anyway. It may slow or stop the progression of weakness in some users, but the underlying condition remains. While approved for every age and for every stage of SMA, it's apparently most effective with kids (and adults with a recent onset of symptoms). So although it might restore a modicum of muscle tone, I may already be too far gone.

I concede that less deterioration sounds desirable. But what of the risks? Listed side effects include possible respiratory infections, kidney toxicity, and blood clots. None of which would faze me if I had nothing to lose, but I do.

Equally daunting, the drug has to be injected directly into the spinal column several times a year. So it's a commitment. It's also an enormous investment, costing as much as $750,000 the first year and $375,000 annually forever after.

To be sure, surmounting fears and obstacles like these is how I've lived much of my life. Even Spinraza's newness—the sense that those who sign on are being guinea pigs—wouldn't stop me if I were hankering for a medical solution to my life's complications. Furthermore, I recognize that I wouldn't have survived as long as I have without medical interventions. So it's not passivity or some kind of technophobia that gives me pause here.

My primary objection comes from my hard-won sense of self-esteem. Long ago I decided that if I was going to like myself, I had to make friends with the disability that was inherently part of me. Living with a disability is not easy. That's why I became an advocate of fair treatment and equal access: I knew deep in my bones that things could be better. It wasn't that I had to pull myself up by my bootstraps. Rather, society had to change, become more inclusive, more open to and validating of people with disabilities.

If instead I'd put my energies into fundraising for medical development, that would've been a betrayal of my core belief—namely, that I and all disabled people are okay as we are.

This resistance to the cure mentality is shared by others and surfaced this month at the South by Southwest festival in Austin, Texas, where the title of a panel on neurotechnology—"The End of Disability?"—angered so many participants that it became a heated topic and hashtag on social media. Some thought it evoked eugenics. "Do they have an #EndOfAbleism session?" someone wrote on Twitter.

The organizers of the panel later apologized, but did they truly understand that this is akin to the difference between saying "the end of racism" and "the end of race"? One takes aim at the problem, the other at the victims of the problem.

To be clear, I have nothing against any advancement that will help others. Not everyone with SMA (or any other disabling condition, for that matter) has the support I've benefited from. But not all of us in the target market are actually seeking this solution. I can't help feeling there's a contradiction between taking pride in one's disability and hankering for a cure. You don't try to cure something you like about yourself.

I acknowledge that as I age with SMA, I am troubled by my increasing difficulties with swallowing and breathing and the now complete loss of use of my hands. Yet even if the drug did help head off further debility, I'd have to face feeling like a traitor to the movement, a turncoat to the cause of disability pride.

None of this is to say that medical science shouldn't be pursued or that those who are drawn to this drug and its potential benefits should not take it. It's just that it will never be the beacon of hope for me that it already is for others. Because I know that even if it did eradicate SMA, the disability community will still be plagued by unnecessary and unfair impediments to equality and justice. Those are ailments that medicine can't do anything about.

Disability and Disease Aren't Interchangeable

After the preceding anticure piece was published, I received some flak on social media. What did I mean that I didn't want this miracle drug? Why would it threaten my sense of disability pride? Couldn't someone have pride and want medicine to help them?

Perhaps I had been hasty in my judgment about medical interventions. Nevertheless, I dug my heels in, so to speak. (A turn of phrase that's distinctly not appropriate for wheelchair users like me, but you get the idea.) It felt important to assert (again) that my disability was an aspect of my life and not a disease that needed curing.

My editor at The Washington Post *liked the idea and encouraged me to write the following.*

Not long ago, I was hired to do a sensitivity reading of a book manuscript, a guide for young adults about how people live with disabilities.... I did my best to make a few gentle suggestions to ensure the text didn't offend. For instance: "Delete 'wheelchair bound'—substitute 'wheelchair user' or equivalent."

But then I came upon a word that gave me pause.

The author, who has SMA, too, had dubbed our shared situation a "disease." There is "no cure for my disease," he wrote. And, "My disease has had an enormous impact on my life, but I try not to let it define me." Good and stirring sentiments, to be sure, and not wrong, exactly. But still ... this wasn't a medical tome. I didn't feel the word *disease* belonged. In fact, I realized it offended me.

Why? Isn't SMA, by definition, a disease? Because of it, he and I and countless others were born with a genetic deficiency that affects the chromosome enabling motor-neuron impulses to travel back and forth to the brain. As a result, muscles atrophy. If the author sees fit to name this a disease—which no doubt many readers and physicians would agree with—who was I to carp?

Politely, I advised substituting *disability*.

Tomato, tomahto? Perhaps. Yet the words are not interchangeable. Disability is the more inclusive choice. A disability can result from illness, injury, accident, genetics, and more. That broad base gives it power. If "my disease" refers to a specific condition within my body, "my disability" connects me with a diverse array of other people, a common cause.

"Disability identifies the group to which I belong and with which I share characteristics," an advocate posted on social media. "Disease caused it in me, but it's no longer active in my life. Disability is."

Then again, a particular diagnosis often captures people's attention, creates fundraising pull. People donate money for muscular dystrophy or Alzheimer's or Parkinson's research, not so much for the vague notion of disability rights. *Disease* equals bucks.

Of course, that's part of the problem. The word conjures tragedy and elicits pity. Maybe it shouldn't. "I don't think the word 'disease' needs to have a negative connotation," posted a second online pundit. "Living with a disease is not necessarily a bad thing."

Indeed, plenty of people need medical assistance as much as equal access to education and employment. They shouldn't be ignored or denigrated for that. To them, the mantle of *disease* drives home the point that they seek and deserve clinical intervention. Here's to Disease Pride!

To my ears, though, *disease* will always be troubling. I'm okay with *disorder*, *impairment*, and other neutral, science-y sounding terms. I'm not a stickler for politically correct language either. Call me a "disabled man" (#SayTheWord) or a "man with a disability" (#PersonFirstLanguage)—I honestly don't care which. Growing up, I was called "handicapped," and that's still fine with me in most contexts (especially because it doesn't come from a begging reference, contrary to popular belief, but from an advantage that's forfeited to make a game fair). I was also taught that *cripple* is a dirty word, yet many of us have reclaimed it with pride.

But *disease* harks back to an outmoded and repressive standard, when we were no longer shunned and feared as monsters and freaks but, alas, studied as biological oddities, as puzzles to solve. Granted, many folks were helped by this approach, as others were harmed. Not until the 1960s and '70s, however, did we progress to the modern paradigm of empowerment. No longer just "patients," we demanded full control over our own lives.

This revolutionary movement culminated in 1990 with the Americans with Disabilities Act. That landmark legislation codified *disability* into law. In so doing, it enshrined the word as a unifying badge of honor.

Today, when I say "disability," it's a way of embracing that cause.

Moreover, I've simply never felt diseased. It doesn't fit how I view myself or my limitations. *Disability*, for me, has always felt natural, an inborn trait as much as my blue eyes and curly brown (okay, graying) hair. That's fundamentally different from a disease, which is an invader, something separate from your essential personhood, an alien presence to get rid of. SMA, on the other hand, is in my DNA. It's part of what makes me *me*.

"Opinion: Disability and Disease Aren't Interchangeable" by Ben Mattlin was first published in The Washington Post *on March 7, 2019."*

A Disabled Life Is a Life Worth Living

Despite all of these words of affirmation, I'm not always so sure I have a good handle on the meaning of my life. For instance, when other disabled people shuck off this mortal coil, it strikes something deep and tender within me. It can make me reevaluate my feelings about vulnerability and mortality. Anyone, whether disabled or not, who has ever faced the passing of a relative, friend, or close colleague—or even the demise of a beloved celebrity—knows a little of what I'm talking about.

Yet somehow, for disabled folks, the shadow of death can often feel intimately near and ever-lurking.

It was in bereavement for two disabled contemporaries—one of whom I'd never met or had any personal connection to whatsoever, the other I barely knew—that I dug down into my soul to write the following piece for The New York Times.

In midsummer, I learned of the death of Laurie Hoirup, a prominent sixty-year-old disability rights advocate in California. Laurie drowned in the Sacramento River after a July 4 celebration. She was well loved and accomplished. She'd served as a chief deputy director of the State Council on Developmental Disabilities for five years and wrote books about living with a disability.

Laurie's sudden and tragic death was not directly caused by her SMA, but it is a stark reminder of the vulnerability of disabled lives. She was deboarding a pleasure boat when the ramp to the dock shifted. The weight of her motorized wheelchair—and the fact that she was strapped into it—pulled her down into the water too rapidly for rescue.

Laurie's death had extra significance for me, in part because we shared a diagnosis.

For people like us, simply enduring can feel like a tremendous victory. One bad cold, though, could spell our end. If our lungs fill with phlegm, we lack the muscle strength to cough them clear. Pneumonia is common. Some treatments help, but respiratory complications—and their impact on the heart—remain a constant threat.

It's not generally acceptable in my segment of the disability community to harp on our defenselessness. Rather, the idea is to assert core competencies, to distance ourselves from the Jerry's Kids model and anything else remotely pitiful. We seek fair treatment, rightful access to everything in society—jobs, romantic prospects, and so on. Highlighting the downside of disabilities seems counterproductive and self-pitying.

But the truth is, to live with a disability is to know an abiding sense of fragility. That isn't always easy, but it's not necessarily all bad either.

I decided long ago that if I'm going to like myself, I have to like the disability that has contributed to who I am. Today, my encroaching decrepitude is frequently a source of emotional strength, a motivator to keep fighting, to exercise my full abilities in whatever way possible. Let's face it, people with disabilities are nothing if not first-class problem solvers. We find all manner of devices to enable us to raise a fork, drive a car or van, go to the beach. I now control my electric wheelchair with my lips, because my hands no longer function. These very words are being written with a voice-recognition computer.

True, it is a hassle having to devise alternative methods for living a normal life. But when it works, oh, how good it feels! How triumphant and liberating! I'm proud of my persistence and creative coping skills.

Of course at times I grow despondent. I fall into what I call "useless cripple syndrome." Most of my nondisabled contemporaries are at the pinnacle of their careers, and I'm just getting by. I shouldn't complain, I tell myself. Unemployment among disabled people is crushingly high.

Because of this, I feel positively driven to make good use of every day that I'm not stuck in bed with a respiratory infection or other ailment. Yes, that may make me an overachiever. I graduated cum laude from a competitive college at twenty-one. I became a financial journalist, and my essays have been featured in major publications, including this one. My second book will be published next year. I don't say all this to boast. The point is, I want to accomplish everything I can while I still have the ability. I may feel fine today, but I can't count on tomorrow—or even an hour from now. I've seen too many friends in the disability community perish too young.

Not long after the shock of Laurie's fatal accident, the news came of a fourteen-year-old Wisconsin girl with SMA, Jerika Bolen, who was planning to end her own life by refusing life-sustaining treatment. Just a few weeks ago, she did, and died. News reports said that Jerika was comforted by the promise of an afterlife in which she would be able to move freely and escape her persistent physical pain.

My reaction to this is strong and difficult to express. Growing up with a disability, I often became isolated. Feeling devalued by my peers, with no confidence in my future, I experienced intermittent but profound depression. One can take only so many surgeries, so many bodily betrayals, so much rejection, before wanting to give up. Even today, I can pivot from utter terror over an itch I can't scratch or a bite of food I can't quite swallow, to almost unbelievable joy if I manage to clear my throat unassisted or zoom my motorized wheelchair through a crowded street. As disabled people, we are endlessly buffeted by circumstances beyond our control.

I dare not judge Jerika Bolen. I don't know the entirety of her situation. But I do wish she had found the will to live. I'm saddened—as were many others with SMA, and some disability rights groups—to think others might grow so weary or apprehensive that they follow her example. I hope she received the same level of intervention any other suicidal fourteen-year-old would. I wish I could have told her about the psychological alchemy that can turn frustration into an internal fuel. If I'd had the chance, I would have told her that society needs its disabled people, too.

The perseverance to live fully with a profound disability comes, I think, in part from honestly facing your own powerlessness and frailty, and recognizing how much worse things have been and could still be. This can instill a delight in the now. In living with a disability, you've already dealt with much of what other people fear most, and if you come out on the other side you are, by definition, a survivor. The resolve required, and begrudging acceptance of what you can't change, may bring a kind of wisdom.

I realize that external conditions can make all the difference. My family has given me unflagging support. My parents fought to get me integrated into regular schools, long before it was mandated, and insisted I could become anything I wanted when I grew up. Today, my family's financial backing allows me to hire the full-time aides I need to live a productive life. My wife provides for my personal maintenance whenever paid staff isn't available. Without all this, I would not be where I am today, but I'd like to think I'd find a way to survive.

Laurie Hoirup lived a full, active life. I wish I could have persuaded Jerika Bolen and others like her to keep striving to do the same, not to put her hopes and dreams into the idea of a heaven of unfettered athleticism. I wish I could have convinced her that she wasn't better off dead than disabled.

Assisted Suicide

(Content warning: This section may be upsetting for some readers.)

Quality of Life Consists of More Than the Physical

For most if not all of us, aid in dying is a controversial and complex topic. It's uncomfortable to even contemplate. But it is a subject I've thought a great deal about, and my view is one I believe in wholeheartedly.

The following piece from the Los Angeles Times *is one of the first essays I wrote about it. At the time, more and more states were considering legislation to legalize doctor-assisted suicide. One prominent champion of the cause was a firebrand of a man named Jack Kevorkian.*

He scared me to . . . life.

If I, a thirty-three-year-old married college graduate with a new baby daughter, threatened to hurl myself off a tall building, would an emergency medical team respond? And if one did, would I be offered counseling—or carbon monoxide?

It's a valid question because of my neuromuscular disability. With all the recent euthanasia news—Dr. Jack Kevorkian's acquittal and new trial and two federal court decisions favoring assisted suicide—I don't feel safe.

It may be constitutionally protected, but the right to die seems dangerous to those of us who are not ideal physical specimens.

I am not terminally ill. Both the April 2 decision by the Second U.S. Circuit Court of Appeals in New York and the March 6 decision by the Ninth U.S. Circuit Court of Appeals in San Francisco permit assisted suicide only for "a competent, terminally ill adult." But Judge Stephen Reinhardt, writing for the majority in San Francisco, went on to say that death is more humane than continuing to live in "a childlike state of helplessness."

They are not the same thing, though, this "state of helplessness" and being terminally ill. I have lived my whole life in such a state, needing assistance for eating, bathing, using the toilet. The humane thing to do is to help, not presume that my life isn't worth living.

Kevorkian isn't concerned with whether or not his clients' conditions are terminal. In October 1991, for example, Kevorkian aided the death of Marjorie Wantz, fifty-eight. Kevorkian himself admits that she was not terminally ill. Rather, Wantz "claimed after a series of surgeries to be suffering intense vaginal pain that [prosecutors] contend was psychosomatic," *The New York Times* reported.

Granted, the people seeking assisted suicide want to die. And I believe in autonomy and self-determination; I am pro-choice. But what happens when nondisabled people attempt suicide? Why is their choice considered irrational? Why is a disabled person's suicide choice more readily judged sane?

Kevorkian would argue that he is ending suffering for people with no options. Tell that to Stephen Hawking, the physicist who has advanced amyotrophic lateral sclerosis, writes best-selling books, travels around the world, and recently divorced his wife to marry his nurse. To say someone has no options just because doctors are stumped is medical arrogance. Quality of life is determined by more than physical condition.

To be sure, not everyone can be a Stephen Hawking. Which is precisely why Kevorkianism is so frightening. Does Kevorkian realize how hard it is for the average disabled person to feel valued in this society?

What I'm calling for is clarity. The right to die is appropriate only if it isn't clouded by fear and ignorance of disabilities. The dangers are potentially enormous. Euthanasia, after all, was one step toward the Holocaust. If doctors, judges, and juries continue to cast doubts on the worth of people with disabilities, I fear for the one in six Americans (according to the census at that time; now it's more like one in four) who has a disability.

If Kevorkian is truly concerned about us, why doesn't he join the cause of disability rights?

Life, and Death, and Who Decides

Eight years later, the subject of legislating the value of disabled lives was still raging. One state after another was passing so-called death-with-dignity laws. I was in one of them: California.

But before California passed a full and binding law, it tried to enact a somewhat different version.

At the end of last month, Governor Arnold Schwarzenegger signed AB 2747, the Terminal Patients' Right to Know End-of-Life Options Act, into law. Supporters hailed it as a victory for Californians in their final days because it requires full disclosure of all options available to terminally ill patients, including euthanasia. Opponents, however, said they worried that the new law would push vulnerable, possibly depressed and uninformed people toward a hasty and ill-considered demise.

I was an agnostic on the question at first. Both sides offered compelling arguments. But after a recent, grueling, three-month hospitalization at the UCLA Medical Center's intensive-care unit, I am sadly drawn to the latter view. It's too easy to tip the severely ill toward craving death above other options.

I know how disoriented and powerless I felt strung up with a variety of tubes, which temporarily rendered me unable to speak. It would have been easy to become very depressed. If not for round-the-clock visits from my wife and other family members to interpret my signals, call for help when necessary, and explain my physical limitations to the hospital staff, I'm certain that I would not have received the quality of treatment I did. My needs—and the very full life I normally enjoy—might have been sorely misjudged.

Under the new law, it's not inconceivable that one of the many doctors, nurses, or medical assistants who looked after me might have deemed me terminally ill—between the blood clots and the low oxygen and the simple fact that, medically speaking, I've been terminally ill my whole life.

What would it have taken for them to begin the process of counseling me about death options? Theoretically, I would have to ask for the information, but would vociferous complaining and moaning have been sufficient to prompt an overly helpful nurse to produce euthanasia literature? Drugged and isolated, possibly depressed, what if I were so miserable that I said, "I wish I were dead"? Would they have instantly appeared with information and counselors to tell me how it could be accomplished?

This is not delusional thinking. I've seen the way harried medical staff can make dangerous errors—innocent misdiagnoses and inadvertent misdosings of prescriptions, for instance. In my own case, though I was well cared for overall, I left UCLA with a terrible bedsore, which I can only attribute to the negligence of an overworked staff—a common side effect of hospitalization, I am told. What's more, many of my nurses had a hard time believing that I normally live the life I do.

What the new law does is make it easier for nonphysicians to recommend death as a valid medical option. It provides no legal standard, nor does a physician have to be involved in the discussions.

It is true, of course, that many severely ill people would like to accelerate an end to their suffering. They see no point in preserving a troubled, limited existence. I do not begrudge those who would find solace in suicide.

But if the law is to guarantee full access to the range of available options, as AB 2747 is intended to do, it should mandate counseling about all nondeath options, too. It should take into account the depression that severely ill people face, the disorientation that comes of isolation in a hospital ward and the vulnerability of patients to the whims and errors of their caregivers. It should provide oversight by doctors to avoid abuse by perhaps well-meaning though misguided medical practitioners.

Granting caregivers who hardly know you the power to question the validity of your life does a serious disservice to an already marginalized population. It could well be the last straw in a life that's barely hanging on.

Suicide by Choice? Not So Fast

As physician-assisted suicide bills kept winding their way through the various state legislatures and courts, I kept developing my arguments against them.

Meanwhile, Jack Kevorkian died. Nevertheless, his cause kept going. So did mine.

This next essay, I'm told, helped convince some voters in Massachusetts to change their minds and vote against a physician-aid-in-dying law. Twelve years later, it still has not passed.

Next week, voters in Massachusetts will decide whether to adopt an assisted-suicide law. As a good pro-choice liberal, I ought to support the effort. But as a lifelong disabled person, I cannot.

There are solid arguments in favor. No one will be coerced into taking a poison pill, supporters insist. The "right to die" will apply only to those with six months or fewer to live. Doctors will take into account the possibility of depression. There is no slippery slope.

Fair enough, but I remain skeptical. There's been scant evidence of abuse so far in Oregon, Washington, and Montana, the three states where physician-assisted death is already legal, but abuse—whether spousal, child, or elder—is notoriously underreported, and evidence is difficult to come by. What's more, Massachusetts registered nearly twenty thousand cases of elder abuse in 2010 alone.

My problem, ultimately, is this: I've lived so close to death for so long that I know how thin and porous the border between coercion and free choice is, how easy it is for someone to inadvertently influence you to feel devalued and hopeless—to pressure you ever so slightly but decidedly into being "reasonable," to unburdening others, to "letting go."

Perhaps, as advocates contend, you can't understand why anyone would push for assisted-suicide legislation until you've seen a loved one suffer. But you also can't truly conceive of the many subtle forces—invariably well meaning, kindhearted, even gentle, yet as persuasive as a tsunami—that emerge when your physical autonomy is hopelessly compromised.

I'm more fragile now than I was in infancy. No longer able to hold a pencil, I'm writing this with a voice-controlled computer. Every swallow of food, sometimes every breath, can become a battle. And a few years ago, when a surgical blunder put me into a coma from septic shock, the doctors seriously questioned whether it was worth trying to extend my life. My existence seemed pretty tenuous anyway, they figured. They didn't know about my family, my career, my aspirations.

Fortunately, they asked my wife, who knows exactly how I feel. She convinced them to proceed "full code," as she's learned to say, to keep me alive using any and all means necessary.

From this I learned how easy it is to be perceived as someone whose quality of life is untenable, even or perhaps especially by doctors. Indeed, I hear it from them all the time—"How have you survived so long? Wow, you must put up with a lot!"—even during routine office visits, when all I've asked for is an antibiotic for a sinus infection. Strangers don't treat me this way, but doctors feel entitled to render judgments and voice their opinions. To them, I suppose, I must represent a failure of their profession, which is shortsighted. As I've said before, I am more than my diagnosis and my prognosis.

This is but one of many invisible forces of coercion. Others include that certain look of exhaustion in a loved one's eyes, or the way nurses and friends sigh in your presence while you're zoned out in a hospital bed. All these can cast a dangerous cloud of depression on even the most cheery of optimists, a situation clinicians might misread since, to them, it seems perfectly rational.

And in a sense, it is rational, given the dearth of alternatives. If nobody wants you at the party, why should you stay? Advocates of Death with Dignity laws who say that patients themselves should decide whether to live or die are fantasizing. Who chooses suicide in a vacuum? We are inexorably affected by our immediate environment. The deck is stacked.

Yes, that may sound paranoid. After all, the Massachusetts proposal calls for the lethal dose to be "self-administered," which it defines as the "patient's act of ingesting." You might wonder how that would apply to those who can't feed themselves—people like me. But as I understand the legislation, there is nothing to prevent the patient from designating just about anyone to feed them the poison pill. Indeed, there is no requirement for oversight of the ingestion at all; no one has to witness how and when the lethal drug is given. Which, to my mind, leaves even more room for abuse.

To be sure, there are noble intentions behind the "assisted death" proposals, but I can't help wondering why we're in such a hurry to ensure the right to die before we've done all we can to ensure that those of us with severe, untreatable, life-threatening conditions are given the same openhearted welcome, the same open-minded respect, and the same open-ended opportunities due everyone else.

POLST

PROTECTING PATIENTS' RIGHTS OR A BAD JOKE?

As more and more assisted suicide laws passed, I've been extra careful about making sure my desire to live is well understood and documented—especially if I'm entering a hospital. "I'm full code," I say from the get-go, and I've signed an advance directive to back that up. I didn't want to do that, but now it feels like I must.

For my next essay on the subject, a commissioned blog post for a nonprofit organization, I addressed a new development—the encroaching use of a novel term in health care: POLST.

Next time a doctor asks to take your pulse, make sure they're not asking for your POLST.

Da-dum!

Unfortunately, POLST (or Physician Orders for Life-Sustaining Treatment) isn't a joke. It's the latest medical form, which follows up on the Living Will and do-not-resuscitate (DNR) instructions, to ensure appropriate measures are taken in the event of a medical crisis—and, needless to say, to protect doctors and clinics from being sued.

But does it truly protect patients' rights? Why are advocates upset?

As Diane Coleman, president of Not Dead Yet, recently blogged: "Though it says 'for' life-sustaining treatment, it would be more accurate to say 'on' or 're(garding).' And if you really want to be accurate in reflecting the medical profession's intent in promoting POLST, you'd say 'against' or 'vs' because there seems to be a far from subtle POLST bias *against* life-sustaining treatment."

One problem with POLST—and what makes it different from other, similar forms—is that medical professionals fill out some or all of it before transferring patients from one facility to another, ostensibly to ensure consistent care. In Maryland, for instance, the form is completed 100 percent by a doctor or nurse practitioner who simply has to indicate that they have discussed various treatment options with the patient. There's no oversight about how that's done—how well the patient understood the options or how clearly the patient answered (a shake of the head, thumbs up or down, a shrug, etc.).

Call me a worrier, but this doesn't make me feel any better about receiving the best possible care. How is a patient—lying in a hospital bed, with his or her very life hanging in the balance—supposed to answer questions about artificial ventilation, blood transfusions, or artificially administered fluids and nutrition? It must feel like having an airplane pilot ask how you want the plane to be flown!

And what happens if you decline to answer? Is silence interpreted as permission to forgo treatment? If you're really in bad shape, chances are you're looking for the medical experts to do whatever they can to usher you to a better state. So if asked, "Would you like to die?" it might sound more like a recommendation than a choice.

In other words, how informed is the "informed consent"? When you're being moved from one facility to another, it's because you're not in the best of shape. It's not the time to answer difficult questions. It's a time when you're easily influenced.

What doctors and other medical do-gooders seem to forget is that we patients are not comfortable in a clinical setting. For the MDs and RNs, its home base. It's the office. For us, it's just about our worst nightmare.

I recognize that many health-care practitioners have our best interests at heart. But that doesn't mean they can't do unintended harm. I'm not just talking about accidental oversights. I'm talking about harm that comes from ignorance, even prejudice, about what life is like on the other side of the examination table or hospital bed.

Coleman goes on to quote a recent NPR piece by Nancy Shute: "Because it's signed by a doctor or other provider, a POLST has teeth. It overrides the legal obligation of an EMT or a hospital to provide CPR and other emergency care."

To be sure, doctors and nurses and hospital administrators have all made sincere attempts to alleviate misunderstandings and honor patients' wishes. But the older I get, and the more complex my medical regimen, the more I'm convinced everyone needs a health-care advocate.

Next time I check into a medical facility, I think I'd better pretend it's a courthouse and bring along a lawyer.

People with Disabilities Often Fear They're a Burden. That's Why Legal Assisted Suicide Scares Me

WE SHOULD FOCUS ON OFFERING BETTER, MORE AFFORDABLE OPTIONS FOR KEEPING PEOPLE ALIVE.

Okay, this section has been heavy. One final attempt to approach the subject from a slightly different angle was published three years later by the online magazine Vox.

It's been nearly ten years since I was rushed to the hospital at 4 a.m., but you don't forget something like that.

Internal bleeding. "It's gone septic," my wife recalls hearing, understanding only that that meant something serious. Something dangerous. Rough translation: blood poisoning.

All I remember is passing out in a hospital bed. My wife says I called out for my mother, who died in 1981. It looked like I was going to join her.

The bleeding was set off a few days earlier by a surgeon's blunder, in another hospital, during an unrelated gastroenterological procedure. In context, I was lucky: I was in a well-equipped, big-city medical center. I was quickly surrounded by medical staff.

But there was a delay. "Is he full code?" someone needed to know.

Again, a rough translation: Should the hospital proceed with lifesaving surgery, or was I DNR? Meaning: Do not resuscitate.

Fortunately, my wife was clear about my desire to live. We'd discussed this possibility before. And, in time, I made a full recovery. But not everyone has a significant other like mine. What happens to them? Does everybody in such dire straits get asked this question?

This is why, a year after the so-called right to die became legal in our nation's most populous state, California, I'm still profoundly uncomfortable with it. The value of my life has been discounted by medical professionals and others more often than I care to remember. That's because even at my healthiest, I am what some would consider terminally ill.

Without extensive daily interventions—hands-on (and expensive) assistance with bathing, dressing, toileting, and feeding, as well as breathing treatments, wheelchair maintenance, and so forth—I wouldn't last long.

The knee-jerk questioning of whether my life is worth saving drives my opposition to the legalization of assisted suicide. And I know I'm not the only one who's experienced this kind of dismissive attitude, the subtle pressures and invisible coercions to unburden others.

California's End of Life Option Act went into effect on June 9 of last year. It was the latest in a string of right-to-die laws. So far, Colorado, Oregon, Vermont, Washington, and Washington, D.C., have instituted similar statutes. That's got me worried.

Months before the California vote, a colleague who has multiple sclerosis asked me to join her in a meeting with a representative of a state legislator (the legislator herself had declined to see us in person) to urge a "no" vote.

Our reasons, simply put: Legalization of assisted suicide unduly threatens people with severe disabilities and health-care costs, like us. In a country where the right to receive health care is under attack and medical costs continue to rise, offering the option of legal suicide is the last thing we need.

Looking back over the past year, I concede that I've felt no ill effects of the law's passage. Yet that doesn't mean I'm put at ease or have changed my mind. I still object to it and see bad things coming from it.

To wit: The state's Department of Public Health recently reported that 111 people died under the act last year—that is, in its first 29 weeks of legislative life. That's roughly one person every two days.

Of those, slightly more than half, or sixty-five of them, had cancer. The rest? It's a mixed bag. Fully twenty had unspecified neuromuscular conditions, perhaps not unlike my own and my fellow advocate's multiple sclerosis.

What's more, the law's so-called safeguards give me scant comfort. They require you to be mentally competent, age eighteen or older, and diagnosed as having six or fewer months to live. I could qualify. If I ever get so depressed about my life that I'd consider ending it—which is not impossible, considering how difficult and expensive it can be for someone like me to survive, not to mention to maintain a good sense of self-esteem in a nondisabled and often inaccessible world—I want to have the same suicide prevention interventions in place that everyone else has. Only fair, right?

Other safeguards also feel like mere lip service. For instance, you must make two separate verbal requests and one written request of a doctor, at least fifteen days apart, though the law doesn't mandate any kind of long-term relationship with that doctor. Furthermore, you must be able to self-administer the poison, but there is no oversight of that. Besides fear of coercion, I have concern about those who down the drug prematurely out of fear of one day being unable to self-administer.

Make no mistake: Fear of debility underlies most support for this law. Consider Brittany Maynard, the twenty-nine-year-old Californian with brain cancer who moved to Oregon in 2014 to take advantage of its right-to-die law before California had one. (The publicity she received is one of the reasons we have the law now.)

In press reports, Maynard's husband, Dan Diaz, said she ultimately ingested her lethal medication when she became afraid she'd soon lose the ability to down it herself: "If a seizure or a stroke occurs as her symptoms get worse, if she loses the ability to self-administer, if she suffers a stroke and she loses the ability to stand, walk or swallow, all of a sudden she's now trapped in her own body, and she's trapped dying the very way she was trying to avoid."

That's a lot of scary "ifs"! I don't judge Maynard, but I can't help wondering whether she would've made the same choice if our society prioritized providing assistive technology, or palliative care and hospice care that ease pain management. How many people like me—people who live full and active lives without the ability to walk or stand or swallow easily—did she talk (and really listen) to?

Proponents of the right to die, such as Matt Whitaker, director of the California chapter of Compassion & Choices (formerly the Hemlock Society), assert the law is "working well." What they mean is that people are using it. But that doesn't really indicate they're better off because of it.

To be clear, my objection has nothing to do with religious belief or a right-to-life philosophy. I am pro-choice when it comes to abortion rights. It has everything to do with economics and equal protection under the law. Conditions such as Maynard's and mine are expensive to treat on an ongoing basis. Death is cheaper. Sure, anybody who tries to push someone toward seeking death under this law is liable for felony prosecution. Yet a lack of adequate health insurance coverage alone sends a pretty strong signal.

To me, just having the state condone the option of unburdening others is tantamount to more than a green light. To the most vulnerable, it's a kick in the pants.

I understand the appeal of letting people on the brink of death have the right to go out on their own terms. But I've personally experienced the myriad often unspoken pressures to move aside, get out of the way, relieve others. And if I had to be kept in a dreary institution—a very real possibility for millions of people like me, if the schemes to slash Medicaid become law—I might request a terminal dosage myself! The struggle to go on living would become too burdensome for me, perhaps even downright impossible.

On days when every breath is a monumental struggle, it can be tempting to give up. I don't want that option to be too easy. Those of us who may be closer to death have as much right to protection from suicidal wishes as anyone else.

A better option, for me, is to ensure that people with ongoing conditions are as welcome and valued as anyone else, and indeed that they are assisted in living their lives to the fullest. Shouldn't that be the first priority?

Health-Care Disparities

People Like Me

IS THERE ROOM IN HEALTH CARE FOR THE DISABLED?

From my rage against the legalization of physician-assisted suicide, I moved on to a rage against our nation's health-care delivery system. In particular, I've found that the disparities in care are maddening, real, and terribly dangerous.

I wrote about how these disparities made me feel for a large metropolitan newspaper that prefers to remain unnamed. Those of you who are paying attention will realize that I springboarded my case with the same example I'd used before in discussing the pressures to off myself: my recent hospital melodrama. It was a good example, I felt, a harrowing experience that deserved retelling in slightly different form.

At its most basic, the disparities are evident in the inaccessibility of many doctors' offices. They are not exempt from the Americans with Disabilities Act and should be at least as accessible as a store or restaurant. But have you ever seen grab bars—the sort found in every accessible bathroom stall—at a medical examination table? What about sign language interpreters?

Beyond that, studies have shown that physicians aren't trained to handle disabled patients. Many would rather not bother. Medical practitioners also harbor a sort of unconscious prejudice about the quality of life for people like me. They assume we're a lot unhappier than most of us actually are.

The result: Disabled people simply don't get the level of care that others do.

It was only in September 2023 that the U.S. Department of Health and Human Services' National Institutes of Health recognized this truth when it officially designated disabled people as a population with health disparities. "This designation recognizes the importance and need for research advances to improve our understanding of the complexities leading to disparate health outcomes and multilevel interventions," said Dr. Eliseo J. Pérez-Stable, direc-

tor of the National Institute on Minority Health and Health Disparities, in a statement.

Last year [when doctors asked my wife if they should bother performing the full measure of life-sustaining care for me], it was clear to her that their uncertainty was due to my physical disabilities.

Was my life worth prolonging? Should the hospital provide me with the same degree of medical intervention it would anyone else?

Please! Don't hold my rag-doll body against me! I have everything to live for.

In fairness, there are patients who don't want medical intervention. Yet too often have I been dismissed out of hand by medical professionals as a lost cause. My disability stems from a genetic aberration that was only pinpointed in the past decade or so. It's still unheard of by many physicians. No cures or treatments are available. [That was soon to change.] That doesn't bother me. I'm used to it. For me, living with a disability is standard operating procedure. But for doctors, I represent a gap in their knowledge, an irritating puzzle, a fearful reminder of the limits of their calling.

Or maybe what I'm perceiving as a stinginess in empathy is truly a case of economics. The simple fact is, those of us with significant disabilities are a bigger draw on the nation's scarce health-care resources than other people. If you're counting dollars and cents, keeping people like me alive and healthy just doesn't add up.

Whatever the cause, I'm not alone in feeling marginalized by our current health system. Who hasn't felt the sting of dismissive and impersonal handling from overworked clinical staff and bureaucratic insurance carriers? Even the pharmaceutical giants, with their glossy TV commercials promising to make your life better, notwithstanding the sometimes outrageous legalese disclaimers about side effects, are in on the act. Health care isn't—cannot be—one-size-fits-all. There are no easy solutions. This is especially a problem for those of us who don't fit the typical model.

Take, for example, the standard examination table. Many friends with disabilities complain that they don't have a step or grab bars or a height adjustment to make climbing up easier, safer. I always have to remind doctors before they prescribe something as mundane as an antibiotic that I weigh only about 113 pounds, because of my lack of muscle tone. The standard dose for a man my age can bowl me over! I've learned this the hard way.

Every day, lawsuit-wary doctors, many with misguided notions about the quality of life for people with disabilities, and the penny-pinching insurance companies who pay them, render judgments about who does and does not receive certain kinds of care. So when the right wing warns about medical rationing as a bleak future possibility, I don't listen. I and countless others on the margins already feel the squeeze. Could the feds really do a worse job?

On the other hand, when the left wing talks about health-care reform as a kind of panacea, I raise a skeptical eyebrow, too. There's more wrong with our current system than Washington can fix. I don't like the outrageously expensive premiums I pay as a "high risk" customer, but the most galling obstacles I face can't be easily legislated away.

The Affordable Act does away with insurance discrimination against preexisting conditions. That's a good start, and it should remain intact. I would also like to incentivize Medicaid programs to offer home- and community-based long-term-care alternatives to costly and unpopular institutionalization. Furthermore, I would extend Medicaid-type coverage to severely disabled adults not poor enough to qualify for Medicaid.

I can't help wishing Washington would also include provisions to guarantee fair and equal access to the full extent of quality care for every American, including the one in five who has a disability, especially those in dire situations, perhaps unconscious on the operating table or otherwise unable to demand [fair consideration for care] ourselves.

Is that asking too much? Perhaps. But we need that reassurance. Not everybody has a wife like mine.

Inaccessible Doctors' Offices? Sometimes Yes, Sometimes No

A couple of years earlier, I wrote a report about the inaccessibility of doctors' offices for a short-lived disability e-magazine called Disaboom. *Reading it now, it strikes me as somewhat simplistic and naive. For one thing, I didn't yet know about the threat of medical rationing during emergencies such as the Covid pandemic—the official protocols that instruct medical centers to triage scarce supplies, so that patients who are younger or healthier can receive care while older folks and those with preexisting conditions go to the back of the line. I didn't yet know about the ordinary disabled people who've suffered permanent damage or even died as a result of parsimonious insurance companies' or physicians' unconscious ableism.*

In a now well-known example, a forty-six-year-old quadriplegic man named Michael Hickson was hospitalized in Austin, Texas, in June 2020. He was diagnosed with a urinary tract infection, sepsis, pneumonia, and Covid symptoms. According to reports, the hospital was not overrun with Covid cases at the time. Nevertheless, his doctors withdrew all life-sustaining treatment, including artificial nutrition and hydration. When the patient's wife, Melissa Hickson, objected, a doctor explained that the decision was based on an assessment of Michael's poor quality of life as a paralyzed man. (You don't have to take my word for it. She recorded the conversation, and it's on YouTube.)

Six days later, Michael died. Afterward, Melissa told the media that their being Black might have contributed to the denial of care, but "the main reason was because of his disabilities."

No matter your disability, one place you might feel you don't have to worry about access is the doctor's office. Unfortunately, studies show that's not always the case.

For example, a 2006 nationwide survey found that three-quarters of people with disabilities have at least a moderate degree of difficulty using examination tables. The tables are often too high, too narrow, too hard (or otherwise uncomfortable), if not impossible to get up onto. Some respondents complained about a shortage of handholds or grab bars to assist with transfers. Many women found the stirrups difficult to use.

Additionally, more than two-thirds of those surveyed reported significant problems with medical-imaging equipment such as x-ray, MRI, mammography, and bone-density machines.

Even low-tech procedures such as getting weighed pose significant physical difficulty for more than half of patients with disabilities.

The survey was published by a consortium that included the Western University of Health Sciences' Center for Disability Issues and the Health Professions (CDIHP) in Pomona, California, and Houston's Independent Living Research Utilization (ILRU).

June Isaacson Kailes, associate director of CDIHP and an independent disability policy consultant, was one of the authors of the report. She has cerebral palsy, gets around mostly in a power scooter, and has enough difficulty with her balance and coordination to find most doctors' exam tables—especially those lacking grab bars—impossible to use. That's not only unfortunate, she maintains; it's illegal and could also be dangerous. Even the most competent doctors, says Kailes, "are missing half the body if they only look at patients who are sitting in a chair."

All this is nothing new. Kailes's survey follows other work, notably *Medical Instrumentation: Accessibility and Usability Considerations*, an overview edited by Jack M. Winters and Molly Follette Story (CRC Press, 2007) and "The Surgeon General's Call to Action to Improve the Health and Wellness of Persons with Disabilities," from the U.S. Department of Health and Human Services (2005).

However, the problem of inaccessible medical equipment became a legal issue with passage of the Americans with Disabilities Act (ADA) in 1990. This landmark civil rights law plainly states that a physician's office is no different from a restaurant, laundromat, bakery, or other public accommodation in terms of its obligation to provide equal access for people with disabilities. This applies not only to external features such as the width of doorways but also to all equipment used to diagnose or treat patients. "People talk about suing inaccessible movie theaters or stores, but they never think about their doctors' offices," observes Kailes.

Some, however, do take action. David Geffen, a disability rights attorney in Los Angeles, filed a suit last year against a medical imaging center in southern California. The center, the suit alleges, had no height-adjustable exam table or lift, and refused to either assist or refer Geffen's quadriplegic client elsewhere, as required by law. "He was unable to transfer himself from his wheelchair onto the ultrasound table due to the table's height," reports Geffen, and the staff denied him any necessary help. In fact, as a matter of policy, they flatly declined to offer any solutions at all, a clear violation of federal and state accessibility codes, Geffen contends. Public facilities, he points out, are required not just to remove barriers but to "avoid policies, practices and procedures that discriminate against disabled persons."

As a result of the lawsuit, the imaging center changed its policies, retrained its staff, and made appropriate accommodations in its facilities.

Many people with disabilities have grown so used to working around the system that they may not notice when their civil rights are being violated. "I need to use a Hoyer hoist [to get up on the examination table], and I must take it with me," says Mary Martz, an art education consultant at the Los Angeles County Museum of Art. Martz, who has post-polio syndrome and uses a wheelchair, brings a strong family member or personal-care assistant to every medical appointment. Still, she never gets weighed. "The medical staff does not want to help because of liability issues," she states.

Ironically, not helping makes the staff more liable to litigation, as well as continuing an unresolved problem. In fact, advocates say quiet acceptance might be the worst problem of all. Do people with disabilities actually deprive themselves of complete medical care out of sheer exhaustion from fighting the system?

Kailes says hopeless complacency is so common she calls it the "Four F experience: frustration, fatigue, fear, and failure. For some people, the effort of seeking health care is just too exhausting and/or degrading," says Kailes.

As a result, people may postpone or avoid medical attention, which can exacerbate undiagnosed problems and even cost lives. "These barriers diminish opportunities for longer, healthier, productive lives for people with disabilities," she says.

A random sample, however, uncovers a mix of opinions and experiences, but scant complaints. Nadia Powers [a visually impaired community activist and former chair of the Los Angeles County Commission on Disabilities] praises the "wonderful, attentive staff" at Cedars-Sinai Medical Center in Los Angeles. Powers always has an assistant with her but rarely needs help during medical visits. "Everything is there for me," she says. "The nurses or staff members always assist me."

Ben Rockwell, a wheelchair user in Long Beach, California, is also satisfied. His primary physician is able to do a full exam while Rockwell remains in his wheelchair. "He finds a way, and is able to do even the prostate exam and everything else," says Rockwell, who has multiple disabilities, including post-polio. Rockwell has even had x-rays at Long Beach Memorial Medical Center without getting out of his wheelchair. "I know they have adjustable-height examination tables there, but they were able to do everything with me in my chair, which I felt was a very reasonable accommodation," he says.

A similar sentiment is echoed by Arnie Pike, of Placentia, California. Pike gets examined in his wheelchair and finds the medical staff helpful when it comes to getting him onto the scale or exam table. Nevertheless, Pike finds the doorways and restrooms at his physician's office too small to accommodate his wheelchair.

Maybe California is more familiar with access needs than other places.

One facility that stands out for its high degree of accessibility is Rancho Los Amigos National Rehabilitation Center, in Downey, California, just south of Los Angeles. Hugh Hallenberg goes there quarterly to check his weight. For other examinations, he's examined elsewhere in his wheelchair. "What's the point of complaining?" he asks, adding that he once did complain, and when his complaints went unanswered he ended up changing physicians. Hallenberg has cerebral palsy.

Ruthee Goldkorn of Moreno Valley, California, sued Riverside Medical Clinic for inaccessibility several years ago. She won her case, but reports that enforcement has been lax. Among her ongoing grievances: the mammography machine is technically accessible, in that it is height-adjustable, but the room it's in is too small to accommodate a wheelchair. The radiology staff is "rude about even considering alternative methods for those who can't stand," she says. And the counters are too high for a person in a wheelchair to check in. "Patients with a disability are not treated with the same respect as other patients," contends Goldkorn, a wheelchair user. "This is a huge problem everywhere."

If you're facing accessibility barriers in your doctor's office or other medical facility, you can discuss ways to do things differently. If an individual doctor or practitioner isn't receptive, bring your issue up with the facility's office manager, patient representative or, if it's a large clinic or hospital, ADA compliance officer. See if you can brainstorm together to arrive at solutions.

There are also catalogs of accessible medical equipment your health providers can consider purchasing. They may be expensive, but they could help avoid a costly lawsuit or even save a life.

And good luck! You might have a battle ahead of you, but it's well worth the fight.

To Hell and Back

DISABILITY WISDOM

To be fair, some medical visits do turn out well. After one surprisingly joyful experience, I was so grateful for modern medicine that I wrote the following upbeat blog post.

This is a story that began like some of the others, with a rush to the emergency room. Fortunately, it had a happy ending, and I felt compelled to give praise where it was due.

In the first few days of this year, I was rushed to the emergency room. "We need help," I'd gasped to my wife before she dialed 911.

I had had a persistent fever and extreme difficulty breathing. My lungs are dangerously weak even on my best days.

The EMTs promptly gave me oxygen, which was continued in the ER. I was also given a nebulizer with levalbuterol, which I'd already tried at home. Nothing was helping. I don't know how much time passed before I started spouting random, nonsensical numbers (or so I'm told). Then I passed out.

When I came to the next morning, I was on a ventilator and a couple of nurses were torturing my nose. Actually, they were inserting a nasogastric (NG) tube to provide nutrition. Same difference. It hurt like hell.

We learned that I had had too much carbon dioxide in my system. Perhaps the problem wasn't so much that I couldn't breathe in as that I couldn't breathe out. In any case, I had the flu—Influenza A, to be precise—plus pneumonia. So much for the flu shot three months earlier.

I was pumped full of antibiotics. Soon I grew bored, antsy, annoyed, and itchy. *Itchy?* One of the antibiotics was causing an allergic reaction.

As for *annoyed*, one of the reasons was that I'd just had a new article in *The New York Times*—a "Modern Love" column I'd been trying to get published for years. I had wanted to savor the moment, respond to the many generous email messages I was sure I'd received. I also had a book coming out in about two weeks, and I wanted to get cracking on publicity. But all that would have to wait.

I weaned off the ventilator as quickly as possible; I know how easy it is to become dependent on one. But that first pneumonia was followed by a second one. More antibiotics. The staff was mostly kind and attentive. But it seemed there were always more hurdles.

For instance, to have the NG tube removed, I had to pass a swallow test. I failed. I knew from previous experience that I swallow better without a tube up my nose and down my throat. So I asked if the tube could be removed before the next test. The lab medic said she would ask the doctor. Later that day I put it to one of the pulmonologists.

His reaction: "You mean they did it with the tube in? That's never done. No wonder you didn't pass."

The next day the tube was removed. I passed.

Not that eating was easy after all that. I couldn't really sit up at all. If I tried, I became dizzy and breathless. All I could handle were very small bites. But I drank a lot of nutritious drinks.

As anyone with a disability who has been in a hospital knows, you tend to be seen not as an active human being but as a collection of symptoms, of problems to solve. No matter how much they smile or make small talk, the personnel can be a tad, well, impersonal and dense. Too often, you don't get listened to. "Do you want the lights left on?" a nurse's aide might ask.

"Yes, please."

"No? Okay." And off they go, no matter what preference you actually expressed.

What's painfully obvious is that they have no idea about the rest of your life, who you really are. I finally told one medico to Google me. I was hoping that whatever pictures and videos I have online would paint a different, fuller, and more accurate image of who I am.

Still, there were several positive aspects to this two-week incarceration that made me smile. First, the beds have alternating-pressure mattress toppers to reduce bedsores, which wasn't true at my last hospitalization ten years ago (when I got a nasty pressure sore). Second, for transfers to, say, a CT scan or the swallow lab, I didn't have to be lifted onto a gurney to get from point A to point B; my hospital bed was rolled through the corridors, making for a much smoother transition. Third, everybody made sure that the right medication went to the right patient, unlike in times past. Nothing was done without first scanning my ID bracelet and checking the computer.

It's been more than two months since I got home. I am still exhausted and frequently short of breath. I looked it up online, in fact, and apparently it's not unusual for pneumonia survivors to take three or even six months to feel back to normal. It so damages the lungs and other body systems that even when the infection itself is gone, it leaves destruction in its wake. And as I said, my lungs weren't so great to begin with!

Nevertheless, I'm thrilled to have survived another close call. As a disabled person, I know that medical (and sometimes technological) interruptions like this happen periodically. But that's all they are. I'll soldier through the ordeal, or adapt my life around it as necessary. It won't derail me from what really matters.

The wisdom of disability? Perhaps. But I think it's just the benefit of experience, mixed with the triumph of hope.

Disabled People Like Me Have Always Been Vulnerable to Disease. Let Us Show You the Ropes.

In a strange way, I have long felt there is a flipside to inaccessibility and even ableism: If you're lucky (read: privileged*), these nasty, sometimes hateful barriers to full inclusion and integration make you tougher. They can force you to become both assertive and flexible. And occasionally, on good days, you can laugh at the absurdity of nondisabled do-gooders' outmoded, nonsensical hypocrisy.*

Are disabled folks scrappy? Perhaps. Inventive? Definitely.

Even during the crisis that was the Covid pandemic—as just about everyone was worried and complaining about the necessary precautions, while many disabled people like me felt especially vulnerable and concerned about being infected by the jerks who refused to wear a mask or were otherwise careless and apathetic—it became clear that some disabled folks actually had a leg up. So to speak.

Anyway, it's always nice if you can maintain a sense of humor even in the worst of times.

I keep hearing about how disabled people are panicked over Covid-19. As a disabled person, I know this is true. But media reports are missing an important point about us.

The fear and outrage are real. My respiratory muscles are so weak that my risk from this dread disease is enormous. What's more, I don't want my right to the best health care to be rationed away to someone younger and healthier and deemed more deserving, as has been reported.

Yet for many disabled people, a strong, stubborn vein of tenacity and even comedy runs through this wrenching sense of menace.

On social media, a kind of bravura greeted the contagion. To some of us, the initial threat almost felt like nothing new. Many disabled people rarely venture outside anyway because of access barriers or environmental sensitivities or the cumbersomeness of lugging an oxygen tank or other apparatus. "Wow! Today I learned that the lifestyle I've always lived is called shelter-in-place or self-quarantining!" joked one online friend.

"I'm really good at not touching my face," said another, referring to the fact that he (like me) has never been able to touch his face. We don't shake hands, either. Plus, those of us in big motorized wheelchairs typically maintain a safe distance from other people—for fear of running over their toes.

Don't get me wrong. We are scared. We know we can't entirely self-isolate. Because many of us rely on outside help, we're always vulnerable to whatever germs our personal-care aides may, despite their best efforts, inadvertently bring into our homes. It's a risk we have to take—always. We don't have a choice.

But we're accustomed to this contagion-phobic territory. Welcome to the club, nondisabled people.

The rationing of scarce medical resources—particularly the idea that ventilators could be given to young, otherwise healthy patients instead of to people like me—has only mobilized us. (Tennessee, for instance, has singled out those with SMA—like me—for exclusion from critical care in an emergency triage.) Online petitions and even lawsuits have ensued to block such blatant and dangerous health-care discrimination. I'm proud of my disabled pals for being among the first to bring this to public attention and taking action.

Like many people with SMA, I already have a lot of medical equipment at home. I have a BiPAP ventilator, an oxygen concentrator, a nebulizer to dilate my airways and loosen secretions, a Cough Assist machine that exercises my lungs and helps to clear them, a tracheostomy, and a suction machine to suck gunk out when I can't cough it up myself. I'm not hoarding this stuff the way some people have stockpiled toilet paper. It's just my standard survival arsenal. Call it disability privilege.

Yes, it's pleasant to joke in the face of terror, to laugh at the nightmare that is before us. But if I do get sick, I hope I can stay out of the hospital. That's vital, because there has been alarming discussion that strained hospitals could end up taking breathing devices away from people who use them regularly so that others can have them. This would be ghastly and unfair. We need and use our devices every day.

So help us not get sick. Keep washing your hands, wearing masks, and coughing into your elbows. It's not fair to make those of us who always have to worry about catching something do all the work.

Indeed, I can't help hoping this crisis leaves some positive long-term changes. Continued widespread telecommuting, for instance, could help reduce the disability unemployment rate, which is twice the national average in the best of times. Expanding the availability of education and entertainment—having more museums open their exhibits to virtual views, say, and more first-run movies released to pay-per-view and streaming services—is another idea disabled people have been clamoring for for years.

In the meantime, though, please don't cry for us. We know all about facing risks, taking precautions, and going on with our lives. That doesn't make us less afraid. But it might make us experts.

Mixed-Up Media

On Halloween, Celebrating Differences of All Types

The disability community has taught me many hard truths about myself and society. Those lessons came (and still come) from conversations, protest demonstrations, memoirs, and social media threads. They filter down from the wisdom of people's experiences and the scholarship of researchers and other academics who give life to the discipline called disability studies.

Among other truths, disability studies has shed light on how civilization has regarded disabled people throughout history—and how those attitudes can impact the way many of us see ourselves.

For example, I knew from my earliest years about pity. I wasn't allowed to have it in regard to myself. "It's no good feeling sorry for yourself," my mother used to tell me. Perhaps it was good advice, perhaps not. But disability studies taught me that this attitude has a history. People my parents' age remember when Franklin Roosevelt was president. He sort of epitomized this idea of not letting a disability get you down. That concept trickled down to me through my mother.

In any case, I certainly experienced other people's pity toward me. I remember old ladies who would accost me on the street with a pat on the head and "What happened to you, dear?"

Unwelcome comments from strangers still happen. "Do you mind if I pray for you?" is one frequent intrusion.

In addition, I'm intimately familiar with fundraising telethons for medical charities that milk pity for all that it's worth, as explained in earlier chapters. And from movies and TV, I'm attuned to the clichés about poor disabled victims. As an adult, though, thanks to disability scholars, I came to recognize the heroic, angelic disabled overachievers whose portrayals are designed to inspire an audience into teary, breathless admiration—and the embittered, scheming, revenge-obsessed disabled villain trope, not to mention the stereotype of limping, one-armed, disfigured disabled monsters.

Fortunately, my editor at NPR's Morning Edition wanted to hear more about this.

I never thought about a connection between disabilities and Halloween until I learned of the once-common fear of deformities—the limping, hunchbacked, hook-handed, or one-eyed monsters of ancient fairy tales and old horror movies. Even the word *creepy* comes from the same word as the oldest term for folks like me, the politically incorrect *cripple.*

As a kid, I tried not to think about what people might make of me, sitting in a wheelchair in my Batman or Lone Ranger costume. A hero who can't walk? Why not? Halloween is a celebration of the imagination, after all.

Sure, some kids teased. But I often scored more candy than my brother, who is not disabled. I saw no reason to complain about being treated differently.

Yet as an adult, I began to feel uneasy about the exhibitionism of Halloween, the way it encourages staring at all things weird. I can't help wondering if Halloween doesn't promote ridiculing differences—and thereby promote a kind of conformity. Yes, I know, for most people Halloween is an *escape* from conformity, but for those of us who don't quite fit the norm, that's nothing special. In fact, demonstrating that you're not exactly what people expect is pretty much what disabled folks do every day.

When I take my own kids—who do not have visible disabilities—trick-or-treating, I often attract as much attention as they do.

It's not the same in daylight. When kids see me on the street, careering in my power wheelchair, they often say things like, "Wow! Can I have one of those?" Hey, my chair *is* an amazing, transformative device.

"Cool, isn't it?" I'll say back. I figure I should do my part to make kids comfortable with people like me. Sometimes I have to tell the adult with them that it's okay, that kids shouldn't be forced to look away. I encourage them to ask questions, to learn.

Maybe I should see Halloween as an opportunity for grown-ups to do that, too. The holiday challenges us to stretch our perceptions. Maybe it can also teach us not to shrink away from the unfamiliar or judge appearances.

This Halloween, I'll try to remember that I really have nothing to fear.

God Bless Us, Every One—No, Really!

A decade later, I revisited disability stereotypes for a guest blog post at Facing-Disability.com. This time, though, my slant was somewhat different.

In Charles Dickens's immortal *A Christmas Carol*, Tiny Tim—the crutch-using young son of Bob Cratchit—is the epitome of a disability trope: He is inspiring, he is cute, he is doomed.

Yet sad and pitiful as he may be, Tiny Tim smiles through the pain and famously says, "God bless us, *every* one." *Every* is stressed, because he's including mean old Mr. Scrooge.

It's inspiration porn at its worst. And yet...

Maybe Tim was onto something. What's wrong with feeling charitable, generous, grateful?

Make no mistake. Inspiration porn *is* harmful. The term, coined by the late disabled Australian comedian and actress Stella Young, refers to using images of ordinary disabled people to make nondisabled people feel better about their lives. It objectifies us, separates us from "real" people who live "normal lives." It seems to say that disabled people's sole purpose is to brighten other people's days.

Such throat-grabbing portrayals remain media (and social media) staples, perhaps especially during the holiday season. They are exploited for all kinds of purposes, from garnering sympathy to raising money.

You know the objections: *Disabled people don't need or want pity. Pity doesn't really help us.* In fact, it's the opposite; it does us a grave disservice.

But there is another, more nuanced problem with treacly fundraising appeals—the sort that inundate us around the holidays. Participating in charity events enables people to think—wrongly—that they've done something important to right an injustice. However well intended, these efforts lull people into a false sense of accomplishment.

I know, this sounds gloomy. It's good for people to give to charity, right? A little charity is better than none. And for many of us, it's easier to donate money than make an ongoing commitment or dedicate time to a cause. We'd rather voluntarily give a few bucks than work hard to undo social injustices. But why stop there?

When people respond to a charitable appeal, they feel good. They pat themselves on the back. They may think they're done. They've done their part. But giving shouldn't absolve you of being kind and fair and generous in general. Moreover, it shouldn't become an excuse for inaction. You can't say, "I gave at the office," and then go out and be a jerk. You ought to continue caring about and doing good deeds for other people. You still have to help those who need help.

In the Dickens story, Scrooge feels sorry for Tiny Tim and is ultimately moved to give the family extra money so Tim can get better and live longer. That's great, but he's not moved to agitate for better social services on a wider scale. He may help one kid, one family, but Tiny Tim isn't the only one who needs help. Scrooge's donation to the Cratchit family doesn't do anyone else any good.

The narrator seems to recognize this flaw. By the end, we're told that Scrooge changes his ways and starts giving to all who need it. Not just at Christmas, but all year long.

That, I think, is the idea. That's a worthy message and goal. Even if it sounds corny, trying to act kindly toward everyone, all the time—to bless everyone, as Tiny Tim says—is the best policy.

What's So Funny About Having a Disability?

As I moved along in my connections with other disabled folks, I found that there is more to disability cultural life than righteous rage.

The following piece about disability humor ran in the New York Daily News.

My family thinks I'm hilarious. It's become my unofficial job at family gatherings like Thanksgiving to make wry, sarcastic remarks—sometimes even at the expense of a family member. I have two brothers, both of whom are fair game, and even our ninety-five-year-old father is usually up for being teased.

I'm not sure I like serving this function in the family, but somehow I can't stop doing it. I never thought that it had to do with my disability, but lately, I've learned about other disabled folks who've made a career of being funny. So I got to wondering what this all means.

Like a lot of disabled folks, I've had strangers stop me on the street and tell me that it's good to see me "out" today. Out of what? Out of bed? Out of the house? Out of the hospital? But of course, I don't say any of that. Typically, I just smile and say thank you. After all, they don't mean any harm. Or, to put it more self-righteously, they know not what they do.

But maybe next time I should respond with pointed humor. "I'm not out," I should say. "I'm closeted." (I'm not, by the way. That was a joke.)

Disabled people seem to know, almost instinctively, that there's no better tool for shaking up the status quo, no better mechanism for upending the zeitgeist, than a good, enduring, eye-opening laugh. Ask any disabled person if there's anything funny about their life, and chances are you'll get an emphatic *yes!* Living with a disability can be rough. It can be maddening, enraging, depressing—sometimes all of the above. Disabled people face constant access barriers—even decades after the Americans with Disabilities Act made those barriers illegal—and myriad other forms of exclusion. They deal with undependable technology, unreliable help staff, and endless government bureaucracy. They cope with poverty and isolation and loneliness.

Yet through all this, their lives can be hilarious.

On any ordinary day, they may experience abundant antics, riotous bodily mishaps, usually without meaning to, or quirks of fate that seem to prove the amateur theologian's assertion that God has a sense of humor.

But I do not think disability humor is a way of coping with disability frustration and rage. Rather, it's a way of coping with other people's prejudices. Honestly, there is nothing quite so uproarious as the mealymouthed ways nondisabled people react to what disabled people call *normal*. They're hysterical in their foot-in-mouth awkwardness.

The practice of laughing in the face of disability has a long lineage, but not always in a good way. "Too often and for too long, people with disabilities have been objectified as a source of amusement," writes Michael Rock, an autistic journalist and blogger. "Since ancient times, they have frequently appeared in such fields of entertainment as circuses."

Today, in its diversity of expression, technique, and subject matter, crip comedy knows few bounds. The humor may be visual or verbal or both. It may be revelatory, scatological, observational, self-deprecating, or offensive. Have you heard the one about the dyslexic agnostic who stayed up nights wondering if there really is a dog?

The most uproarious aspect of all this is how disability humor surprises ableds. The shock on their faces when they realize their own prejudices adds an extra chuckle to the impact we're having. Because besides being comical, we're also acute observers of other folks' faux pas. Call it a special ability.

Wheelchair Guys Are All Alike

I'll be honest with you: I prefer writing stuff that makes people smile. I've published a lot of terribly serious and somewhat depressing advocacy pieces, but it's the funny side of disabled life that I would really prefer to focus on and share.

Sometimes, a random item in the news will give me cause to chuckle. And even the dour old New York Times *seemed to agree. The following lighthearted piece was my first in the* Times, *and it remains a personal favorite.*

According to recent media reports, the esteemed British physicist and author Stephen Hawking has been frequenting a Southern California sex club.

My reaction to that news: Are you sure it was him?

Not that Professor Hawking couldn't or shouldn't go to what one paper called a "jiggle joint." Rather, my skepticism stems from the fact that I'm often mistaken for Stephen Hawking.

But it wasn't me. Honest. Strangers frequently mistake one wheelchair user for another, and I'm often mistaken for him. We both use sophisticated, customized wheelchairs, because of different but similar disabilities. And we both wear glasses. But there the resemblance ends.

Even before Stephen Hawking was world famous, it wasn't uncommon for me to hear something like, "Didn't I see you on TV the other day?" Or "Aren't you that guy from the church outing last year?" Sorry. Must have been some other guy on wheels.

What's really funny is when people don't take no for an answer. "Oh, come on. You *are* that guy! Or at least you know him, right?"

I don't take this kind of stuff too personally. (A) I'm used to it. And (B) I'm certain other folks in wheelchairs experience it, too. In fact, remarks like these are so common that a friend recently suggested we start a Twitter feed about it. Like "Bleep my dad says," only it would be stuff the nondisabled say to people with disabilities. It'd be a gold mine.

Why do people do this? Do we really all look alike?

What hurts the most is when the mistaken identity becomes a judgment, a remark about *how* people perceive me. How am I supposed to feel when a stranger says, "It's so beautiful to see you outside today," which I recently heard at a busy street corner and puzzled over. All I can think to say in response is, "You, too!"

To be sure, there are plenty of neutral and even backhandedly flattering examples. Jokes about my equipment are especially frequent, as in, "You got a license to drive that chair, buddy?" And I've been called heroic and inspirational more times than Moses, Jesus, and Muhammad combined.

More irksome are the random, uninvited prescriptions. Being told how to drive my chair, for instance—"Turn around and back into the elevator," say—by someone who's never used a wheelchair. Or if I only tried vitamin E or accepted Jesus Christ, I'd rise up and dance!

Worse still are the remarks directed at whoever is with me that demean us both. The people who ask my African American friends if they're my nurse. Or ask my wife if I'm her brother—or even, once, her son!—based on an assumption that someone like me wouldn't have friends or a spouse.

Once, several years ago, I was riding in the park with my wife on my lap when a guy on a bench shouted, "Who says *you* ain't gonna get lucky tonight!" Only not in those exact words.

People shouldn't comment about strangers, especially if the comments are unkind. The worst of them reveal that, in these strangers' eyes, I'm not a person but an object. An oddity, a noble sufferer, or a needy specimen who's burdening others. At best, I'm mistaken for someone familiar—a celebrity, like Stephen Hawking.

Perhaps I should take advantage of this by doing something naughty. I'd get away with it because no one would believe it was me.

Why I Will Miss Trevor Noah's Daily Show

I confess: Despite being periodically mistaken for certain disabled celebrities, I have had occasional fantasies of appearing on TV. Who hasn't? I have dreamed of wowing the world with my wit—and perhaps elevating the discourse about disabled people.

Alas, one of my dream interviewers resigned from his post before I had a chance. The disappointment, however, inspired the next blog post.

When the popular comedian and TV host Trevor Noah recently announced that he's leaving *The Daily Show* after seven years, perhaps no group was more disappointed than the disability community.

Noah might not have realized he's a kind of hero to many of us. Perhaps not all disabled folks would agree, but to me, he's done more for those whose bodies and minds function in ways that society deems shameful, who've struggled to feel comfortable in their own skin, than almost any other entertainer today.

Consider this: Back in March 2020, under Noah's stewardship, *The Daily Show* featured [the late] Judy Heumann, often called the mother of disability rights, to promote her memoir *Being Heumann* and the documentary film *Crip Camp*. She didn't appear in a tight head-and-shoulders shot either, as other live shows have done to hide a wheelchair user's disability; she was shown on-screen in all her post-polio glory, photographed like any other guest.

Then, this past August, blind YouTuber Molly Burke was Noah's guest for no particular reason other than to explain the many prejudices and access obstacles she routinely faces.

More recently, when certain people on the right suggested that John Fetterman, then a Democratic candidate for the U.S. Senate from Pennsylvania, was unfit to hold office because of his poststroke language-processing disability, Noah said that was "trash, especially since America already has disabled lawmakers serving right now. It shouldn't be a disqualifier."

Noah has proved himself happy to give time on camera to those deemed different, to amplify the voices of the oppressed and outcast alongside the shiny and famous.

I think the reason that Noah seems to identify with disabled folks—and perhaps vice versa—is that he, too, was born into a society where discrimination against people like him was completely legal as recently as the early 1990s. In fact, South African apartheid officially ended at about the same time the Americans with Disabilities Act (ADA) of 1990 went into effect.

In his best-selling book *Born a Crime*, Noah, now thirty-eight, describes his boyhood under apartheid and how his life—and, more importantly, his expectations for his life—changed after apartheid.

I grew up years before disabled kids like me were allowed in regular schools, let alone protected from discrimination in stores, restaurants, and movie theaters. It's sort of a similar trajectory.

Like Noah's mother, my parents told me I could grow up to be and do anything I wanted. It wasn't quite true, though the subsequent Education for All Handicapped Children Act of 1975 (later renewed as the Individuals with Disabilities Education Act) and, later, the ADA brought that dream closer to reality.

Noah, I believe, understands how you can be grateful for gaining your rights but also angry because you should've had those rights all along, just by virtue of being a living human being! Moreover, though the government says you're now legally protected against prejudice and entitled to all society has to offer, you can't help feeling that promise is not yet fully realized.

"Trevor," I'd say, if I were ever lucky enough to be on his program, "you wouldn't believe what I went through to get here! The New York subway is about the most inaccessible and unaccommodating place left in America, second only to airplanes!"

He would get my drift. Noah knows what it's like to be unjustly locked out of society and told you don't belong.

To be sure, there are other enlightened talk show hosts. But Noah clearly leans in to people who speak up, who assert their right to social justice and fair representation. I can only hope that his successor will see the beauty in this vision of diversity—one that includes all body types and ways of functioning.

The need for this acceptance, this endorsement, is palpable. Disabled people are done with hiding, minimizing, or apologizing for our differences, limitations, and necessities. We want and deserve to be seen, which is something that Trevor Noah seems to understand.

Stigma and Reputation

It's Just a Wheelchair, Not a Batmobile

Many people think disability rights and its later incarnation, disability justice, are all about ramps, sign language interpreters, Braille signage, closed captioning, descriptive video, and other accommodations for equal access. But there is another element that may be equally important.

Changing prejudicial attitudes, to put it euphemistically.

Unfortunately, attitudes can't be legislated. Sometimes they're difficult to define. They can be deep-seated and are often unconscious. Those who harbor any form of bigotry probably aren't aware of it, and they would certainly deny it. They may conscientiously use the right language and meet all the legally required standards—but still miss the point. A simple test to judge whether you're one of these people: How would you feel if a disabled person moved in next door or were a coworker? What about if that disabled person were your boss or were engaged to your child or sibling?

The truth, I believe, is that most if not all of us have some unconscious prejudices. We tend to be more comfortable with people who are basically like ourselves, or like what we aspire to be. Alas, it seems to be part of human nature to be wary of differences.

When it comes to ableism, the discrimination may be so subtle as to appear harmless. I've never heard anybody say, "I hate those damn disabled people!" In fact, most folks want to help disabled people. But what if a disabled person doesn't want your help? Is that okay with you? Can you respect a disabled person's autonomy?

No matter how diligent and kindhearted you may be, unless disabled people are empowered or at least treated as equals in any given situation, there is still a problem.

I really can't blame people for having a bad attitude toward disabilities. There's a lot of stigma around them. And to be honest, even the staunchest disability advocates didn't exactly ask for their disabilities. But they've come to terms with them, even learned to celebrate them, as they realize that most of the problems come not from their own bodies and minds but from external obstructions and impediments that can and should be rectified.

From early on, I've recognized the power of words. I've tried to use them to call out offensive tropes and clichés, to identify them and help people recognize not only the stigmas that exist but also their own unconscious prejudices. I've tried, too, to instill in readers' minds a sort of picture of disabled people that's more fair and accurate. It's almost as if all we really need is better PR.

One of my earliest published pieces tried to do just that. Like most of the essays here, I wrote it completely on spec. Unlike most of the essays in this collection, I sent my draft to just one publication, Newsweek, *instead of my usual scattershot approach. I remember thinking up sentences while shopping with my kids for new clothes, because I was obsessed with making it perfect. I was going out on a limb, communicating my own notions instead of mimicking something I'd picked up from my comrades in disability activism. This one would be all mine.*

Naturally, I was delighted when it was accepted. The magazine even sent out a photographer to take my portrait. Though the piece feels somewhat dated now, it still holds a special place in my heart.

For as long as I can remember, people have told me my life would make a good book. I suppose people envision a sort of *My Left Foot* meets *The Paper Chase*.

I couldn't see writing a book about my life. I've always rejected being an "inspiration." Like most people with a disability, I've simply lived my life using whatever resources were at my disposal. It's not like I had any choice. Besides, there are dangers in being put on a pedestal. It may be flattering, but it can also be marginalizing. You're too lofty to date or get job offers, yet not free to feel bad, sad, or angry. You can easily be left out, segregated, and trampled on.

Yet several months ago I began writing my memoirs. Why did I change my mind? Now officially middle-aged, I'm seeing my experiences in a different light. I worry more about what legacy I'll leave my kids than what other people think of me.

The truth is, I'm not the only one who has to deal with physical problems. I've had friends my age die. And last summer, at my twenty-fifth high-school reunion in New York City, nearly everyone had some sort of health-related restriction. No fat, please. No salt. I'd like to say they all looked great, but honestly, there were wide variations. The funniest were the ones who had facial features—noses and ears, especially—that seemed to have stretched to clownish proportions with age. Our bodies betray us.

Even mine. If I ever thought I was exempt from acquiring other ailments—I've paid my dues, haven't I?—I was embarrassingly, emphatically wrong. Two years ago I developed ulcerative colitis, an incurable digestive disorder. It's manageable, but figuring out which drugs to take and at what dosages is a grueling ordeal. Plus, there are still awful flare-ups.

But dealing with life's curveballs is not entirely unfamiliar. At my lowest points, I wonder if my wife and I will remain healthy enough to enjoy the rest of our lives. But my mood always bounces back. Somehow I'm able to draw on an ever-filling well of optimism. It's a coping mechanism that I've learned from years of living with disability.

Reflecting on this and other lessons I've gleaned from my unusual life is precisely what motivates me to write about it. I know all about accepting, even embracing, variations from the norm. Some limitations are maddening, of course, but others become opportunities for flexing my creativity. For example, when someone is trying to help me but doesn't understand what I'm asking, I can't demonstrate. I'm forced to come up with different words to explain it. "Please move my right hand forward. No, to the front more. Uh, toward the table . . ." I think of this when my computer suddenly doesn't do something it's supposed to do. From a distance, my elderly father marvels at my [technological] know-how. But the reason I'm able to solve [software] glitches is that I'm conditioned not to give up hope.

For me, persistence has been necessary—lifesaving, in a sense. I've had to learn to absorb what's thrown at me and go on. That doesn't make me anything special. Many, many people face extraordinary odds every day. It's entirely feasible to keep going. Don't get me wrong. I'm too cynical and smart-alecky to be anyone's idea of a Pollyanna; I get angry and depressed. Yet I know firsthand that anything is possible, and so, deep down, how could I be anything but hopeful?

In an era of terrorist attacks, unthinkably high gas prices, and a tight job market, perhaps this is a worthy message. As a nation we feel vulnerable, confused, enraged. A sort of nihilism besets our days. How many were killed today in Iraq? What's the latest verdict in the Enron/Tyco/DeLay case? Which hot author is under fire for plagiarism now?

Part of what keeps me optimistic is knowing I've benefited from incredible progress in technology, which has enabled me to drive a motorized wheelchair with the slightest of finger or lip movements and use a computer by voice. I've seen the flowering of the disability rights movement and the enactment of access regulations. Perhaps most of all, I've managed to find love and have a family. Why shouldn't my luck continue?

And if other people find my story inspirational, I guess I'll just have to live with it.

I Am Not Your Supercrip

It's hard to believe, but sixteen years later I was still complaining about the problem of being inspirational. Not surprising that I was still complaining; that's par for the course for me. But it boggles the mind that this was still an issue, that people had still not learned better.

The following essay is from a blog post I wrote for FacingDisability.com. It draws on concepts I developed more fully in the book I was writing at the time, so a few passages may sound familiar.

In June, CBS News showed a young paraplegic man walking—yes! walking! (with the aid of a walker and leg braces)—at his high school graduation.

In August, NBC News did a feature about a man who had allegedly overcome quadriplegia(!). To prove it, he swam from Alcatraz to the San Francisco shore.

These stories were not tabloid sensationalism. They were part of serious news broadcasts. Human interest items, to be sure. But to me, they're offensive and do a serious disservice to the disability community.

Such representations are common. Though the network producers clearly felt these events were newsworthy, you see similar depictions all the time. They make people feel good. Yet as a lifelong disabled person, I have to ask: Why do disabled folks have to do extraordinary things to be taken seriously? Why do we have to, in effect, imitate nondisabled people to gain respect?

Don't get me wrong. I have nothing against either of the gentlemen depicted in these stories. It's not their fault the media lionize (read: *exploit*) them. I know that if you're disabled and feeling downtrodden, if people treat you as *less than* because of your disability, it's only natural to want to prove them wrong. You want to show that you can do anything anybody else can do, that you're just as good.

But why make a spectacle of yourself?

In disability circles, we call these media portrayals "supercrip" stories. I was guilty of trying to be a supercrip myself at one time. I felt I had to work twice as hard as anyone else to be treated normally. I had to prove that I was exceptional to disprove ableist prejudices, many of which I had internalized.

"'Supercrip' stories can act as a defense mechanism for the status quo," says Shailee Koranne, a Toronto-based writer, in a blog post for the Canadian Broadcasting Corp. They effectively say that if one "disabled person could beat the odds and live happily in our current society," she continues, then all disabled people "should have it within themselves to do the same."

Supercrip stories are a subset of "inspiration porn"—that is, portrayals of disabled people that treat them as inspirations (rather than as individuals) in ways that effectively say disabled people only exist, or are only worthy of photographing and writing about, to inspire or motivate nondisabled people.

For a lot of disabled people, there's no choice. To be inspiring for others seems the only way we can be accepted.

The first group of disabled folks to gain widespread acceptance—other than breakout stars such as Ray Charles and Stevie Wonder—tended to be rugged, muscular, and white. Many were wheelchair basketball or wheelchair tennis players, their beefy arms propelling their stripped-down, aerodynamic sports chairs to great speeds and an almost brutal rigorousness. Very macho, they were considered strong, independent, autonomous, tough, sexy—and they helped put at ease anyone who might be a little uncomfortable around atypical bodies. (They were also almost uniformly cisgender men.) That is, their pursuits were more recognizable and legible to the nondisabled world. Remember the popular 2005 documentary *Murderball*, about quadriplegic jocks who play full-contact rugby? Remember Oscar Pistorius, the Olympic and Paralympic sprinter from South Africa whose prosthetic "racing blades" helped make him famous (and who was later convicted of murdering his girlfriend)?

Society's preference for disabled people who are able to, in a sense, impersonate nondisabled people, or otherwise fit nondisabled expectations, has a long history.

The problem is, the message of the brave, miraculous, heroic disabled person trickles down to those of us far from the spotlight.

I don't know how many times I've been applauded for just going to the grocery store or the movies (pre-Covid, that is). Most times, I try to smile and answer pleasantly. I figure they're trying to be nice and mean no harm. They don't know they've been conditioned by inspiration porn and supercrip stereotypes.

The harm these portrayals do, though, can be significant. They tell ordinary disabled people that they're not good enough. Worse still, they give the impression that if you work hard, you might be able to overcome your disability. In other words, your disability is your own fault.

People really do say this. Strangers constantly tell me, "You should try . . ." Fill in the blank. Hyperbaric oxygen therapy. Vitamin E. Passive exercise. Prayer. Do whatever it is, they insist, and you will be cured. It's a sort of ableist equivalent of mansplaining, in which nondisabled people think they know better than you do. Call it "ablesplaining."

I know better. There's nothing wrong with me as I am. And if that's not good enough for you, then you're the one who needs to work harder.

Adapted from Disability Pride: Dispatches from a Post-ADA World *(Beacon Press, 2022).*

Disability After Dark

After my 2022 book, Disability Pride, *came out, I was interviewed by Toronto-based disability activist, consultant, and sexuality guru Andrew Gurza for his podcast, which explores stereotypes, self-image, and society's shortcomings toward disabled folks. What follows are edited excerpts.*

Andrew: On the show today, I sit down with my new friend, Ben Mattlin. He wanted to reconnect with his cripdom and his disability community more, because he felt as a white, cisgender, straight, disabled man, he really wasn't connecting with the new generation of disabled people out there. And I really, really love that he wanted to learn more and he wanted to grow more. Welcome, Ben.

Ben: Hi, Andrew. Great to be with you.

Andrew: Let's just dive into it. Because you highlight queer disabled people and people of color who are disabled and a bunch of different identities, because you're using your privilege as a white disabled person to highlight that, I think that's really important, because you're saying, "I don't want to be the center of this. I want to use my platform to lend it to someone else." This highlights that we all have to do that. We all have to take a step back a little bit and be like, "Yep, my disability is important, too, but there are other people that need the spotlight."

Ben: I appreciate your saying that. I really wanted to [be inclusive], and if someone out there goes, "Nah, you messed up," let me know, you know? I want to hear it.

Andrew: One of the things I heard you say was the word *cripple*, and I love that word, because it's what I use to describe myself. I wonder what does that word mean for you, and why do you use it personally?

Ben: It's a word that seems to shock nondisabled people, but I think most of us feel connected to it. It connects you to the community.

Andrew: I do feel the shock value part. I certainly use it when I do talks and when I talk about my life and I do presentations. I'm constantly saying, "I'm going to use the words *queer* and *cripple* today," and people are always . . .

Ben: It shocks people, right?

Andrew: Yeah. But I love that, because it means that they're going to pay attention. And maybe they'll listen to what I have to say after I say, "I'm a queer cripple." They're going to go, "Oh, no. That's such a scary word," but then they're going to listen to what I say afterwards.

Ben: Right.

Andrew: I also really like it when people just kind of use it in everyday conversation, because it means they get it. They're one of us. They understand. [But] some people don't have disability pride. Some people don't see their disability as something to have pride over. It's important to highlight those things because we are met with a lot of toxic positivity, such as, "You can do anything. Don't worry about it." But also some disabled people are like, "I'm not proud of it at all. It sucks and I hate it." Ben, how do you feel in respect to disability pride within yourself? What brings you disability pride?

Ben: Good questions. As I might've mentioned before, back in the olden days I thought I could pass, you know? I didn't think about it—

Andrew: I'm giggling, because how did twenty-year-old Ben Mattlin be like, "Oh, yeah, I can pass. I don't look disabled." How?

Ben: Right, right. Until I came to a bump in the road. I didn't think of it as a form of self-hatred. It was just a way to operate. It seemed the only choice, really, if you wanted to get anywhere in life or do anything. Like you had to follow this pattern. It was a paradigm that I think went back to President Franklin Roosevelt, who hid his disability as much as possible. I felt you had to put on a brave face, be tough, be resourceful, and all those things.

Andrew: Rise above and all that stuff.

Ben: Exactly! That was the only way people would respect you. Otherwise, you're feeling sorry for yourself. I probably got that from my parents, but it was out there.

I think it's really only when you connect to the disability community and learn to understand some of these messages that you've internalized, that you didn't even realize, that you can begin to get past that. I heard another disabled person talk about trying to pass, and that's when I first recognized it. "Oh, yeah. I'm doing that," I thought. And then as I learned more about what other disabled people are capable of doing, have always done, and continue to do, the ways that we contribute and have always contributed to society, well, you almost can't help but feel proud, you know?

So, to me, it's partly a matter of self-esteem and not feeling ashamed of yourself, but it's also about feeling connected to the broad and diverse disability community. I don't want to oversimplify or kind of reduce it to—

Andrew: That's okay. You can reduce whatever you need to.

Ben: Okay. Well, in a way, ableism is about a system that presumes there is a right way to be, a right way to look and think and communicate—maybe a few right ways. There's a little latitude there. But only a little. Basically, anything that varies from that is judged a problem, is wrong, and needs to be fixed. When you begin to understand that and the repercussions of that, you say, "Hey, I don't buy into it. I'm okay the way I am."

That's a kind of disability pride.

There are people who say, "What? How can I be proud of things I can't do?" Well, you may not like aspects of your disability, but you don't have to hate yourself because of them.

Andrew: Yeah.

Ben: We all have aspects of our lives that we don't like. And most of us disabled folks have been on an ongoing journey to understand, to really feel disability pride. It's a common theme that's not often explored.

Andrew: Disability pride—two words that aren't supposed to go together. And so, when they do, people go, "What is that? I better pay attention!" There's this overarching belief that if you're disabled, you shouldn't be proud. So saying it, the two words together, is kind of like a big "fuck you" to anybody who thinks, "You can't be proud of your disability."

Ben: And it means different things to different people, of course. But, yeah, it's a good concept.

Andrew: What would you say back to someone who says you shouldn't have disability pride?

Ben: We're all entitled to our own opinion, of course. But the more you understand what it means, and the contributions and role of disabled people throughout history, the more the idea of being ashamed of it seems kind of absurd. I mean, the more you know, the more pride you'll feel.

Andrew: Amazing, amazing. I think the more nondisabled people—or people who are not disabled yet—learn about disability pride, well, it will give them something to hold onto when disability becomes a part of their story.

Ben: True. It's important for newly disabled folks, too.

Andrew: Yes. Now, when you were growing up, what media appealed to you as a disabled person, and where do you want to see disabled media go today?

Ben: When I was growing up, we had telethons, like the Jerry Lewis Muscular Dystrophy Association telethon. Not a very good example of disability pride. We used to laugh at it—but again, no wonder I wanted to try and pass! Who wants to be a Jerry's kid, you know?

Andrew: True.

Ben: I hope people know what that is. It's been years, but there used to be a telethon, a fundraiser for charity, and Jerry Lewis, the comedian, would bring out these kids in wheelchairs and talk about how terrible their lives were and how they were all going to die unless you send some money.

There was also a TV show I loved called *Ironside*, starring Raymond Burr as a police detective in a wheelchair. Because he'd been shot. It was extremely unrealistic, but he had a van with a lift and a ramp into his office. There were little things like that, little moments, that meant so much to me—to see a guy sitting in a wheelchair bossing everybody around. It always inspired me.

Andrew: Didn't they try to remake the show a couple years ago?

Ben: Yes, they did. It was terrible. Had like three episodes before it got cancelled.

More recently, there are TV shows like *Speechless* and *Special*, and others, that seem to have much better portrayals of disability, to me. There are performers and entertainers with highly visible disabilities. That's important, because it shows that disability is part of the multicultural mix. We need more of that, I think, whether it's main characters or just in the background—

Andrew: I would love to see more disabled folks in the background. Sometimes, when they make the disabled person the main character, the story becomes tragic and sad and horrible. I would like to see a guy in a wheelchair on TV or in the movies who's just hanging out or talking to his friends or just being there. That'd be cool.

Ben: There are more examples than there used to be, but still it's so rare that when you see it you've got to go, at least I do, "Oh, look, there's a cripple!" It doesn't happen often enough. There are more in Britian, I'm noticing—English actors with disabilities who are getting more attention.

Andrew: Yeah. I think they do a lot more representation over there than they do in North America. A separate question, about health care: Does lack of health-care support for you as a disabled man in his sixties concern you?

Ben: Sure. You bet. The Covid years really accentuated the vulnerability. Yes, I get angry, frustrated. Why aren't more people wearing masks? Why do people pretend it's all over? Why is it thrown entirely on me to take precautions? If other people would be more careful about not spreading germs and stuff, we could be more equal. You see, I have difficulty wearing a mask. It's hard enough for me to breathe without a mask, never mind with one. Plus, I now drive my wheelchair with a little, itty-bitty joystick I control with my lips. If I wear a mask, it becomes impossible to drive my chair. My wife has created a mask for me that's more flexible, so I can drive somewhat better, but it's not exactly an N95, not the safest mask in the world.

We take risks all the time, but going out into the world now seems extra risky from a health perspective. I have been very isolated for three years now, like a lot of my fellow crips, just to stay safe and healthy. I'm getting a little tired of it.

Andrew: I like how you said, why do you have to be the one to make the concessions? Wearing a mask is a sign of respect. If you wear a mask, you're giving somebody who can't wear a mask the chance to go out and feel safe.

Ben: Exactly. Also, there are masks that have transparent panels for those who are lip readers. You don't see them very often, but if you really want to show respect for others, that would be ideal.

Andrew: Let's shift to a different question: I want to know, Ben, what brings you disability joy?

Ben: That's a good question! How about humor? A lot of crips have some pretty funny experiences. Afterward, you laugh about it, but it's stuff that we all know or have experienced in some way. That's a good laugh I think we can all share. Other kinds of joy? I get joy seeing disabled people who are comfortable with themselves in their own skin. That's great. Even sometimes a good blog post, a good podcast.

Andrew: Like this one?

Ben: Definitely.

Not All Crips Are Creeps

What happens when an inspirational role model disappoints? A couple of back-to-back news items in 2018 raised that question for many of us—and, for me anyway, the larger issue of disability exceptionalism.

It's sort of the flipside of being a supercrip. If you're judged remarkably impressive for accomplishing ordinary things as a disabled person, does that give you the liberty to take advantage of your status, to believe that perhaps normal rules don't apply to you? Of course not!

This is another blog post that was commissioned by FacingDisability.com.

What's happening with my people?

In late December, in separate allegations, the esteemed Public Radio host John Hockenberry and world-famous artist Chuck Close were both accused of sexual improprieties. So were many others, of course. But these men both use wheelchairs.

I do, too, but apparently I'm much nicer.

I realize that people with disabilities have been saying for years that they can do anything anybody else can, but this? Do you have to prove it in such a creepy, criminal way? It's no laughing matter, to be sure. And the accusations against them aren't entirely identical—Hockenberry (often called "Hock") reportedly insulted and bullied female coworkers, while Close is accused of making women he hired as models undress and then uttering unwarranted comments about their body parts.

Yet the cases are similar enough that, in the current climate, the public is likely to conflate the two examples.

I don't know Close, but I've met Hock. I interviewed him and his wife, Alison, for a book about interabled romance—that is, unions between people with disabilities and people without them. With their full consent and cooperation, I'd delved into the details of their twenty-year marriage. How had I missed the clues that there was trouble in their paradise?

Frankly, I'd come to think of Hockenberry as a kind of role model. Yes, a rolling role model. Hadn't he braved Middle East war zones as an NPR reporter, wheels and catheters and all? Hadn't he written a best-selling memoir (its title, *Moving Violations*, now rings with haunting irony) and performed a well-received one-man show off-Broadway?

Neither Hock nor Close ever made a secret of their disabilities. Without shame or the usual disguises of the paraplegic (framing camera angles for head-and-shoulders-only shots, for instance, or magically appearing behind a desk with no visible means of entrance or exit), Hock had been in front of TV cameras many times, chalking up multiple Emmys. Close was often shown in full-body portraits.

For me, now, these brave images carry the smell of deceit.

Perhaps that's not entirely fair. Still, how should I square my admiration for these men's myriad accomplishments with my revulsion at their alleged depredations? Can I still feel proud of, even inspired by, their examples?

Reluctantly, I search through my Hockenberry interview notes. Hock talked about the emotional bubble he put around himself as a defense against feeling overlooked, discounted, or negated. Did that mean something more sinister? Alison told me that his insistence on being strong and independent was a turn-on, initially, though later it became a hindrance. She needed him to learn to be vulnerable, to confide in her, to share his feelings, and participate in the give-and-take that's essential to a good, lasting relationship.

At the time, I took these frank confessions as typical relationship chatter. But should I have read between the lines?

What's most galling to me, though, are the explanations both men have made. "As a quadriplegic, I try to live a complete, full life to the extent possible," Close reportedly said. "But given my extreme physical limitations, I have found that utter frankness is the only way to have a personal life."

What on earth does that mean? Does anybody believe it?

Hock's public apology wasn't much better. It included this: "Having to deal with my own physical limitations has given me an understanding of powerlessness, and I should have been more aware."

No, guys, your disabilities aren't a license to fondle, bully, tease, or otherwise abuse. Your physical limitations are irrelevant—and, please, don't give the rest of us wheelchair guys a bad rep. It's your behavior, not your bodies, that are in question. If disability isn't pertinent to your professional capabilities, then it isn't to your wrongdoings either. You can't have it both ways.

I concede that many of us with disabilities may harbor deep-seated feelings of inadequacy. Some disabled people—men, women, and nonbinary folks alike—are sexually insecure, starved for physical affection. The late cartoonist John Callahan, a quadriplegic, used to talk about living at a nipples-eye view of the world, which I took as a comic expression of his horniness.

But such frustrations are no excuse. True, we can and often do get away with stuff. Probably every disabled person has taken advantage of others' pity at some point. I've accepted discount tickets to movies and plays. At Disneyland, I've used my wheelchair to cut to the front of the line. Whether or not such perks are justified is debatable. But sexual harassment isn't among the items signified under the Twitter hashtag #cripswag.

I hope the general public doesn't come away from these recent news items thinking all crips are creeps. And for those of us with disabilities, the message should be loud and clear: Don't even think about it. If we don't want special treatment, then we're not entitled to special dispensation either.

This is true even if you're considered a role model.

When Wheelchairs Are Cool

On the subject of role models and icons, the following essay about a certain popstar addresses something I've always felt very deeply: Everything is what you make of it. For example, because of my many personal-care needs, I've always had someone around to help me. As a kid, I hated it when someone referred to my assistant as a "nurse" or "caregiver." For some reason those words sounded more embarrassing and stigmatizing than, perhaps, "valet," "butler," or even "chauffeur." Yet a lot of the job was the same as those more suave-seeming professions. "Attendant" was sort of okay, but "personal-care assistant" was my favorite term.

Similarly, disability activists prefer "wheelchair using" to "wheelchair bound." "Nondisabled" has replaced the old, slightly threatening "temporarily able-bodied," or "TABby," because it's considered more accurate. To my mind, there's a difference between "able-bodied" and "nondisabled." Many people with autism or dyslexia or some other invisible disability may be able-bodied but are not nondisabled. So the words aren't really interchangeable. Anyway, beyond language, context and perspective can make a tremendous difference in how we see and judge the world around us—including what we think of those of us who get around in wheelchairs.

This piece ran in The New York Times.

Last week, the celebrity gossip site TMZ posted pictures of Justin Bieber in a wheelchair. He was not at a hospital. He was at Disneyland. As everyone knows, Disney patrons in wheelchairs get to cut to the front of the lines. But as a dispute flared over whether this was Mr. Bieber's intent, becoming a trending topic on Twitter, one fact remained unassailable: I was there first.

One of the great perks of being in a wheelchair—as I have been since age [three or] four [before that it was a baby carriage, or just being carried in someone's arms]—is being able to cut lines. Sometimes people let you go ahead of them at the grocery store. Sometimes theater and sports arena box offices give you discount tickets. When I was a kid, I often got backstage passes. In short, you get to take advantage of others' pity—or at least their desire to keep things simple and not cause a scene. You get treated like a VIP. You get treated like Justin Bieber, except without the screaming fans.

The teen heartthrob's publicists said that he was just resting an injured knee, not trying to pretend he was, well, like me. But I prefer to think otherwise. After all, they also acknowledged that even without the wheelchair, he would still get to circumvent the endless queues, to avert a riot. The point is that he was not afraid to be seen in a wheelchair, which, to me, is a point for my team.

I've never pretended to be in a wheelchair to curry favor, of course, but I've often felt that I can play the disability card for all it's worth. I have, I confess, used it to hustle my kids through Disney lines, even though I knew full well that I wasn't actually going to get on the ride myself.

Besides, sometimes you can't help it. People offer you stuff. Strangers smile at you, give you a thumbs-up, pat you on the shoulder. (I can never quite decide whether that's complimentary or condescending—or both.)

The mantra of disability rights is "no pity." Yet the truth is, taking advantage of one's disability—or rather, of other people's solicitousness—is one of the true joys of life on wheels. When I was a kid, before equal-access laws attempted to level the playing field, I often got into movies free. I never asked for it, but I never refused it either. "I'll just stay in my wheelchair," I sometimes said, as if it were a consolation for not taking an actual seat from a paying customer. (Still, I had my limits. When sweet old ladies offered to buy me candy or a cookie, it was decidedly creepy. I never once said yes.)

This kind of cloying generosity was a great source of laughter when I was growing up. My older, nondisabled brother and I used to joke that if we were ever orphaned, or simply needed some extra spending money, we could clean up by begging on street corners. He would accost passersby while I would act, well, as "handicapped" as possible, moaning and drooling and contorting my face. Sure, this gallows humor was a sort of defense mechanism. But the constant clash between what others thought they knew about me just from glancing at my skinny, floppy, wheelchair-riding limbs and what we actually knew about me—that I was a smart, alert, regular guy who happened to require a lot of assistance—occasioned much familial hilarity.

Now I know better, of course. It wasn't really funny. And if I want fairness and equality, I have to pay the price—even if it's full price.

But many well-meaning [nondisabled] folks remain frustratingly ignorant about people with disabilities. We even have a term for it now—"ableism"—though I'm not sure how much it helps. People may know that it's wrong to exclude or underestimate the disabled, but I fear they're rarely clear on exactly what that entails or how to behave. For many people, there is still something hopelessly "other" about folks with disabilities. Wheelie Justin may be a hopeful sign for the future, when the very image of disability no longer stigmatizes.

I've long believed in disability pride, [or] Crip Cool. To me, that has never meant being an awe-inspiring overachiever, someone who succeeds despite a disability. Rather, it's the opposite—someone who embraces their disability and isn't afraid to show it. Wheelchairs can be fun. Voice-recognition technology is a blast. Vans with automatic ramps are awesome. And don't forget our coveted parking spaces. All of which help mitigate the bad stuff.

So go ahead and play disabled. As long as it's done with joy and respect—not to tease or poke fun—I won't be offended. Just don't do it for the freebies, which are harder and harder to find these days anyway. Do it as you do anything else, because you think it's cool.

And if Mr. Bieber wants to give me a call, I'd be happy to show him how to pop wheelies.

Ongoing Issues and Irritations

No Straws? No Thanks!

When someone who isn't used to making accessibility accommodations asks me about my requirements—door widths, ramp slopes, toileting needs, and so on—a funny thing tends to happen. All of a sudden they start noticing access barriers everywhere, they tell me. As if these obstacles had been hiding in plain sight.

The truth is, the same thing happens to disabled folks when they learn about the issues facing other disabled folks. Or at least it's happened to me. I've learned, for instance, that it's not just about architectural barriers. Atmospheric affronts, such as strong fragrances, are intolerable to some people with extreme environmental sensitivities. Low lighting or ambient noise can severely interfere with how folks with sensory disabilities function. Jarring images or sounds may trigger dangerous discomfort or even seizures among some of my disabled pals who have neurological, autistic, or emotional disabilities.

Then there are the pats on the head, the averted eyes, the political pandering, the systemic medical arrogance, the I-don't-care-about-what-you-need dismissiveness, or even the malicious, anti-access backlash.

The specific issues may change, and sometimes it's hard to keep up with what is causing outcry at any particular time. Indeed, any number and variety of offenses might spark justifiable, righteous rage. But I believe we can learn from one another. I trust the wisdom of my peers, whether they're elders, ancestors, or younger advocates.

The next piece is a reaction to news items I might not have been aware of without the advocacy of younger colleagues. But the issue at hand is something I know personally, something that directly affects me, and I feared wasn't well understood by the general public.

Recently, when Starbucks announced it would stop giving out disposable plastic straws by 2020, it drew a line in the sand.

For people like me, it was bad enough that municipalities such as Oakland, Berkeley, Malibu, Miami Beach, and Seattle had banned the bendy drinking tubes. Proposals for similar ordinances have also appeared in New York, San Francisco, and parts of Europe. But I don't live in those places. Starbucks, on the other hand, is right down the block. And up the block. Wherever I go, there is a Starbucks nearby. They're everywhere! So to me, Starbucks banning plastic straws was the last "last straw."

Granted, I shouldn't feel offended. I'm in favor of clean beaches, safe water, and breathable air. I'm not anti-Green. It's just that I depend on single-use straws every day, all day long, for my sustenance.

I can't hold a cup or raise a spoon. As a kid, I'd bite the edge of plastic tumblers (and sometimes glass ones) to hold them to my lips with the proper tilt. In time, though, that maneuver proved awkward. My jaw grew weaker, plus too many cups collapsed, slipped, or shattered.

Having other people lift and tip cups to my lips was a recipe for disaster, too. Bendable straws became my perfect solution.

In college, I endured razzing over this method. (No, it's not true that drinking beer through a straw gets you drunk faster!) But I didn't care. For me, straws weren't for fun. I used them because I had to.

These days, they deliver my morning coffee; the pliable conduits are unfazed by piping hot beverages [unlike paper straws, which disintegrate]. Midday, they channel vocal-cord-restoring juice and water to my parched and frequently catarrh-inflamed throat. They're also useful for the evening cocktail or wine, and for slurping broth.

What's more, they enable me to direct the flow of liquid to just the right spot in my esophagus to push food down. This is key, because my disability affects my ability to swallow. I'm also at high risk for aspiration—meaning edibles and beverages easily go down the wrong pipe, blocking airways. If that happens, I don't have the muscles to cough stuff out. So I have to swallow just right.

Could other types of straws perform the same miracles? Not nearly as well. I frequently have to grip the tip of a straw with my lips and teeth to steady it. Paper straws collapse and degrade under that pressure, and metal ones are too firm and distort taste.

Make no mistake: I'm far from the only one who feels alienated, even threatened, by the #StrawBan trend. In a Greenpeace blog last spring, disability activist Jamie Szymkowiak wrote, "A soggy paper straw increases the risk of choking. Most paper and silicone alternatives are not flexible, and this is an important feature for people with mobility related impairments. Metal, glass and bamboo straws present obvious dangers for people who have difficulty controlling their bite. . . . In addition, re-useable straws in public places are not always hygienic or easy to clean."

On Facebook, my disabled allies go so far as to dub the straw-banning movement ableism. One wag posted, "Ahh, the joys of being nondisabled, and the freedom it gives to tell disabled people what they should and should not be able to do."

I prefer to think it's blithe ignorance, not downright meanness. But then I hear environmental activists such as Dune Ives from the advocacy group "Strawless in Seattle" tell NPR, "Imagine drinking a glass of water without a straw in it. It actually is possible."

Not for me.

To be sure, no one is proposing outlawing my trusty straws completely. I can still carry around my own stash, which I do anyway, like a quiver of arrows. One day, I might need special permission to buy and use a plastic straw, like a doctor's prescription. If so, will straws then acquire the stigma of medical equipment, complete with higher pricing and insurance claim forms?

More pressing, though, for me, is that these strictures further marginalize an already marginalized population. However well-intentioned, these bans become forms of discrimination because they don't allow for reasonable access to plastic straws for people whose disabilities require that they use them.

As for Starbucks, I have a counterproposal: Why not, instead, ban plastic bottles that are just a little too tall for standard straws?

Grounded by My Disability

In a small motel, on my way to my elder child's college graduation, I saw something startling on TV that prompted the following essay and, in time, an entire book. This piece became my first contribution to the New York Daily News.

I was in a motel room when Ali Stroker won her Tony, making history as the first wheelchair user to be so honored. "This award is for every kid who is watching tonight who has a disability, who has a limitation or a challenge," she said.

As a lifelong wheelchair user, I was thrilled; the feeling buoyed my spirits through the remainder of my four-thousand-mile road trip. But the irony did not escape me.

Stroker's triumph was a beaming example of disability integration, advancement, and power. But the reason I was driving to my child's graduation from college, a college I'd never been able to visit before, was that air travel remains prohibitively inaccessible for people like me.

In fairness, people with disabilities have made incredible progress. A year before Stroker's victory, a giant Times Square billboard for Olay, the skincare brand, featured the silky smooth face of Jillian Mercado, who was born with a variation of muscular dystrophy, like me. Never before had New Yorkers witnessed a bigger, more prominent image of disability outside of a fundraising telethon.

Around the same time, apparel retailer American Eagle promoted its Aerie lingerie brand with unretouched photos of barely dressed women of all shapes, sizes, colors—and impairments. One was on crutches, one in a wheelchair, another brandished a colostomy bag, yet another wore an insulin pump.

More recently, Aariana Philip, an eighteen-year-old transgender woman with cerebral palsy, appeared in ads for Sephora and Dove, a Miley Cyrus video, and elsewhere.

This new visibility goes beyond fashion and commerce. Last year, Senator Tammy Duckworth rolled her wheelchair into the Capitol with baby in tow. Moreover, in July a study by Rutgers University found that the disabled now represent 20 percent of the voting population.

In response to a lawsuit, New York City just agreed to make all 162,000 street corners in the five boroughs fully accessible within fifteen years. The subway's transformation is slower going, but even that's showing signs of long-overdue progress.

Twenty-nine years after the passage of the Americans with Disabilities Act, why can't the airlines get with the program?

Sure, they've made attempts to accommodate. But they're held to a lower standard. They are exempt from the Americans with Disabilities Act, bound instead to the looser Air Carrier Access Act.

Consequently, no one can stay on board an airplane in a wheelchair, unlike with most city buses. We must transfer out—often at great personal peril. Airlines rationalize this with terms such as *safety* and *crash testing*, but isn't all airline travel intrinsically risky? Surely we can find ways to secure wheelchairs and the people in them on airplanes.

Most wheelchairs are then whisked away and shoved into the cargo hold, unless they can fit into a cabinet in the cabin. Problem is, many of today's motorized wheelchairs don't fit easily into the cargo hold either. That doesn't stop cargo handlers from pigeonholing them in any way they can, though. The result: your chair may emerge more like a pretzel than an essential mobility aid, if it emerges at all.

In fact, in May 2019 alone some 951 wheelchairs and scooters were lost or damaged by the major air carriers, according to the U.S. Department of Transportation. That's 31 per day.

Will the airlines finally yield to the jet-setting demands of the new disabled glitterati, not to mention the rest of us? No such luck yet. After my return from commencement, Jillian Mercado, the model, posted on social media that she'd just landed at JFK International Airport to find her wheelchair in pieces.

She tweeted: "THEY [airport handlers] have no consideration at all that these devices is our way of living and moving forward, literally through life.

It has happened to me almost 4 to 6 times in the last two years . . . AND I HAVE HAD IT!"

Stroker got a standing ovation. I'll give that tweet a sitting one.

Mastering the "Pee Math"

Another ongoing problem for many of us that may surprise you is finding an accessible public bathroom. It's hard enough for anybody to locate a decent, available public facility. But one that's wheelchair friendly can be inexcusably difficult.

Worse still, what do you do if you need help in there, as I do? Suppose I'm with my wife or another female helper. Do we go into the men's room or the women's?

To cope, to compensate, folks like me control their liquid intake and calculate how long it will be till relief is possible. All this would be eased, though not completely solved, with more accessible, unisex facilities. But until that happens, or until I start sporting a catheter with a leg bag, or find some better solution, I have to remain very careful.

I had never heard the term pee math *until I encountered it on disability social media, but I got it immediately. So I wrote a blog about it.*

A while back, I encountered the term *pee math* online. Kooky as it sounds, I instantly understood what it means.

Those of us with certain types of disabilities are all too familiar with the need to ration our bathroom output. For some it means controlling the intake of liquids. For others, it's more a matter of calculating how much you've had to drink, how long it's been since you last emptied your bladder, and how long it will be till you can find the necessary assistance and/or accessible facility to do so again.

I've always needed help in the bathroom. I vividly recall when I was in first grade, "mainstreamed" in a normal school, how my teacher was more than willing to assist me to "go potty." The problem was letting her know when. I couldn't wheel myself over and whisper in her ear. So if I had to go, I had to announce it publicly. Which I was unwilling to do. Accidents ensued.

It was suggested that I devise some other signal, a code word that my teacher would understand, but no one else would. I was just six years old, and the best I could come up with was "Judy one two three." (It was the swinging '60s, and my teachers were on a first-name basis.)

It worked!

Over the years, there would still be some accidents as I resisted the inconvenience of interrupting my day to urinate. It was just such a hassle, asking someone for help and getting undressed enough to position a portable urinal. Perhaps if I'd been able to do it as easily and quickly as others, it would have seemed less annoying.

But all in all, my needs were fairly well under control until about ten years ago, in my mid-forties. I had colostomy surgery and, thanks to complications, an indwelling catheter for about three months. Afterward, between the cath and the surgery, I ended up with some nerve damage. It became harder to tell when I had to go.

Around that time, I also tried to stay healthier. I began drinking a lot of water. You know where this is going.

For a time, my urinary habits seemed uncontrollable. I went to a number of urologists, underwent tests. I tried Flomax to make it easier to empty my bladder fully. Then pills for overactive bladder syndrome. That's when a urological surgeon recommended a suprapubic catheter.

For those who don't know, it's an external cath that connects to a hole in the lower abdomen. It has to be changed periodically by a nurse. But, the doctor assured me, it would solve all my troubles.

I wasn't convinced. For one thing, I already had a surgical opening in my lower abdomen for my colostomy pouch. For another, I didn't like the maintenance. The incision had to be kept clean and infection-free. And suprapubic catheters can and do come loose sometimes. I wasn't convinced this would simplify my life. In fact, quite the opposite.

Surgeons, I've found, favor surgical solutions. I sought another opinion.

Somehow, online, I found a nearby urologist who claimed to have worked with quadriplegics. I immediately made an appointment.

Dr. Kim reviewed my tests and medication history. "You still have bladder control. It's just that it's a little wonky," he said, or words to that effect. "The difficulty is getting your medications right."

He upped my dosage of Flomax to 8 mg daily to ensure that when I peed I got out as much as possible so there wouldn't be a buildup of what he called "residuals." At the same time, he changed my overactive bladder medication to a strong dose (50 mg) of Myrbetriq, which was then a new drug. This removed (or at least eased) the sudden, reflexive "vacating" of my bladder without warning.

The result borders on the miraculous.

Someday, I may still need to go the catheter route, whether internal or external. But in the meantime, this balance of meds—at once calming and facilitating the outflow—remains effective.

To be completely honest, it's not quite that simple. I need someone to press hard on my bladder while holding a urinal in place. That's partly because of that nerve damage from ten years ago, partly from weak abdominal muscles due to the progression of my disability. But if I can get that, most days go pretty well.

Provided, that is, that I keep track of how much I drink and when I last went.

Marriage Penalties

A lot of disabled folks have difficulty securing the government benefits to which they're entitled. Ever the nonconformist, I had the opposite problem.

I could not stop receiving benefits to which I wasn't technically entitled.

I tried and tried to get the government to cease sending me checks, yet every month they kept coming. You might think I shouldn't have complained. But I knew that if I didn't, the Feds would catch up with me and demand a repayment. Perhaps with a nasty penalty.

As you will see in the next essay, which was accepted for publication but never ran, my worst fear was more or less what ended up happening.

When my mother died, I inherited a debt of $70,000.

Okay, that's not entirely fair. It wasn't her fault, and it was more than twenty years later. The money was owed to her Social Security account. The reason? It's a long story, but an important one that, if enough people know about it, could help change public policy.

Here's the backstory: Because I was not yet twenty-one when Mom succumbed to ovarian cancer—I was a sophomore in college—I started receiving "survivor's benefits" from Social Security, under its Social Security Disability Insurance (SSDI) program. The checks, which started at about $300 a month and, even with annual cost-of-living increases, never exceeded $450, were drawn on her Social Security account. It was money she would've received if she'd lived long enough.

My local Social Security Administration (SSA) representative said I would keep receiving benefits until I was no longer disabled (which was impossible) or earned too much money (which seemed unlikely). But there was another disqualifying factor he failed to mention.

In time, after graduation, my intermittent earnings from freelance writing grew big enough that I thought I'd better notify SSA. To my surprise, the rep (a different rep) wasn't fazed. "How much do you spend on wheelchair maintenance, personal-care help, and other equipment required for your work?" he asked.

It was a good point. My earnings minus my disability- and work-related expenses amounted to negative income. The only way I was surviving was from generous family support.

The government checks kept coming.

Years later, I was with a group of disability-rights friends. Someone brought up the "marriage penalty" in Supplemental Security Income (SSI), which is the separate federal benefits program that many disabled people rely on. I was never eligible because I have more than $2,000 in savings, the qualification cutoff. The aforementioned marriage penalty is that this threshold shrinks to $1,500 per person if you're married. Which is why many recipients lie about their marital status.

"Glad I'm not on SSI," I said, since I'd recently married.

Quizzical looks ensued. So I explained about the benefits program I did have, the Survivors' Benefits. No one was aware of it, except for one knowledgeable wheelchair-using friend who rolled closer.

"For SSDI Survivors' Benefits, you *have* to remain single," he said. It was a kind of warning.

I was puzzled. I had made no secret of my marriage. I'd even mentioned it in articles that were published in national magazines! Surely my friend was wrong. But he wasn't. When my next check arrived, I cut it in half and sent it back with a note: "I no longer want this." I didn't divulge why, for fear of being billed for past due. Or arrested.

No one at SSA reads notes, apparently. It took several years before anyone noticed I wasn't actually cashing my checks. Then I finally got a phone call from an SSA official asking why.

"I'm earning more money, and I got married," I said quickly.

The SSA agent only heard the first half. She asked how *much* I was earning and again went over my necessary expenses. She did the math quickly and declared me still eligible.

A decade later, out of the blue, a bill showed up in the mail. I had allegedly been overpaid more than $70,000 and had to pay it back right away.

The amount was so absurd I couldn't even panic. I mean, who has an extra $70,000 lying around? An arrangement would have to be made.

First, I filed an appeal. Not my fault, I protested. I had never lied about my marital status, nor tried to keep it a secret. Furthermore, I had never received an official warning about staying single. But it was no dice. Ignorance of the law is no excuse.

So I had to discuss terms. A nice woman at the SSA Overpayment Office (yes, it was a whole separate office, with its own phone number) explained that I could pay monthly installments, with zero interest. "How much can you afford every month?" she asked.

"I don't know," I said, trying to do rapid calculations in my head. "Maybe a hundred..."

She repeated it back to me, making certain it was okay. Something in her tone prompted me to ask ever so politely if $50 a month would be permissible. She said sure.

I was stymied. Nevertheless, every month for the past fifteen years and counting, I've been sending $50 to my late mother's Social Security account. I tried once more to secure a waiver, without success. I figure, at this rate, I'll have it paid off when I'm 101 years old—unless, somehow, I manage to get the rules changed. (Are you listening, Mr. Trump?) Otherwise, my kids will inherit my debt. Just like I did, in a way. Call it a cockeyed family tradition.

Why I Hate Buying a New Wheelchair

Money and benefits are constant problems for a lot of disabled folks. Perhaps that's no surprise. But you might not believe how hard it is to acquire necessary assistive devices, including wheelchairs. And I'm not talking about the exorbitant prices for this stuff! I'm talking about finding a device that's comfortable and works with your particular needs.

Whatever anger and embarrassment I felt over my struggles to find a new wheelchair that fit my body type, suited my lifestyle, and otherwise met my specific requirements was greatly eased when I discovered that I'm not the only one going through this kind of ordeal. This helped me extract humor from my aggravation. Fortunately, my editor at The Washington Post *liked my story.*

Its upholstery is cracking. Its motors are gunked up with mud, cat fur, and other detritus. But deep down I really don't want to replace my fourteen-year-old wheelchair.

Not that it's a better ride than its many predecessors. Over my lifetime, I've acquired a new chariot every seven years or so, till this time. The process always feels monumental, but now that I'm middle-aged, it feels nothing short of dispiriting.

Purchasing a wheelchair is not like buying a car or bicycle. Any wheelchair rider will tell you: Rarely do you get to see the chair beforehand, let alone take it for a test drive. You may get a demonstration, but chances are the demo wheelchair won't be the right size or meet your other particular requirements. Most wheelchairs, at least ones for people such as me, are custom-built.

In fact, you don't really choose your wheelchair so much as have it chosen for you—by physical therapists and sales reps. You can express preferences, of course, or refuse to follow their expert advice. But you'd better have a good reason, and play by the rules, if you want insurance to foot the bill—$15,000 is a steal for high-tech electric-powered models such as mine. After all, what do *you* know? You're just the patient.

My first wheelchair was a traditional, manually pushed one, and it was a thrill. [It] was a definite step up from the baby stroller I'd been cruising around in. I got to pick the upholstery color (green) and named it Wheelie Bird.

I was ten before I was allowed a motorized Wheelie Bird. By "allowed," I mean that my neurologist determined that I wasn't actually getting any exercise from the manual conveyance, since I lacked sufficient muscles to propel it. A power chair, he reasoned, would give me greater autonomy and self-confidence. And indeed, it did. It also gave me a way to chase my older, non-disabled brother around our apartment, at least until he learned to shut it off.

But that first power chair was too ungainly to take outside. A manual job remained my primary means of transport. Wheelchairs have come a long way since then. The manual models are lighter and more aerodynamic; the power chairs faster, quieter, and tougher, and they can be programmed for different environments and purposes. You might load one "driving profile" for indoors and another, zippier one for outdoor terrain. There are add-ons for tilting, reclining, elevating all or individual body parts, even standing.

But innovation certainly hasn't led to shopping ease. Before selecting my current chair, I did everything the right way. Instead of going to a wheelchair store, as I had previously—where, in memory, a fast-talking, brochure-brandishing salesman took one look at my insurance and decided I needed "the Cadillac of power chairs"—I approached a specialized wheelchair clinic at an in-hospital rehabilitation facility.

In weekly visits over six months, I was measured and evaluated by a horde of physical and occupational therapists who showed me various options, brands, and accessories to accommodate my slackening muscles. My disability had progressed, as it's wont to do, to a point where a standard joystick control was no longer an option.

Just about everything else, however, felt like a fight.

"You need a different type of headrest," I was told.

"But I like the kind I have."

"No. It hurts you."

It didn't. But I followed most of their recommendations, and when the new chair arrived, almost everything had to be changed. Seat cushion, armrest, and, yes, the headrest. The monster chair didn't fit in my apartment elevator, so the footrests had to be modified. The driving harness had to be propped up with dense foam or I couldn't reach it. On my first drive, I crashed in my living room. Then the powerful chair tipped over backward at the first incline, so the center of gravity had to be shifted forward.

In short, until myriad alterations were made, my brand-new, state-of-the-art machine had effectively immobilized—dare I say "crippled"?—me. It took another year of tinkering to get it right.

Is it any wonder I'm averse to rebooting this grueling procedure? I acknowledge that age has made me impatient. And perhaps I'm uncommonly complicated and picky. But a quick online survey of wheelchair-using pals suggests I'm far from alone. "My two-and-a-half-year-old 'new' wheelchair is still unusable, other than being a coatrack," one friend said.

But it's a losing battle. Sooner or later, this chair will give out. If by then I still haven't mustered the energy, patience, and courage to replace it, well, I suppose I can always use the backup Wheelie Bird I keep in a closet for emergencies. It's only thirty-seven years old.

"Opinion: Why I Hate Buying a New Wheelchair" by Ben Mattlin was first published in The Washington Post *on September 8, 2017.*

Help! I Think I Created a Word!

Language is a constant source of fascination to me. I'm in the language business, you might say. For activists, though, it can incite much ire. A short while back, one new term in particular seemed to be gaining a degree of mainstream acceptance, which raised hackles among a lot of my disabled colleagues. I'm not particularly emotional about nomenclature. Sticks and stones, and all that. What's in a name, after all? But in this case, I understood the objections all too well. What was worse, I thought I had actually helped popularize the controversial expression.

Here's my confession.

Watch the *Today* show. Watch *Dr. Phil.* Read the *Chicago Tribune*. Go on YouTube. You'll see a new word that's causing a mild uproar.

It's *interabled*, a shorthand description of a relationship between a person with a disability and a person without one.

I fear I'm at least partly responsible.

It was mid-2015 when I originally used the expression. I was pitching a possible book that would explore this specific type of mixed romantic union. To make it work, the book would be only partly about *my* marriage. I sought out—and easily found—other couples like us.

I honestly don't recall how I came up with the expression. Maybe I'd read or heard it somewhere (it's not in the *Oxford English Dictionary*... not yet anyway). It just sprang naturally from *interfaith* and *interracial*, with a hint of *ableism* thrown in. As soon as I said it to myself, it seemed to fit.

As a defense mechanism, I guess, I hyphenated it at first (*inter-abled*), put it in quotation marks, and added "for lack of a better term." I knew even then it was new or newish and kind of awkward. I knew it might offend.

And indeed, it did:

"A qualifier is pointless," carped an online post which objected to using *interabled* as an adjective. "It's highlighting that one person is disabled when it doesn't need to.... Who cares what kind of relationship it is? And what business is it of anyone's?"

Nonetheless, it was instantly understood. I'd inadvertently hit upon something that resonated with a lot of people. So I kept it.

I'll admit, I struggled with contradictory impulses about using it to describe my own marriage: There is nothing special about us; we *are* just an ordinary couple. For years, I insisted that no one should make a fuss about my wife and me. Ours was just a marriage like any other. We worked out our differences in our own private ways, just like anyone else.

But I also came to see that we in the interabled club do have extraordinary stories to tell, stories that enlighten everyone who wants to hear or read them. We were worth identifying as a particular phenomenon, a specific facet of our society.

When you say "interabled," people know what you mean. Some have suggested alternatives, such as "crip curious" or "crip mates," though these are less understandable by the general public and only describe half of the equation.

What prompted me to make "interabled romance" part of the title of my book were articles about Michael J. Fox and Tracy Pollan, or ex-congresswoman Gabrielle Giffords and her husband, Mark Kelly, which dubbed these couples "amazing" and "remarkable," with "a special kind of love." The assumptions of otherness were plainly out there, if a bit saccharine.

Honestly, though, I didn't need to see *People* magazine to realize that people think relationships like ours are somehow different. I can tell by the way strangers stare at us. By the stupid comments and inappropriate questions. My wife and I are frequently assaulted with praise from strangers—"you two are so inspirational!" Or they assume... worse things.

Such experiences, I soon learned, are not unique to us. I heard similar stories from every couple I interviewed. I came to see that many of us do have a shared perspective. We do face prejudices and laughs that other couples don't. So why not find a handy term for it?

The need to zero in on this often misunderstood issue became painfully clear in a recent episode of *Dr. Phil.* The host insisted—with folksy certainty—that interabled couples are doomed to failure. I and a gazillion others firmly disagree. If you don't believe me, look up #1000outof100 to see the storm of criticism his comments provoked.

Better yet, join me in celebrating interability—and the many good relationships it describes.

Invisible but Present

Harvard and Its Minorities

DIVERSITY ISN'T JUST SKIN DEEP

The more disabled folks you get to know, the more you realize the diversity of the community. I'm not just talking about race, skin color, religion, gender identity, sexual orientation, socioeconomic status, or any of the other usual markers of diversity, equity, and inclusion. The breadth and depth I'm referring to in this case concern the many different types and degrees of disability.

Some disabilities are from birth, like mine; others are acquired later. Some are permanent, others temporary. Disabilities may be progressive or stable, treatable or not so much. But sometimes the biggest divider, at least in terms of how society treats you, seems to be whether a disability is visible or not. And if it is visible, how visible and where.

Any number of disabilities may be less obvious to an outsider. Deafness, dyslexia, lupus, Crohn's, depression, bipolar disorder, autism—to name a few. The international access symbol is a stick figure in a wheelchair, but there's no reason that those of us who get around on wheels should be considered the standard. In fact, though emotional disabilities aren't always obvious, they are far more widespread than we realize. And they are often blamed for all kinds of evil behavior that should not actually be attributed to them.

In this next piece, I wrote about how disability, in all its variations, is often left out of diversity discussions.

I have watched the trial against Harvard for alleged admissions biases with great personal interest. To me, what both sides—and indeed, most of the media—failed to consider is the role of our nation's single biggest minority group: people with disabilities.

The U.S. census puts us at nearly 57 million, which is more than the various racial minorities who are laying claim to the ivy gates. Yet as the only wheelchair-using member of the Harvard class of 1984, I was part of a very small minority constituency. How small? Considering how few of the campus' accommodations were barrier-free in those days, I can say with great confidence that, besides me, there was only one other physically disabled student in my grade—a woman in the adjacent suite of our freshman dorm who used crutches. (We also had a classmate with bipolar disorder who sadly died during our freshman year.)

Later, as a volunteer coordinator for students with disabilities, I learned of others within the university system: a hearing-impaired lip reader in the law school, for instance. As a sophomore, I became a resident of the exact same dorm room that had housed another quadriplegic before me, who had since graduated. The school had no other place to put quads.

In the circuitous back-elevator and through-the-kitchen path to the otherwise inaccessible dining hall, I met a friendly senior who was born with spina bifida. But mine was the only wheelchair I ever saw on campus. No doubt I benefited from an unspoken affirmative action policy. I wasn't a bad high school student; my SATs were above average but not outstanding. I was also a "legacy"—that is, my dad was an alum.

Yet what really tipped the scales in my favor was Section 504 of the Rehabilitation Act of 1973, which required institutions not to discriminate against the disabled. The year I entered college, 1980, was the first year that standard was enforced.

Lucky me! I got into every school to which I applied. I had my pick. At my admissions interview for one of them, the dean told me I was accepted before I'd even applied! How many ethnic minorities have had that kind of special treatment?

Nevertheless, even if Harvard and the rest do practice a kind of quota system to ensure diversity, as the lawsuit alleges, too few remember to add disability to the mix. My dad says that when he attended the school in the 1940s, it limited the number of Jewish students. Nobody seems to be counting Jews in colleges today. That's progress.

But the demographics of disability in higher education should not be overlooked. I'm all for ethnic diversity. I'm for diversity of all kinds. I don't want my kids going to schools where every child has straight or curly hair, a bulbous or retrousse nose, and so on, let alone shares the same background or belief system. To me, diversity should go beyond race and socioeconomic markers. It should extend to perspectives, opinions, even politics—assuming it stays safe for all viewpoints to be respected.

Speaking of which, it's ironic that the high-profile lawsuit over insufficient diversity—or is it actually about too much diversity? Not quite clear, in the legal double-talk—is transpiring at the same time the Trump administration seeks to eliminate "transgender" as an official consideration, a qualifying trait, in federal standards. Erasing a minority category is not a shortcut for establishing diversity. In fact, it does a grave disservice not just to members of that minority but to everyone else who would be enriched by their inclusion.

In all honesty, I can't claim to know how to solve diversity, or the lack thereof. I didn't set out to be a pioneer of disability inclusion. I still wish I could've done more in college—accessed other dorms besides my own, for instance, and more common areas where students congregate. I wish more admissions directors—and employers, for that matter—would view disability in a positive light, even as an asset. But at least I know that, for a time, I had my alma mater's attention.

Today, to be sure, there are many more undergrads in wheelchairs. I don't know how many, but some of them have emailed me for advice. They shouldn't have to reinvent the wheel . . . uh, wheelchair ramp. Yet many of them still feel pretty isolated and challenged by a sometimes unwelcoming environment. They still feel underrepresented.

But there is a silver lining. Now that I'm facing my thirty-fifth reunion, I'm no longer the only one asking about wheelchair access. There's nothing like aging to increase the representation of those of us with disabilities.

Naomi Osaka's Withdrawal from the French Open Was a Stand for Disability Rights

Misunderstandings about disabilities are common. Yet some disabilities may be more misunderstood than others. For instance, most people think they have a pretty good idea of what a wheelchair user or blind person might want or need. They might be dead wrong, but that doesn't stop strangers from touching you or telling you which way to go.

When it comes to disabilities such as autism or anxiety, however, the average nondisabled citizen seems pretty perplexed. In fact, some disabilities aren't commonly recognized as disabilities at all. But they should be, as I argued in this essay for the Los Angeles Times.

Before you get to that, though, you should know that this one got me in a little hot water. "Who are you to write this?" said an online critic. "Don't take up print space from others who are more appropriate and deserving," said another. More accusations piled on in a similar vein.

In retrospect, the subject would've been better coming from someone more closely and personally aligned with it. I apologize. As a white cisgender male who doesn't truly struggle much with mental health myself, I was not the best person to write about it. But I saw no other mainstream coverage of the issue in this context, which I felt should be brought to light for the good of everybody, including some family members who are close to my heart. I hope and believe that my voluntary contribution, which I submitted as an ally of the cause, and for which I received no money, did not prevent anyone else from stepping up.

When Naomi Osaka exited the French Open this week, the tennis champion wasn't just shielding herself; she was defending her rights as a disabled person.

She may not have put it that way. But Osaka is a perfect example of how one can be both able-bodied and disabled.

Under the Americans with Disabilities Act (ADA), emotional and psychiatric impairments such as depression and anxiety are disabilities. If you're treated unfairly in a public place or employment situation because of these impairments, you have a valid discrimination suit. Of course, the French Open is not within the ADA's jurisdiction. But if it were, the French Open, along with the Women's Tennis Association and the International Tennis Federation, could be liable for failing to make a reasonable accommodation for Osaka's emotional needs.

Osaka announced last week that she would not participate in the French Open's news conferences due to a "disregard for athletes' mental health." She then won her first round of the tournament and skipped the postmatch press conference. She was fined $15,000 by Grand Slam tournament administrators. They also threatened her with expulsion from future matches if she continued to ignore media obligations. After her subsequent withdrawal from the French Open and announcement that she has suffered from depression, officials walked back their previous statement and gave vague offers of support and sympathy.

But what Osaka deserves isn't pity or even kindness. She needs a modification to make these events accessible for her, such as being allowed to compete without participating in postmatch press conferences. As someone who is physically disabled, I know firsthand that when such a change is not granted, it sends a chilling message to all members of the disability community.

According to the World Health Organization, an estimated 264 million people globally have depression. In the U.S., roughly 26 percent of Americans eighteen and over have diagnosable mental disorders, reports Johns Hopkins Medical Center. Accommodating Osaka's depression and anxiety would not be a special privilege but a reasonable accommodation for an all too ordinary condition that more people should recognize.

Press conferences are required of most professional athletes by the leagues to which they belong. The players are considered representatives of their sports, and more media attention to a specific league or team helps draw bigger audiences and sell more merchandise. But effectively forcing Osaka to drop out doesn't do the tennis world's bottom line any good either.

To be sure, the ADA is a complicated document, and it might be difficult for other governing bodies to adopt their own versions. Still, the landmark law broadly defines disability as any "physical or mental impairment that substantially limits one or more major life activities." Specific diagnoses are irrelevant: It's about an inability to accomplish tasks in traditional ways, as well as any stigmas related to being physically or mentally different.

Its applicability to mental illnesses was established by the Supreme Court in 1999 in the case of *Olmstead v. L.C.* That case involved two Georgia women who each had diagnoses of different mental health conditions and intellectual disabilities. They sued the state of Georgia to permit them to receive their periodic treatments in their home communities rather than having to live in state-run institutions to be treated. The case was heard by the Supreme Court, which ruled in their favor, establishing for legal purposes that mental illnesses are ADA-protected forms of disabilities. (Olmstead was the name of the state official. Some community members have pointed out that the plaintiffs, Lois Curtis and Elaine Wilson, were the real heroes of the story. Their names should not be erased from retellings of the case and its significance to the disability community.)

The decision was about institutionalization, not tennis. But since then, there have been many other cases in which employees have gone to court to get their employers to make necessary modifications for their mental health needs.

The ADA challenges both employers and employees to think about accommodations—ideally, they work together to come up with fair solutions. Disabled employees (or job candidates) must be clear about what they need to be able to perform the essential duties. They should put in specific requests, such as fatigue breaks, or telecommuting when possible, or, as with Osaka, the right to wear headphones to "dull my social anxiety," as she said on social media.

For employers, the challenge is to specify the necessary requirements of the job. For example, if an administrative assistant can manage a calendar and input data as required, does it matter if they lack the dexterity to serve coffee?

If Gilles Moretton, the president of the French Federation of Tennis, is sincere about being "committed to all athletes' well-being and to continually improving every aspect of players' experience in our Tournament, including with the Media," the least he and the other leaders of the sports world could do is reconsider the essential tasks required of players. Is it truly necessary that Osaka participate in press conferences?

Naomi Osaka and others like her should be accommodated not because they are "spoiled brats" with unreasonable needs but because they are human —and humans have disabilities.

I Have a Disability That Is Obvious—and One That's Not

Writing about less visible disabilities made me realize that I'd better come clean about one of my own, a not obvious disability that I had unthinkingly sought to minimize or hide. I wrote about it for Invisible Disabilities Week, and CNN published it.

My wheelchair hides my worst disability.

Most people probably think that having spinal muscular atrophy is the nastiest thing that ever happened to me. It isn't. It isn't even my most irritating, aggravating, or vexingly incurable medical problem.

That dubious honor goes to . . . ulcerative colitis (UC).

My UC is more or less well managed, thanks to a lot of effort. But its symptoms are maddeningly erratic and unpredictable. It's considered an autoimmune disease, a still-evolving classification thought to include lupus, rheumatoid arthritis, multiple sclerosis, celiac disease, Graves' disease, Lyme disease, and many more, according to Meghan O'Rourke's *The Invisible Kingdom*. These and other chronic illnesses disrupt the lives of nearly two hundred million Americans according to the Centers for Disease Control and Prevention (CDC)—not including another sixteen million with long Covid, according to the Brookings Institution.

Such disorders are often considered "invisible" because they're not apparent to onlookers. But that doesn't mean they don't hurt and don't impact people daily. That's why, in 2014, the Invisible Disabilities Association designated the third week of October as Invisible Disabilities Week, to help raise awareness and build support for those of us who are coping with complex chronic diseases.

Frankly, when you also have the opposite sort of debility—one that's highly visible, as I do—it's easy to forget about or at least minimize other infirmities. That is, until an awful flare-up reminds you.

A lot of disabled people like me have multiple conditions, some of which may go undiagnosed. The CDC estimates that more than 38 percent of disabled American adults are also obese, 16 percent also have diabetes, and 12 percent also have heart disease.

Many people, even including many in the disability rights movement, often overlook less visible disabilities, including mental illnesses. But they're just as important—and as stigmatizing.

In fairness, I've been complicit in keeping my less obvious malady under wraps. Despite publishing several books and essays about almost every embarrassing detail of my life as a proud disabled person—someone who has learned to love his emaciated arms and legs and crooked spine—I've unwittingly neglected to divulge the full extent of my ongoing battle with gut inflammation.

The reasons for this deception seem obvious: First, it's embarrassing, and, second, it's no one's business. But perhaps in acknowledging the beast, I can hereby soften its fangs.

After all, ulcerative colitis and other inflammatory bowel ailments such as Crohn's disease are nothing to be ashamed of. Like all autoimmune diseases, they can be treated but not cured. Doctors offer a number of therapies, including aminosalicylates (pills, suppositories, or enemas), antibiotics, and steroids. Perhaps the most effective treatments are immunosuppressants, which lower your ability to fight infections, something I really don't want in the age of Covid.

Surgery only helped me to a degree. Years ago, after a life-threatening colitis-related *Clostridioides difficile* infection, I had my colon removed. Ever since, I've sported a colostomy pouch under my clothes. The little bit of my rectum the surgeon left can still become inflamed, however, and leak odorless mucus that intermittently stains my pants. I have no control over it. Flare-ups can be excruciatingly painful, too, like a bad cramp that presses against the bladder. And yes, accidents do occur every now and then.

But usually, the only outward sign is a frown on my face, and maybe my grumpy mood. The fact that I'm always sitting helps. No one knows if my pants are soiled. But if I ever have to get out of my chair—at, say, the dentist or to board an airplane—I panic. I envision dying of shame.

In online forums you read about various pseudoscientific remedies—raw kombucha, aloe vera jelly, even belly exercises. Believe me, I've tried many of them. But I have doubts about advice from strangers. Which may be another reason I've kept my intestinal affliction on the down-low. I don't want to attract hucksters.

A more honest explanation is that very little of my life is private, so I've been protective of the few secrets I have. Anyone who sees me instantly knows a number of big and personal facts about me. For instance, not only can't I walk, but I clearly need help with all manner of daily activities. Wrongheaded assumptions are common, too, of course—such as, that I can't make up my own mind at restaurants. But even if I can't pretend that walking is an option, I can make believe my bowels are fine.

Make no mistake: My spinal muscular atrophy impacts my whole life. But that's not all there is to me. And when it comes to what can most upend my day and my sense of well-being, there's no contest. Ulcerative colitis is far more intrusive because it sneaks up on me, and nobody understands when I suddenly wince for no apparent cause.

I only wish more people realized that disabilities come in all types—even if you can't tell by looking. Learning about invisible disabilities is an important first step in creating a better understanding and, ultimately, building a more inclusive society.

I Have a Disability Everyone Can See. My Bipolar Friend Who Died by Suicide Did Not.

From talking to a variety of disabled folks, I've gotten the definite impression that everyone who has a less visible disability finds it socially or professionally advantageous at times to "pass" for nondisabled. It's unfortunate that they feel the need to do this, but I don't judge them for it. We all cope how we must.

Several years ago, I learned a hard lesson about the secret struggles that some people go through, as the following story that ran in USA Today *illustrates. (Content warning: This piece discusses suicide.)*

At my last birthday, I received a cheery pink-and-white card from a close colleague who had died months before.

Startled, confused, I checked the handwriting and the return address. All legit. I immediately emailed a mutual friend. She had received one on her birthday, too.

No, this isn't the prelude to a tawdry murder mystery. Our well-wisher had apparently hired a mailing service, which to my knowledge she had never done before. I had to wonder whether she was already planning her exit when she signed the cards.

Like Kate Spade and Anthony Bourdain, whose suicides last June preceded my friend's by only a matter of weeks, she struggled with her mental health. The day of my friend's passing, I learned she was diagnosed with bipolar disorder, but I should've already known. As a longtime wheelchair user and disability-rights advocate, I might have recognized the telltale signs.

A vibrant fifty-year-old with her own business, a new boyfriend, and no kids, she was prone to intermittent bursts of brilliant brainstorming energy followed by long, frustrating periods of solemn silence. She never told me why, and I never asked.

Not that my knowing would've made any difference. She had other friends who did know, as do many of the estimated ten million American adults who experience bipolar disorder at some point in their lives, at least a quarter of whom attempt suicide. It's thought to be caused by a combination of biological and environmental factors. New treatments such as ketamine [an overdose of which has been blamed for the death of *Friends* star Matthew Perry in 2023] are said to help, but there is no cure.

I can't pretend to understand this implacable, erratic psychiatric disability. The International Society for Bipolar Disorders, which is marking its sixth annual World Bipolar Day this month, hopes that awareness and acceptance can lead to earlier, better diagnoses. Eliminating the stigma could help avert some suicides. I believe it, though it's hard to be aware and accepting if we can't see it.

The stigma surrounding disability is certainly real. For me, it can be as big a problem as steps or narrow doorways. Sometimes, I'm embarrassed by my appearance. I have to dig deep inside to bolster my self-esteem, especially when others stare at me or, worse, look right through me.

In a way, though, I have an advantage. My disabilities are obvious. Meet me and you know most of them instantly. This has forced me to develop coping mechanisms. It has forced me to accept what can't be denied. I can't pretend to pass.

My late friend, however, could pass. Whatever issues she faced were opaque, cryptic. Her mental illness was probably not easy to ignore, but easy to hide.

I wish she had shared a little of her struggle with me, if only because I inevitably shared some of mine with her. We might have bonded over it, two kindred spirits. Then again, maybe our shared but unstated experience of otherness explains why our professional relationship evolved into a heartfelt friendship.

It might just be that I'm going through survivor's guilt. I'm no stranger to grieving. You can't live in the disability community long without losing a few friends. Every year my holiday mailing list grows shorter, though I can never delete the names of the no longer living from my Facebook or email contacts. Cyber immortality does no harm, I figure.

Nonetheless, the way her posthumous note wishes me a wonderful year to come reopens my emotional wound. I so wish I could say the same back to her.

On the anniversary of her suicide in a few months, I'll probably post a remembrance on her Facebook page so her loved ones know she's not forgotten. Perhaps I'll donate to a charity in her honor. Yet none of this will truly wash away the sting.

Alas, even the old Jewish bromide "may the memory be a blessing" seems to miss the point.

To me, her death and the deaths of others like her should be a wake-up call for societal change. Those of us with obvious physical disabilities have too often left our psychiatric counterparts behind in the pursuit of an inclusive and accessible world. Their issues may be invisible, but they should be neither hidden nor forgotten.

Mental Illness Is a Disability, Not a Public Threat

Around the same time, in a blog post for FacingDisability.com, I again tried to emphasize that people with mental illness are part of the big disability tent. A close family member had helped make me particularly aware of this. But also, the subject seemed especially significant considering the unfair, prejudicial news flow around mental health at the time.

May was supposed to be mental health awareness month. That's ironic, considering how much depressing news there was—and how frequently mental illness was blamed for that.

In May, mass shootings rocked the country: In Buffalo, New York, ten people were gunned down in a supermarket. Not long after, a Laguna Woods, California, church was shot up, taking one life and severely injuring at least five others. Then came the elementary school shooting in Uvalde, Texas, that slaughtered twenty-one human beings, including nineteen children. And finally, yesterday's hospital shooting in Tulsa, Oklahoma [in which four people died and countless others were injured].

This spate of horrific carnage inevitably led to much hand-wringing about gun control and mental illness. The first makes sense; the second doesn't.

I don't have a mental illness, at least not at the moment, not as far as I know. But many people I know and care about do.

A mental illness does not automatically make a person dangerous or violent. Yet many people—some of whom are influential—equate the two. For instance, in the wake of the Texas school slaughter, Texas governor Greg Abbott explained the situation this way: "We have a problem with mental illness in this community."

Such views are unfair, misinformed, and ableist.

By ableist, I mean prejudiced against disabled people. Mental illness is a disability. Depression, anxiety, and other mental health ailments can severely limit major life activities. But that doesn't mean people with these sorts of conditions are dangerous to other people.

To better understand, realize that mental illness is extremely common. According to U.S. government statistics, nearly 53 million Americans or 20 percent of the population live with mental illness. Such emotional or psychological disabilities may not be permanent. About 18 percent of workers in the U.S. report having a mental health condition in any given month. The vast majority of them do get better thanks to improved treatments and services.

Rather than being the perpetrators of crimes, many folks with mental health issues are actually victims of discrimination. "Stigma, prejudice and discrimination against people with mental illness can be subtle or it can be obvious—but no matter the magnitude, it can lead to harm," says the American Psychiatric Association.

In the disability community, there is a very real fear that if people with mental illness are profiled as dangerous and blamed for rampant violence, many innocent people will be reviled and targeted by law enforcement.

Scapegoating people with mental illness calls to mind age-old prejudices against disabled people. In centuries past, people with disabilities were feared and shunned as evil. Disabilities were considered marks of the devil, or at least manifestations of sin. Think of all the hunchbacked, peg-legged, hook-handed, deformed, or scarred villains of myth. Come to think of it, such characteristics are still common in movie bad guys.

The same fear and loathing surrounds invisible disabilities. People with anxiety or depression are sometimes seen as unattractive and weak. People with PTSD are often portrayed as tightly wound, enraged monsters or sympathetic antiheroes who just can't control themselves.

Let's be clear: Bad behavior cannot and should not be tolerated. Bad behavior is not a disability. But mental illness *is* a disability. Having a mental illness is not synonymous with being dangerous or violent.

Meltzer Center for Diversity, Inclusion, and Belonging, New York University School of Law

During the Covid pandemic—so roughly 2020 through 2023—I wrote a book about the disability community as it seemed to me at that point. My research filled me in on a lot of aspects of how the activist movement had evolved since I'd become less involved. A professor at the New York University School of Law wanted to interview me about my findings. I suggested there were other people in the community who would be better to talk to, more representative of the community's diversity, but he insisted on chatting with me. Our conversation was open to the public, thanks to Zoom. Here is an edited transcript.

Prof. Kenji Yoshino: Good afternoon. I'd like to welcome you to our final speaker series event for the academic year. . . . I'm thrilled to introduce our distinguished guest, Ben Mattlin. Ben, just to set the scene for our audience today, you've written that "the disability tent is much bigger" than you had realized. Who is in this tent of the disability community, and how did your work expand on your prior understanding?

Ben: Yes, it's true. But let me start by describing myself, for those who can't see. This is something I've learned to do, and is a pretty good example of trying to be inclusive for the big tent of disabled folks.

I'm an old white guy with not enough graying hair. I'm wearing tortoiseshell glasses and a headset microphone. Behind me is assorted mess. I'm actually talking to you from bed today, which I had not planned on doing. But I've been going through some medical stuff, and this was much more comfortable for me. It's kind of relevant to our discussion, because I've wrestled with it. My vanity—or some would say my "internalized ableism"—told me

I ought to, you know, be upright with a bookshelf behind me and in a nice blazer and shirt. But I realized that if I truly embrace disability pride, I've got to be accepting of what I need to feel comfortable, what accommodations I need. I reasoned that I could do this talk better and more comfortably if I did it this way, from bed.

That kind of speaks to your question because the disability community, if we really understand what it means, is not just people in wheelchairs or people who are Deaf or blind. It's a whole range of neurodiversities and autoimmune disorders, people with lupus or fibromyalgia or on and on. And it's not just about diagnoses really. It includes anyone who is impaired in a major life-affecting way, as well as their family members and anyone perceived as such. So that's pretty broad in itself.

But I think even more important is understanding the idea that there is no standard, no right way to be. We are a diverse population, and we function in different ways and have different needs in order to be able to function and be comfortable. So that's sort of what I mean by the broad tent. There are temporary disabilities, too—you break a leg skiing or something—and there are permanent ones that are from birth, from disease, from accidents. There are all kinds of stories, all kinds of biographies in the disability community, and all kinds of needs and requirements. There are even those who have to be, who are, activists from bed. You don't have to go marching in public to be an activist.

There are also folks who may not label themselves as disabled but maybe ought to. If they felt disability pride, they wouldn't be afraid to call themselves disabled.

It can be very liberating to accept your disability as an identity, to accept that you are part of this club. You can stop pretending that you're something you're not.

Kenji: Thank you for that personal note. On intersectionality, you've talked about how individuals belong to multiple identities in addition to the identity of having a disability. Can you tell us a little bit more about the connections between the disability rights movement and other struggles for social justice and equality?

Ben: Sure. I think it's fair to say some of the early activists for the [Americans with Disabilities Act] were inspired by the African-American Civil Rights Movement. In fact, some of the early protestors were joined by members of the Black Panther movement. Got a lot of assistance and were working together. As the disability cause has developed, one of the key elements going forward is allyship with other social justice movements. There is overlap or interconnection. Again, the idea of rejecting a standard for what a person must be to be deserving of respect and full access to all of society. We throw that out and talk about how people really are.

Within the disability community there are people of color and white folks like me and everything in between. There are people who are queer, and so on. We have to embrace all these causes if we're going to really move forward. You can't say we accept this kind but not that kind. I confess I made that mistake several years ago. We were protesting when Jerry Lewis was getting an honorary Oscar for his allegedly charitable work, and a bunch of us were offended because we thought his so-called charitable work was bad for disabled folks. Insulting to many of us. Well, somebody brought up that he makes fun of gay people, too. And I'm afraid my reaction was, "Let's not confuse the issue. Stick to one agenda, one cause, at a time." But I was wrong. I've learned my lesson. We have to take a broad social justice perspective if we're going to move the needle, move things along and try to create a truly inclusive society for all people.

Kenji: Thank you for that. Again on this big tent idea, you've written about inclusion of neurodiversity and the autistic community, [how] we should expand the lens in order to understand other forms of less apparent disability. Could you talk a little bit more about the specific challenges that people in the neurodiverse community face, and what organizations can do to be more inclusive on issues of neurodiversity?

Ben: That's a tricky one for me, because I'm not autistic. I'm neurotypical, as they say. It's not really appropriate for me to speak about that community, to speak for that community. But I don't want to exclude them from our conversation either. They are an important part of the community. Autistic self-advocacy is crucially important.

From talking to autistic people and reading what they have said, I've come to understand that just as people's bodies function in different ways, so do their brains. Their minds function differently. I think a lot of people would qualify as neurodivergent who might not recognize themselves as such. There are all these stories about the so-called geeks, the techno-wizards who might, in fact, be autistic to a degree, given their ability to concentrate and focus on things.

But it's hard to talk, for me anyway, about accessible environments for autistic people. There is some work on this [that I've researched]. For some folks, transitioning is difficult, so gradual transitions in scheduling and space, in the physical environment [can be helpful]. Also, some folks need a quiet space, a quiet room to collect their thoughts. Somewhat related, I think, are things like trigger warnings. There are people who have been traumatized. That's a little different, but if people are able to have a smoother transition and to be sort of better prepared for situations, it can be helpful. But I find it hard to come up with an easy checklist—do this, do that—to be more accessible for autistic people. It's just important to realize and to respect that people do things and need to do things in different ways, even if it's not physically obvious to you that they need those things.

There are some horrible examples of people who have been killed by law enforcement because their neurodivergent behavior was misunderstood. It's apparently very common, not always well reported, but it can get very bad, very dangerous for people. We need to be aware of that, I think, too.

Kenji: Sure. Shifting gears, you have argued that there are not only systemic, structural disparities in health care but also problems with attitudes and the habits of individual medical practitioners. How would you describe these issues?

Ben: Big topic. But let me give you a recent example. I was in the hospital in December for about eight days, and on the second day, I was lying in the hospital bed, and my wife, who had been by my bedside almost 'round the clock, stepped out to get a cup of coffee. Just then, two nurses came in to check my skin for pressure sores. And rather than tell me what they were going to do or ask me if it was okay, they started moving my body around. They looked behind my ankles, behind my ears. Then they lifted my head in a way that pressed my chin down to my chest, closing off my breathing. I couldn't breathe and I couldn't open my mouth to talk because they had pushed my head forward so far. Then they rolled me over and it got worse. My throat and jaw were really squeezed, and all I could do was sort of groan. Their reaction was, "Don't worry. It'll be over soon. We're almost done." But I passed out. I could not breathe.

Next thing I know, I'm waking up and everything is rapid. It was like a movie on fast forward. I'm surrounded by doctors and nurses. They bring out an Ambu bag, which basically puffs air into your lungs. My wife, meanwhile, was down in the cafeteria, and she heard over the loudspeaker, "Code Blue in Room . . ." whatever the room number was. She knew right away what was going on. She raced back upstairs, but she was stopped by security because it was early in the morning and she still had yesterday's visitor's ID badge on. They updated her badge, and she finally got upstairs, where she saw a crowd at my door. They didn't want to let her in. They finally did, and she knew what to do—kind of lift my neck up and tilt my head back to open my airways.

I also have a little trach, an unusual kind that's very small, called a stoma stent. She knew to open that up and do a little suctioning, and I was fine. Afterward, as I recovered, I laughed about it when I thought about those two poor [pressure checkers] who were just checking my skin. I bet they learned a lesson! I hope they did.

Could they know in advance not to do that to me? Maybe. But I am unique, we all are, and my body isn't like anybody else's. Still, a little more respect for my bodily integrity might have helped, you know? In any case, if you don't have experience with disabled bodies or minds, as most medical practitioners frankly don't, you can become harmfully dismissive. I know hospital people are overworked, but this lack of consideration and perhaps lack of adequate training can be very dangerous. I know of cases where disabled people have died because of inadequate treatment, or penny-pinching insurance coverage, or frankly the presumption that disabled people aren't worth the full measure of medical intervention. My life is worth saving, you know? Disabled people should not be considered less than, should not be considered sort of expendable or less deserving of full care and respect.

Wow, that's a mouthful!

Kenji: Not at all. Thank you for sharing with us. . . . I'm going to move on now to audience questions. First, how do you gently correct well-intentioned people who call you an inspiration, especially strangers? Second, how do you personally define the difference between being inspiring as an activist and being subjected to inspiration porn.

Ben: Good questions. Part of me always felt flattered to be called inspirational, but, yeah, it can be dangerous. It puts you up on a pedestal, like you're not a regular person anymore. What do I say to people? Oh, I might say, "Oh, come on. I'm just living my life, doing my thing. What choice have I had?" Stuff like that. I try to come up with clever responses, but I usually fail. Yes, if I'm going to be inspirational, I'd prefer that it be related to something I've done, other than just surviving and living a normal life. But honestly, at some point I just began thinking, "Whatever. You want to think of me as inspiring, then be inspired. I don't care. That's *your* problem." I'm going to go on and do my own thing and not let it upset me too much.

Worse, perhaps, is when people tell my wife, who is nondisabled, that she's inspirational for being with me. That feels more offensive. I think my wife is worthy of all kinds of praise, but sometimes it gets a little silly. And she'll always try to divert people, switch it around. "Well, I'm lucky to be with him," not just "He's lucky to be with me." We get a lot of that, too. I find that more irksome.

At the same time, there are many examples of inspiration porn in media and online that only add to the problem—you know, where a disabled person is portrayed solely for the purpose of inspiring others, to make other people feel good. It doesn't really help the community. There are—how do I say this?—a lot of disabled folks on social media or with their own YouTube channels who are raising awareness about various issues, and I guess that's good. But too often I feel like they're just saying, "Hey, I count. I'm important. Don't undersell or underrate me and my life and my worth." I understand that, but some of them seem like they're just out to help themselves. I'm not sure they have a community consciousness.

That to me is part of the problem of the inspirational business, inspiration porn. It tends to be about one person, without recognizing the systemic issues that are part of what all of us deal with.

I think, too, there is a tendency for some of us, I've certainly been there, to be overachievers. You know, you have to be the best at something to really impress people. That's a mistake. I don't think you have to . . . "mistake" isn't the word I want. We need to be, we are, we should be valued by virtue of being human beings, not by what we accomplish in a material sense or economic sense.

Portrait of the Cripple as a Middle-Aged Man

Coming to Terms with Survival

When I was younger, I remember noticing how my dad and my aunt, and others of their "advanced" age, invariably talked to each other about their health. Not that they were especially sickly or even unwell. Updates on wellness simply comprised a curious topic of seemingly bottomless fascination. Not unlike the weather.

Now that I'm past sixty, I get why.

As we age, health concerns become bigger parts of our lives. It's inevitable. Little annoyances become impossible to ignore. People of a certain maturity know this. They see it as something they have in common with one another. Irritations they share. Similarly, a lot of disabled people I know, no matter how old or young, speak very frankly to one another about specific health and wellness issues because they are points of commonality. We understand, without judgment, and might even be able to offer useful advice. That's not true of outsiders—that is, nondisabled people—who we fear might be put off or overwhelmed by our candor about our bodies. Griping becomes a means of bonding.

Put the two together—age and disability—and you get a whole new level of worry. You grow more keenly aware of how you're doing and how you could be doing. You acquire a more pronounced sense of vulnerability. Or at least I have.

To reach my current age, with a disability like mine, feels a little like living on borrowed time. Some doctors thought I wouldn't make it through my teens, and in all honesty, I have had a few narrow escapes. I can't help occasionally wondering if I'm the oldest living human with my particular brand of infantile-onset spinal muscular atrophy. (I'm not. But I might be headed there. God willing.)

When a body works as hard as mine does to breathe and swallow and fight off infection—that is, to stay alive—it tires out more quickly than a nondisabled body might. The wear and tear is more intense. Parts are more likely to degrade. My physique, inherently weak to begin with, sometimes feels as if it's falling apart, coming unglued. Nobody has studied the effects of my particular diagnosis over the long term. Whatever I experience is the research, or a piece of it, to date. So if, like my forebears, I tend to sit around and talk about my ailments, take note. It just might be medically significant!

In a sense, I am a pioneer again. As I was when I was the only disabled student in my school.

Incidentally, as I write this, I'm in the midst of my latest little medical crisis. An infected intra-abdominal abscess landed me in the hospital. A medical drain was inserted into my body to empty the abscess of fluid and pus. Why this happened is still somewhat unclear. Surgery would've been the best solution, my doctors tell me, but they weren't sure that I would survive such surgery, given my disability. I've been home now for eight months, yet I'm still recovering from the invasive drain, which only came out a month ago. I'm still spending more time in bed than usual.

This sort of indignity might have been easier to bear when I was younger. Yet I believe it will pass, as so many other maladies have. Each one takes something out of you, but such setbacks can also grant a kind of wisdom.

Here are some reflections I put down more than a decade ago, after my lengthy hospitalization for C. diff infection and colon surgery, which appeared in an online literary-arts magazine called Tryst. *I've edited it to avoid repetition, though some of the facts might be familiar.*

Last year my wife saved my life. Literally, and repeatedly. First, emergency gastrointestinal surgery went wrong, and I ended up in septic shock—so near death, in fact, that the doctors asked her if she was sure I wanted every measure taken to rescue me. That's when we learned the term *full code.*

This was no rinky-dink hospital. The original, botched surgery was done at the star-studded Cedars-Sinai Medical Center near Beverly Hills; the "full code" question—and subsequent three months in intensive care, with a grueling succession of multiple pneumonias, scattered blood clots, and other complications—at the Ronald Reagan UCLA Medical Center, to where I was transferred by ambulance at 4 a.m., when my incision started hemorrhaging, after Cedars had sent me home.

After parking our two kids with her brother and then an overnight babysitter, my indefatigable wife kept bedside vigil. I couldn't speak because of a tracheostomy and was too weak to press the call button. She read my facial expressions and monitored my machines. Often, when their alarms sounded, she alerted the overworked nurses. That was life-saving gallantry Number 2.

Then came six months' rehab at home. I was still tethered to a ventilator and feeding tube, with round-the-clock nursing care. Shockingly, however, the home health workers—not full-fledged RNs but less qualified CNAs and LPNs—proved almost without exception frighteningly incompetent. Medications were switched, supplied at the wrong times and in incorrect doses; my wife's eagle eye caught most errors before any real harm could be done. Injections were sprayed across my skin instead of into it—and when I, by then able to talk, politely pointed this out, the ill-equipped medic acted like I'd called her un-American. Dirty water was reused to wash me, despite my protests. And so on.

My wife couldn't bear to watch and frequently stepped in. She became so good at, well, doing everything that these junior nurses began asking if she was a doctor! In time, we reduced their shifts to a bare minimum, which of course meant my exhausted wife took on more and more. My survival was in her hands once more.

Now I am myself again, perhaps even better than before, and my wife is back to work at a neighborhood boutique. But even a year later, the repercussions remain with us. The shock, fear, and gratitude. Life is back to normal, but is it? Can it ever feel fully normal again?

I told our story to a physician friend who practices in another state. I felt my wife and I had gone through something extraordinary. "It's not uncommon," he said to my surprise. "Family often has to be involved. The fact is, patients who are surrounded by family always get better care."

"You mean patients need an advocate, someone looking out for you?"

"No," he responded blithely. "Having loved ones around signals the staff that this person is important and deserves our special attention. It may sound terrible, but it's true."

I shuddered to think about those who are alone, or whose spouses can't take the time off work, as my wife did. How do they cope?

Perhaps at this point I should disclose that my wife and I aren't exactly your typical couple. We're a mixed marriage, but not in the way you probably think.

Because of my disability, I retain the musculature of a rag doll. My wife is nondisabled—or at least as nondisabled as you might expect a midlife mother of two to be.

Looking out for my well-being isn't exactly new to her. To be sure, my disability complicates our relationship. At times I rely on her too much for assistance with basic tasks. I maintain full-time hired help (attendants, not nurses) so we can pursue separate careers and enjoy a degree of autonomy from each other. She, in turn, has gotten in the habit of defining her life in terms of being needed—by me, our kids, her boss. It's a balancing act for both of us, but usually it goes quite smoothly. Until a snag arises.

Hey, don't knock it till you've tried it!

We like to think our interdependence gives us a tighter emotional bond than other couples. We have few secrets. And sometimes needing each other as we do keeps us from flying apart over minor disagreements. We're also allies against an often unfair world. Access barriers such as a flight of stairs can draw us nearer together, the unity of facing a common enemy. When other people treat me as an object of pity—appalling, really, in this day and age—it impacts her, too. She gets caught in the spatter of prejudice about me, an inadvertent victim. She's collateral damage.

We keep a wedding portrait prominently displayed in our living room, like newlyweds, just to underscore the point that she married me aluminum casters and all. We are not noble, triumph-over-tragedy types. Don't take us for the late Mr. and Mrs. Christopher Reeve, thank you! Even so, some have been heard to mumble that I must be rich to have won her hand.

You learn not to care what other people say or think. At least you try to. From my earliest memories I developed a guise of plucky good humor, peppered with barbed sarcasm. Yet I confess, there are times I want to shout, "I am not my disability!" But I also know that my disability is part of me. I can't conceive of myself, or of life, without it.

My wife is more practical-minded than philosophical, though she understands where I'm coming from. So honestly I wasn't all that stunned by her devotion during my illness. She's used to helping me, to taking care of what needs to be taken care of, and has always been incredible in a crisis.

What I am having trouble with, however, is how long it seems to be taking her to bounce back. I've gained a keener sense of personal fragility than before, perhaps, but even a year later I'm like the island castaway returned to civilization. Everything is intense, brilliant, and tasty. Look at the sky! Feel the air!

She, on the other hand, is like one still lost at sea. Despite my doctors' reassurances about my health, she often still sleeps in clothes in case, she explains, of a middle-of-the-night dash to the emergency room.

Worrying is not uncharacteristic for her, but this particular anxiety is clearly an emotional fallout from our ordeal.

With my demands on her down to prehospital levels, and the adrenaline rush dwindled to a trickle, it's as if there's a vacuum in her life. She's searching for a sense of direction, struggling to regain her equilibrium. In fairness, my brush with the hereafter left her weary in a way I'm not. I mostly slept for eight months while she kept our home and me going. So why can't she sleep now? Outwardly all is fine, but at her weakest moments the inescapable shadows of vulnerability haunt her like post-traumatic ghosts.

"You almost died," she reminds me when I bring this up. "It was very scary."

She's right, of course. And perhaps I'm too quick to put a silver sheen on the inky cloud. That's not exactly an uncharacteristic coping strategy for me, either.

"But it's all past," I insist, scrounging to heal her spirit as she helped mend my body. Perhaps that's it. The twin G's—guilt and gratitude. I want to repay her.

Lately, it's occurred to me that it's not up to me to ease her pain. Time will provide an answer. It's up to me only to be patient. This is one of those things she must do for herself, no matter how long it takes. However much time it turns out to be must be accepted without resentment, like a spouse's hobby you can't relate to or share in.

Not that I've stopped wondering how a marriage survives the kind of stress we underwent—the desperate, one-sided dependence over so many months. Recovery is not a light thing like an avocation. It's a rougher trial. Yet I'm beginning to see that getting through this will be like handling any other rough spot in a marriage. You go slow, with tolerance and humility.

Ironically, it's only afterward, as the tensions and white-knuckle worries abate, that you begin to recognize what's revealed. For us, our disparate reactions—my delight in having a second chance at life, her once-burned-twice-shy caution—are symptoms of fundamentally different perspectives on the world. Simply put, it's a half-full-half-empty conundrum. The truth doubtless lies somewhere in between, but unless both viewpoints are brought into focus, it's impossible to grasp it.

I recall a discussion we had months before my surgery that had left me feeling confused, lost. I was reflecting on how fortunate I'd been. A good upbringing, good education—every advantage a person could ask for.

"How can you say that?" my wife replied. "You were born with a severe disability, your parents divorced when you were nine, and your mom died when you were eighteen! Your life's been rough."

I'd been thinking about how my parents had the intellectual, emotional, and financial resources to take care of me when many other kids with disabilities were carted off to institutions . . . to insist on my being integrated in regular schools a decade before "mainstreaming" became law . . . to instill me with a sense of entitlement and rights, even when I had none legally. I'd been thinking about how I'd beaten the odds medically and in countless other ways.

Still, I could see her point. "Yes," I said. "But given all that, consider what I might have become, where I might have ended up."

In retrospect, I probably should have added, "I was lucky enough to marry you, wasn't I?"

Alive at 55!

Several years later, I again reflected on my experiences of aging with a disability, this time from a different perspective. I don't think I could write these same thoughts today. This was before the pandemic and other recent health events. Still, I like its joie de vivre.

In late November, I turned fifty-five. For someone like me—born with a dubious life expectancy—that feels like a big milestone.

Yes, I'm fifty-five and still alive!

Not that I don't feel my age. I have the usual aches and pains and dietary restrictions and health worries that anyone my age might have, plus the relentless, albeit gradual, weakening that defines so much of my disability. I don't necessarily grow weaker every year. It's more like every ten or twenty years that I find I've suddenly lost some small ability I used to have. For instance, I haven't been able to feed myself since the 1990s. For the past dozen years, I've been driving my motorized wheelchair with a lip-controlled mini joystick because my hands finally gave out.

What next? Who knows? Within the next decade, if I live that long, I'll probably have a BiPAP or other ventilator attached to my wheelchair. And I'll be glad of it, too. Sure beats not breathing.

Funny thing is, the more debilitated I become the more productive I seem to be. Perhaps it's got something to do with intimations of mortality. On a good day—when I'm breathing well and my machinery is working correctly and my attendant has shown up on time, and so forth—I try to use the opportunity constructively. I schedule appointments, answer old emails, shop online, and write articles and essays that I've been putting off. After all, tomorrow I may be stuck in bed.

Just as each birthday can remind me of the miracle of my continued existence, it also encourages me to believe that there will be a *next* birthday, a tomorrow . . . a useful tomorrow, that is. Even if twenty-four hours hence things go awry, there will come another day that goes well.

I can't say why turning fifty-five makes me believe that I'll turn fifty-six, but it certainly makes that possibility more likely. I mean, I couldn't turn fifty-six without first turning fifty-five, right? And beyond that, the sky's the limit.

Some time ago, an online friend with roughly the same diagnosis I have put the question to a Facebook group for people with neuromuscular conditions: "Am I the oldest person with SMA?" He wasn't. I had him beat by eight years. Sadly, he only made it one more year.

But since he raised the question, I know I am not the oldest survivor either. There is (or was) someone a good ten years my senior online who also has SMA. But only one, as far as I know.

To be clear, SMA doesn't affect longevity per se. It just keeps making you weaker. Sometimes that means the heart just gives out. More often, people with SMA die because of respiratory complications. We are susceptible to pneumonia and other upper respiratory infections. Our lungs become too weak to go on.

That's why, for someone like me, paying attention to breathing is so important. I keep in close touch with my pulmonologist and my allergist, and always try to maintain a supply of respiratory meds, even when my insurance fights it. You're only supposed to get a thirty-day supply at a time, but the way some of the drugs are packaged allows for just twenty-four doses per month (the boxes hold four pouches of six vials). At the same time, I keep a spare nebulizer machine (though, come to think of it, I'm not sure where it is at the moment) so that I can keep sucking in the bronco-dilators that open my airways and the corticosteroid that keeps my lungs from becoming inflamed. Recently, my doctor told me not to use the corticosteroid more than twice a day. I'm trying to comply, but I'd swear that, just a few years ago, I was told I could use it up to four times a day as needed.

Keeping up with medical advances becomes almost second nature. The same could be said of technology. I love the ultrasensitive mini joystick that drives my wheelchair, but now I'm told that the Belgian manufacturer has gone out of business. A new model that's locally built should be out any day now. Or so I've been told for the past five months.

Similarly, my hunt for a new wheelchair after nearly fifteen years has uncovered an alarming development. The chair my dealer says I need does not come with detachable, swing-away footrests. Not clear why. I have always had detachable, swing-away footrests. They're great for reducing the overall depth of the chair, if it needs to fit in tight spaces. They're great for pulling up to a table that has a central pedestal; you just swing one footrest out of the way and roll in. They're great for parking close to your bed, knees against mattress, for . . . oh, never mind. You get the idea.

I have agreed to try the new footrest design; I'm trying to keep an open mind. But that's one problem with living as long as I have. You get set in your ways. You think you've solved all of your problems, only to find that the old solutions might not be available anymore.

A Wheel in Two Worlds

That same year, a random memory prompted a deeper, more literary, perhaps more pretentious rumination on some epiphanies I'd experienced over my more than half a century of living with what's reductively called a "genetic muscle-wasting disease."

My hands were in a cold sweat as I entered my wife's third-grade classroom at a small private school in the San Fernando Valley. It was a hot, dusty afternoon, I recall, though my palms had their own thermostat. The school was informal in that Hollywood way; I knew many of the teachers by first name, and I enjoyed the pervasive echo of kids at educational play. My wife greeted me with a perfunctory peck on the cheek.

Then I took my position at the front of the colorful, glue-smelling room—my eyes darting from bulletin board to bulletin board to glean what the kids had been learning—and began what was truly a double mission. My wife had asked me to talk to her kids—as we referred to them in those days, before we had our own children and she gave up teaching—about my career as a budding freelance writer *and* my life as a permanent wheelchair user. To me, the two facts were seamlessly braided. But would this motley crew of eight- and nine-year-olds get that?

It was the early 1990s, and the Americans with Disabilities Act was still new. Most of it wasn't even implemented yet. Diversity curricula were just starting to include the disabled as a genuine minority classification. I spoke to a lot of schools and community centers at the time, making the case for our movement, but my wife's class was the only presentation where I was both cripple and career guy.

Everyone bears multiple identities: We have intersecting familial ties (parent/spouse/offspring/sibling) and professional designations. Sometimes they overlap, such as "stay-at-home dad/mom." But in case you haven't been in this sort of dual-label situation, you should understand how disconcerting it can be to feel one side of you battling for validation against the other—or at least it was for me.

To my relief, the kids made a good audience. They'd been visited by other adults—parents—about careers, so they knew how to be respectful of guests. My technology captivated their attention. "How do you drive your chair?" was a not-unexpected query. (Answer: "With this tiny, super-sensitive joystick... see how it moves?") I loved that something I took for granted, something often stigmatized as pitiful or medical, was for them so cool. I was also unfazed by off-topic questions such as, "What's your favorite color?" (Answer: whatever color that particular kid was wearing.) And the reliably giggle-inducing, "How do you go to the bathroom?" ("Same as you, but with help.")

Then one squirmy little girl looked me in the eye and asked, "What was the name of your *first* agent?" Not my second or third or current one—just the first! Somehow she'd picked up on my tale of publishing woes.

"Why? You want her number?" I felt like responding. Instead, I gave the name, which seemed to satisfy, and moved on to the next question. But I never forgot that moment. Not just the baffling specificity of the question, or the evident fact that she'd actually been listening, but the recognition of my dual status resonated. She was relating to me not as a physical curiosity but as a person, a professional, a sort of veteran of the literary trade. Or so it felt anyway.

Afterward, I began to wonder where my embarrassment, my awkwardness about this split sense of personality, came from. I'd grown up thinking my disability didn't matter. It was a private concern, perhaps, but not relevant to the rest of my life. Then I learned the world didn't really work that way. And I learned to keep my cripitude as hidden as possible in professional situations.

I became a regular contributor to financial magazines and websites, always working from home by phone, fax, and email. Disability became my secret identity—except once, when I had to visit a boutique investment bank to interview its research director in person. Donning jacket and tie, I nervously plotted how best to present myself. But when I met the balding, middle-aged man I was to profile, he was gracious, warm, and kind—and, I quickly noticed, had the shaking hands of early-stage Parkinson's. We bonded instantly.

I know many disabled job seekers still debate whether to mention their "reasonable accommodations" on their résumés and cover letters. There is, I think, an advantage to being up-front, but even today it can close off a lot of opportunities.

The only career alternative I could see to the one I had chosen was to be a "professional cripple"—that is, someone who advises on or advocates for accessibility *all the time*. But that never interested me. I never felt my disability should define what I do or who I am. So my alter ego remained hidden.

In truth, there were a few overlaps in my discrete worlds. For instance, financial magazines wanted stories about the need for caregivers for the aging population. There were insurance articles, too, addressing long-term care. I brought my insider's authority to bear on such subjects.

Then, with age, my own hypocrisy began to eat at me. How can I argue that disabilities should be accepted as a normal part of life and society while simultaneously trying to cover up mine? Maybe, I dared hope, I had sufficiently established myself as a journalist by now that my other identity might be deemed acceptable, even interesting, rather than a deficit. Maybe.

Look at my website and résumé now and you'll see the full variety of my publishing achievements. From my essays about disability issues to my stories about financial subjects, they're all there. I have online followers from both camps, too. I no longer seek to disregard my disability, but I don't want to be judged by it either. My explanation, if anyone asks, is that I am a writer active in both worlds, proud of my versatility, the diversity of my accomplishments. That's the unifying theme.

This doesn't mean I'm immune to the old panic, however. The other day, a financial PR man I've worked with by phone and email was in town and invited me to lunch. I delayed answering. Unless he'd Googled me, he didn't know about my disability.

We never did meet. By the time I responded, scheduling became too crazy. Next time, I promise, I won't hesitate. All I have to do is remember that little girl who, with her odd question about my first agent, saw the whole me.

Brockton Public Library

More recently, I spoke to a virtual gathering under the auspices of the Brockton Public Library in Massachusetts about my latest project. It was essentially a research project, a mission to reacquaint myself with the activist disability community.

I had begun to realize that I'd completely lost touch with the disability activism of today. A whole generation of crips had grown up while I wasn't looking, and I wanted to understand them better, to understand the current issues facing the disability community, my community.

I decided to write about what I had learned.

A lot of people write about their feelings and experiences. They just feel compelled to put down words, I guess, hoping someone else will read them and get something out of the reading. If you're lucky, these scribblings get published. If you're luckier still, your words generate enough interest to get you interviewed on radio programs and podcasts (usually without pay, but if you're on this lucky streak, well, you never know).

Here, then, is an edited transcript of the talk I gave to Brockton library fans after completing and publishing my research on the new generation of disability activism.

Warren: Thank you, Ben, for joining us. Without further ado, I'll let Ben take over.

Ben: Thank you, and hello to everyone. I'd like to say it's great to be back in Massachusetts, virtually anyway. Let me start, though, by describing myself for those who can't see very well. . . . Access isn't just about ramps and elevators, after all. It's important to be as accessible as possible. I hope when this recording is done that there'll be closed-captioning and such.

Warren: Yeah, we'll have that.

Ben: Oh, good, good. Okay, well, I'm old enough to remember the world before the Americans with Disabilities Act [ADA], remember it quite well. But after it passed, or not long after, my wife and I had a couple of kids, and I got involved in the domestic life and my other career. I got away from disability activism, and really from the disability community. I realized that the new generation of disabled folks were doing things that I dare say my generation never imagined. I needed to catch up.

So I did my research. The most important part was talking to or emailing—let's say communicating—with as many disabled folks, folks with chronic health conditions, primarily those under age forty, as I could. When I couldn't connect with somebody personally, I would read up on what they'd been blogging and articles they'd written and other interviews they'd done. I felt it was important for me to step back and provide space for these folks to explain themselves in their own words, in their own way. Obviously, I'm not entirely objective on the subject. I understood what I was learning from my perspective as a fellow disabled person.

I learned a lot. I thought I knew what disabled people wanted, what activism was all about, but I was wrong. I had a lot to learn about my own community and about what the new ideas of fairness and justice were all about. There are a lot of aspects to the disability community and disability history that I didn't know because they had been sort of made invisible or erased from the mainstream record, particularly disabled people of color, queer and trans disabled people—heck, even the lives and contributions of disabled women.

So much of what I knew was from the perspective of white men in wheelchairs, people like me. I'd also never thought much about mental health issues, psychiatric and cognitive disabilities, neurodiversity, and on and on. I mean, we're a pretty diverse bunch, the disability community, and I feel that once you understand that, once you know a bit more about the history and the diversity, you as a—I as a disabled person can begin to feel better about myself, too. This knowledge helps engender feelings of disability pride. I realized that I've struggled with it. I've gone through times when I've tried to hide my disability, which is sort of impossible. It's pretty darned obvious. I've tried to minimize my limitations. But why?

As I interviewed people, I asked them about this, and every single person had a story to tell about how they had been ashamed or felt uncomfortable about their own bodies, and the journeys they'd been on to feel okay with themselves as they are, and how it helped when they connected with other folks like themselves. They came to understand the roots of some of that shame, that it was coming from without, from a society that celebrates certain norms and makes you feel bad if you vary from those norms in any way.

Anyway, that's a long, roundabout way of explaining what my talking to more people taught me. I hope others get a similar understanding of the community, the history, the issues, but also what it means to feel disability pride. Now to catch my breath. Any questions or anything else I can address? I can ramble on.

Warren: All right, let me ask if there are any specific people who particularly stood out to you or that you'd like to highlight?

Ben: I'd hate to highlight someone and leave someone else out. I mean, there are so many folks past and present who struggled against prejudices and difficulties, and it's nice to know that they existed.... It can be a problem that sometimes disability stories are seen as inspirational and amazing instead of just plain real life. People still think that disability rights is about being nice and charitable, but that's not really the point. It's about civil rights and justice.

That's actually a newish wrinkle in disability activism. It started actually fifteen or twenty years ago, sort of the second wave called *disability justice*, which a lot of people misunderstand. I misunderstood it at first. I thought it was just a cool term. I'm not totally appropriate to describe it, because it's not about people like me. It's about fairness and justice for the most marginalized disabled folks who have not really had a seat at the table. It's about reinventing society to be more fair to all types of people. The Americans with Disabilities Act [ADA] and civil rights are great and all, but they only go so far. Disability justice folks have pointed out, for instance, how incarceration is fundamentally linked to ableism. [Many of the people in prison are actually disabled in some way.] That kind of harmful unfairness goes beyond access to employment or access to theaters and shopping malls.

There are a lot of issues like that that I was not really aware of. But there is this new generation, new strain of activism, new framework for thinking about what an accessible society should be like. To me, it's thought-provoking and it gives me hope, because I confess I had a fear that the new generation had grown complacent, resting on the laurels of what previous generations had accomplished. Not so, not so. Disability activists all over the world are doing all kinds of things to move the cause along.

Warren: Would you mind talking a little bit more about your background? Did you participate in protests or things like that when you were growing up?

Ben: Growing up, no. I grew up in New York [in the] sixties and seventies to upper-middle-class, intellectual parents. That was a time when there wasn't very much for them or us in terms of disability awareness in a political sense. There was medical stuff. The Muscular Dystrophy Association, for instance, was my parents' only source of information, of context, which was unfortunate because that was all about pity and fundraising. But in the late seventies I began to read in the paper about disability activists. I guess I thought they were all radical weirdos or something.

Warren: And later, you struggled to find a job after college?

Ben: Yes. No one would hire me, so I started writing for myself, with mixed success. I never got a full-time job until last year at the age of fifty-nine, and that's at least partly thanks to the Zoom revolution. All of a sudden it was acceptable for me to work from home with equipment that I had made accessible for myself—a voice-recognition computer and a mouse I can operate by mouth. All of a sudden, I was employable. A benefit of the pandemic, and I really hope that doesn't roll back. I mean, the virtual access to events and to employment opportunities, it's huge for a lot of disabled folks. That's kind of the silver lining of the Covid pandemic, I guess you could say. We all like silver linings.

Warren: We have a question from a listener whose wife has MS and they're having trouble finding affordable help for repairing her wheelchair and other equipment. I don't know if you have suggestions.

Ben: Hmmm. Not specifically, I'm sorry to say. I wish I did. But I get it. It's always a problem everywhere. The common, ordinary stuff that disabled people struggle with [doesn't get enough attention]. And it's as mundane as that. Getting a wheelchair that is comfortable and affordable, or a van, finding romance, finding sex, finding accessible affordable housing—these are huge basic issues. I think that sometimes activists get so full of big ideas and systemic issues that they kind of lose touch a little bit. A lot of folks have some pretty basic issues around funding and just getting by day to day.

Having funds, financial resources, makes a big difference. It can turn a disability into an inconvenience, in many cases. Not all. I mean, there are people with chronic pain and no amount of money will help. But not having to worry about money, being able to afford the stuff you need, that makes a profound difference. Whether it's daily personal-care assistance or devices or medicines, these are huge financial issues that should be talked about. Not charity but basic fairness, if that makes sense.

Warren: Yeah. I have many friends who use wheelchairs and other mobility devices, and often they've made the point that, "If I have my wheelchair, then I can actually go to work." It's not so much, "I feel like society owes me something," but "I'd like to have the funding and equipment so I can contribute."

Ben: Right. Thank you to your listener for the comment.

Warren: That about wraps it up.

Ben: Thank you for having me. And thank you all for joining in and listening, and for your interest. Buy my books, buy other disabled people's books, because the more the publishers, the gatekeepers of media, realize that there is interest, that there is a market, the better for all of us.

Reflections

Quiet Activism

Somebody asked me once, not too long ago, if I thought capitalism was antithetical to a disabled-friendly society. For me, it's a complex question. Opposing capitalist principles is indeed a component of the disability justice framework, as I understand it, but it's a hard idea to get my head around. I grew up with liberal parents who nevertheless had a capitalist mindset. I'm indoctrinated in the capitalism ethos, so to speak, and I have a hard time shucking that off. That doesn't mean I look down on people who are not rich and "successful." But I think people have a natural instinct to strive for better, and I'm not sure that's a bad thing. Plus, I've done a lot of work over the years for financial publications that are all about competitive strategies and that celebrate monetary worth. I don't always agree with the people I interview and write about, but I enjoy learning about the game, even if I don't live by its rules.

Then again, the capitalist imperative to meet certain milestones in order to achieve status, to gain respect, is not too friendly to the disability lifestyle. Some of us are less able to compete, to produce goods and services that others consider valuable. That doesn't mean we are not deserving of an equal place in society. People should be valued just by virtue of being human beings.

The disabled writer, activist, and MacArthur Fellow Alice Wong published an essay in Yes *magazine that expresses the uncapitalistic disability justice ideal with stirring clarity: "If we lived in a world that placed access above all, creating access would be a collective responsibility. In this world . . . people, not profits, would be the priority; care would flow generously without restrictions from the state; and people like me would be secure knowing we are valued and wanted not for what we can produce but for who we are."*

Wong alludes to another unfortunate truth about disabled people that doesn't fit with capitalist standards: We can be expensive. Full-time care and necessary equipment cost more than most of us can earn. We draw a lot from society's resources. Scholars say the Nazis referred to us as "useless eaters" to justify the sterilization and extermination of disabled people in a program that preceded the genocide of Jews and other groups. To Hitler and his cronies, our expensiveness was hard if not impossible to justify.

Certainly that's an extreme example. Nobody would dare express such views today. Still, why do so many of my disabled peers who live in our capitalist society feel a subtle pressure to justify their existence?

There is nothing wrong with not being fabulous, rich, athletic, competitive. It doesn't make you less of a person to be stuck in bed, if that's where you need to be. Some of us just aren't cut out to be on the scene, to hustle or raise a ruckus. Being quiet or nonconfrontational doesn't make you a failure—nor a traitor to the cause of disability empowerment. You still matter. Sometimes just surviving despite the myriad pressures to give up is a rebellious act in itself.

I tried to make the case for this sort of quiet activism in a blog post for FacingDisability.com.

Earlier this summer, social media (and a smattering of conventional media, too) were filled with images of disability-rights activists protesting against certain proposed health-care reforms. Witnessing these events from the safety of my home, I felt profoundly proud of my colleagues and allies in disability rights. I was also a bit sad and guilty that I couldn't join them.

What I saw next, however, caused my feelings to shift in a disturbing way. Somewhere deep within me, I began to question what I was witnessing. And this, in turn, made me question myself and my loyalties.

In the biggest demonstration, some sixty activists—mostly people with disabilities—had gathered at Senate Majority Leader Mitch McConnell's D.C. office. Between chants I couldn't quite make out, they laid their bodies on the floor like corpses, disrupting the space in what they called a "die-in."

As [activist] Stephanie Woodward later explained, the idea was to represent "the harm that the bill would do to so many disabled people." A good and righteous cause, to be sure. Fear of being bumped off the life-sustaining Medicaid rosters runs far and deep. Swift and dramatic action was needed.

What I saw, though, were the faces of the overworked guards. To me, they appeared overwhelmed. They didn't like what they knew they had to do. They might've even agreed with the protesters, but their job was to clear the passageways and keep the peace. I felt for the peacekeepers. I wasn't supposed to, perhaps, but I did.

For me, the problem was that the protesters had effectively made these cops the accidental targets of their wrath instead of the politicos they'd intended to confront or persuade. I couldn't view the guards as part of the enemy because all I could see were honest hardworking men and women who were caught in a bad spot.

My next reaction was remorse. Whose side was I on anyway? The proposals under debate would cut millions from the roster of Medicaid recipients, many of whom are people like me, people I consider friends and heroes!

Having considered myself a disability-rights activist, I support the message, the goal. I also support the means to that end. It's just that noisy activism isn't my style.

Make no mistake: I have participated in protest demonstrations. Years ago, I joined the throngs outside the Hollywood studio that was broadcasting the late Jerry Lewis's MDA Labor Day telethon. I festooned my wheelchair with signs decrying the annual charity fundraiser. "Piss on pity!" we chanted.

For the most part, however, I prefer to express my political righteousness in writing. My first published op-ed was an open letter to Jerry Lewis about that charity's message. As I began to get more essays published in newspapers around the country, on various disability issues, I realized I'd found my métier. I could do a better job of getting the disability-inclusion message across through my writing than I ever could through waving banners and joining in protest actions.

Okay, that's just me. I'm a man of thoughts, of words, not banners and chants. I believe in dialogue and discourse.

So sometimes I still feel guilty about that. But who's to say which method is more effective? Perhaps it takes all kinds. Perhaps to someone in political power, one protest march looks a lot like another. Or maybe essays, even those published in the *Washington Post* and *New York Times*, are all too easily tossed in the trash bin. I don't know.

The hope, though, is that someone's mind will be enlightened or even turned. Someone who just may cast a vote next time and so, in turn, may affect outcomes.

Don't get me wrong. I still support activists. People are legitimately frightened by the course of political events. They need to protest, to shout in righteous rage. I bear them no ill will. Yet like the old song says, it ain't me.

I may be mistaken. It may be that my methods are too calm, too nonconfrontational, even too cowardly. Written words only go so far. Sometimes you have to put muscle behind them. But deep down I'm not an in-your-face kind of guy. I'm a spinner of words.

I may not always join the crowds of protesters, but you won't shut me up either.

My '70s Show

Staying out of the fray has advantages. For one thing, you have time to contemplate life and its meaning. But you also have time to write whatever the hell you want.

One day, I was looking through some old home movies. I had an ulterior motive. I wanted to get a clear sense of how much my disability had progressed since childhood. I saw my parents carrying me around when I was small, as you would any baby. Only in my case, that went on longer than usual.

But then, from about age three or four, I was in a manual wheelchair. Never could propel it myself, so I was pushed everywhere. When I turned six, we had a game of Pin the Tail on the Donkey for my birthday party. Actually, it was Pin the Six-Shooter on the Lone Ranger. Anyway, there I am, blindfolded, directing my mother how to position my chair and hold up my arm to where I thought the paper gun should go. I'm sure I thought I was doing it myself, in a way, but I clearly didn't have the muscles for it.

A few years later, at another birthday party (did little boys really wear neckties at birthday parties in those days?), we played a game of Hot Potato. My wheelchair was parked in the circle of kids. But as each well-dressed child passed along the ticking time bomb of a potato (or whatever it was) to the next kid in the circle, I grinned with eager anticipation of when it would come to me. When it did, the child on my right simply placed the spheroid in my cupped hands, which were motionless in my lap. Then the child on my left grabbed it from there and kept it moving along. Thus I got to participate. In memory, though, I had performed as every other child did.

Then there was another forgotten gem from when I was twelve years old, which prompted the following essay. I was delighted when a small online literary magazine called The Write Place at the Write Time *offered to publish it.*

It was shocking to behold. Not only a blatantly offensive stereotype, but it was me, at the impressionable age of twelve!

To be sure, my family and I didn't know any better at the time. As I recall, it started as an innocent attempt to enliven a boring Sunday in early autumn 1975. My parents had separated three years before, and Dad was still struggling to reingratiate himself with my brother and me, determined to make his weekends (which alternated with Mom's) as fun as possible. "Let's make a movie!" he suggested.

My big brother, Alec, then fifteen, looked up from his *Doonesbury*. "Where? How?" he asked with a combination of suspicion and eagerness.

We were not in a filmmaking habit. YouTube was still decades off. But somewhere at the back of Dad's closet in his new West End Avenue pad was an old Super 8 movie camera—the kind with blinding lights and no audio. He'd used it for our birthday parties when we were younger. We hadn't seen it in years.

"Silent movies are corny," I complained. But nobody listened to me, as usual (or so it felt at twelve).

Dad suggested we start by sketching out a basic story arc, revealing his latent Hollywood aspirations. "It'll only be five minutes long," he said, to temper our unrealistic hopes and outsized fears.

Sure enough, ideas started flying like sparks off a spinning film reel. At length we came up with a storyline. A simple crime drama, with a cynical New York twist.

After roping in a friend of my brother's—our story called for a cast of four, not three—we set out for Riverside Park. It was a lovely sunny day, and the natural light would solve most of the squinting problem that had characterized our past indoor birthday party footage.

To watch the clip today—which Dad converted to VHS tape a few years ago and I transferred to DVD and the cloud for posterity—is to laugh at the bushy 1970s hairstyles and flowery, tight-fitting clothes. Also the hurried, half-baked costumes: specifically, my six-foot-three-inch father squeezed into my five-foot-two-inch brother's trench coat to become the Detective. Why Alec didn't play that part himself is a question lost to history.

To me, though, there's something even more disturbing on display.

Picture this: a park bench. All is peaceful. Enter the Mugger. He snatches a wallet and runs off. The Detective appears, scratches his head. In comes the Witness, pointing as if to say, "He went thataway." The Detective gives chase. A struggle ensues, during which the purloined wallet falls unnoticed to the ground. The triumphant Detective presents the subdued Mugger to the Victim for positive identification. But where is the wallet? The Witness has found it—and pocketed it! In the final shot the duplicitous Witness walks off gleefully, leaving everyone else flummoxed.

Alec plainly relished being the thief, for reasons that would surely land him on the psychologist's couch years later. His friend Michael could win an Oscar for his portrayal of the double-crossing Witness. Leaving me as—what else?—the Victim. The muggee.

There I am with a headful of unruly blondish curls and huge Elton John glasses, sitting in my wheelchair utterly defenseless as my evil big brother in a bandanna mask seizes the wallet from my lap. All I can do is shake my head, wiggle my fingers, and open my mouth in a pantomime scream. It'd be funny if it weren't so pitiful.

No doubt I owe my lifelong determination to beat the odds of my disability to my pioneering—dare I say "maverick"?—parents, who insisted on integrating me in regular schools. Which is why this revelation of familial disability stereotyping was so startling.

I may have wanted to be the muggee. I don't remember. I'm certain we all assumed I had no choice. Physically, I couldn't reach out to steal the wallet and run away, couldn't chase after and tackle the bad guy, and couldn't bend down to pilfer the forgotten wallet from the bushes, pocket it, and walk away.

We didn't think about how we were perpetuating a kind of bigotry. We hadn't connected the patronizing dots between, say, Laura Wingfield, the physically and emotionally damaged young woman of *The Glass Menagerie*; the old woman cast down the stairs—wheelchair and all—by Richard Widmark in *Kiss of Death*; bedridden Barbara Stanwyck during a break-in in *Sorry, Wrong Number*; the struggling, blind Audrey Hepburn in *Wait Until Dark*, and so forth. (Male "crippled victims," for some reason, are generally so frustrated and embittered they turn into another stereotype, crippled villains—Quasimodo, Richard III, the Phantom of the Opera, Captain Hook, or any number of Batman bad guys, to name a few.)

I'd like to think we had some realization of the cliché at least. I'd like to think we were riffing on people's misconceptions about me, lampooning a prejudice we were aware of but hadn't actually identified as such. But that's probably revisionist history.

It's just one event, of course. Yet seeing the clip after so many years, I couldn't help wondering if it reflected a larger pattern—a subtext of my upbringing.

I phoned my dad to ask. He merely laughed. Like me, he has only a vague recollection of a pleasant, lighthearted afternoon together. Indeed, we were blissful in our ignorance of the larger political repercussions of the portrayal.

I showed my wife the clip, for a second opinion.

"You didn't have to be the victim," she said. "You could have been the detective, rolling after the bad guy and tripping him with your footrests. Or the thief, perhaps a criminal mastermind with henchmen. Or the witness, tucking the wallet into the crevices of your wheelchair. You could have been anything!"

Why hadn't any of us thought of that?

Even in my nostalgic haze, two undeniable facts came into sharp focus: Perceptions of people with disabilities, though still far from perfect, have surely evolved. After all, you now see us everywhere—on the bus, in shopping malls, at voting booths. Secondly, I married well.

My Dad Was the Ideal Father for a Kid in a Wheelchair

As my dad kept aging (as I write this, he's ninety-six), I felt compelled to pen a tribute for Father's Day. My motivation, I confess, wasn't entirety filial devotion. I was trying to promote my second book, which dealt partly with family issues related to disability.

I was doubly pleased when The Washington Post *agreed to publish it. My dad had moved to the D.C. area some years before, so he and his friends there would be sure to see it.*

Do you remember being carried in your father's arms? No? I do.

That's because my dad was still lifting me when I was in college. See, I can't walk. Never could, never will. I have full sensation, a big and opinionated mouth, and zero muscles.

Tall and broad-shouldered as he is, Dad only stopped lifting me when his back gave out. And I moved out, though not for that reason. I was twenty.

Before I got my first wheelchair, I moved about primarily on my mom's slim hip. But after that, as I got bigger, Dad took over moving me in and out of my chair, the bathtub, the car, and elsewhere. He'd still be doing it—I can tell he wants to by the way he sometimes reaches for me—but he's now over ninety years old.

I've never been all that heavy—ninety pounds at present—due to my lack of musculature. My petite wife can lift me. Still, I recall feeling especially secure in Dad's embrace. Even when he almost lost hold of me in an amusement park ride a lifetime ago, a story he frequently recounts with horror. My memory: He held on; I was safe.

I've thought a lot about what makes the ideal father for a kid in a wheelchair. Dad, a Harvard-educated Fulbright scholar, might seem an unlikely candidate.

Before my birth, he gave up academia to become the first editor of a fledgling magazine soon known the world over as *GQ*. (He still calls it *Gentlemen's Quarterly*.) He knew nothing about fashion, but he possessed a definite sense of what it meant to be a gentleman. And that boded well for me.

Of the thirteen years he stayed at *GQ* (before metamorphosing, again, into a financial journalist), he's not proudest of his celebrity encounters—though I love hearing about Fred Astaire's disdain for being photographed as a clothing model, Cary Grant's insistence that war was caused by sexual frustration, and how Farley Granger made a pass at Dad.

Rather, Dad points to being an early publisher of George Plimpton (October 1958 and April 1959), Joan Didion (October 1959 and October 1962), and Joseph Heller (December 1959).

To him, a gentleman should be not just well dressed but well read. That was a key lesson for me, on whom clothes never quite fit right because of my skinny limbs and scoliotic spine. It told me that I could nonetheless bring something valuable to the table. My ideas. My wit.

Throughout my childhood, Dad always proved willing to experiment. He kept an eye out for gadgets that might assist me in performing daily tasks. To this day, I am a keen user of the latest high-tech assistive devices.

Not that things were always great between us. Looking back, I see that Dad had a hard time accepting my disability. For a while, he went down a rabbit hole of pseudomedical craziness in search of a cure. (There is none.) He took me to a spiritualist who promised to commune with the Other Side on my behalf. And we almost went to Europe for an experimental transplant of sheep cells, purported to help generate new motor neurons. (I still have his extensive notes on the project.)

Crazy, yes. But as a father now myself, I can only applaud his efforts. If he'll never exactly be an advocate for disability pride, he has always been an advocate for me.

My late mother was equally supportive, to be sure. But Dad's insistence that things can and should be better became a transformative spark for me. It spurred me to keep striving, to prove the pessimists wrong.

Let's face it: I'm a cripple who can't scratch his own nose. Yet that was never going to define me.

Dad not only had confidence in my potential; he instilled in me a driving sense of ambition, a hunger to achieve. I credit this, in part, with helping propel me to graduate from Harvard (just like Dad), to move across country, to marry and have kids, and to write articles [and books!] such as this one.

Many other disabled people I've met tell me their parents either discouraged them from trying to live a normal life, for fear of disappointment, or set unachievably high expectations. The results are as you might expect. I'm eternally grateful that my upbringing fell somewhere in between.

"Opinion: My Dad Was the Ideal Father for a Kid in a Wheelchair" by Ben Mattlin was first published in The Washington Post *on June 15, 2018.*

I Remember Life Before the Americans with Disabilities Act. Now, We Need to Do More.

Every year before the anniversary of the signing of the Americans with Disabilities Act on July 26, I think about writing some sort of tribute. A few years ago, in anticipation of the thirtieth anniversary, I was successful. I cobbled together this essay, which USA Today *thankfully picked up. It's been edited to avoid repetition.*

Sunday marks thirty years since passage of the Americans with Disabilities Act (ADA). The landmark civil rights legislation secured unprecedented freedoms and civil rights for the disability community—estimated to comprise nearly 20 percent of the United States population. But is that enough?

I remember what life was like before the ADA. I've seen improvements that surpassed my wildest hopes and expectations. Yet the disability revolution is far from over. We may have laws against discrimination, but we still have discrimination. We may have rights, but we don't always have justice.

As much progress as the disability community has made, it's not where it ought to be.

Unemployment among disabled people remains at roughly twice the rate of those who are not disabled. In 2016, the Ruderman Family Foundation, a nonprofit disability advocacy organization, found that almost half of the people killed by police had a disability.

The disparities facing disabled people have never been clearer than during the coronavirus pandemic. In the early days of the panic, certain state and medical authorities considered rationing vital resources such as ventilators, which were drastically in short supply. Disabled and elderly people feared being deprived of needed care because they are considered the most expendable, or at least the least likely to benefit.

For instance, in June, a Texas hospital withheld treatment for six days from Michael Hickson, a quadriplegic who contracted coronavirus, because the people in the facility judged he would have poor quality of life. It's as if the value of somebody's life with a disability is considered less.

The inequity became even clearer as a disproportionate number of those who died were living or working in nursing homes and long-term-care facilities. They couldn't secure an adequate supply of personal protective equipment, and in such close quarters social distancing was often impossible. In late June 2020, the number of U.S. coronavirus-linked deaths in long-term-care facilities had surpassed 54,000, or 43 percent of Covid fatalities. Some called these institutions the epicenter of the disease.

Such dangerous disparities are beyond the purview of the ADA. But they underscore the difference between having rights—at least on paper—and having fairness, having justice.

Ever since the ADA passed, businesses and politicians have tried to gut the requirements. They don't want to force stores to become accessible or employers to be more accommodating.

But the disability community—much of which only came of age since the ADA—remains strong and defiant. Beyond fighting the backlash, we've raised awareness of invisible disabilities such as bipolar disorder, learning disabilities, and mental health conditions. We've had a rise in autistic self-advocacy and improved the understanding of neurodiversity, acknowledging that just as some people move or communicate differently from others, so too do some think differently and react differently to stimuli—and there's nothing wrong with that.

We've seen the birth of the disability justice movement, which aims to fill the gaps the ADA left, in part by addressing discrimination against disabled people of color, disabled Indigenous people, disabled queer people, and others who proudly claim intersectional identities.

I thought I knew what the disability movement was all about: respect, jobs, access, fairness, an end to medicalizing us, enshrining our civil rights. But our cause and our community have emerged as broader and more diverse than that. The ADA was just the beginning.

What I Learned from the Generation of Disabled Activists Who Came After Me

Not long after the previous piece was published, I received an email from a small literary magazine about contributing a long essay on disability as a cultural identity. I was intrigued—plus I would be well paid for it.

I confess that I had doubts about the legitimacy of the offer, but it was a good challenge. I spent months drafting a long essay, which I attempted to substantiate with examples from the research I was doing. It took a while to hear back from the editors, who ultimately rejected my submission because they were opposed to "identity politics."

It turns out that it was a politically and religiously conservative publication, which I didn't know going in. Of course, I thought my submission was politically neutral and not objectionable, but there was no appeasing the editors. They paid me half the original offer as a kill fee. Which was fair and decent—but now what was I going to do with this four-thousand-word masterpiece? Where else could I submit it?

After some minor revisions, I sent it everywhere I could think of. Imagine my delight when I received an unexpected email back from Time *magazine. Could I possibly shorten the piece? Maybe cut out the carefully researched examples and stick to my opinions and impressions. Of course I could! I had never been published in* Time *before.*

My shortened and revised draft about disability culture appeared both on the Time *website and in the print magazine. Here it is, again edited to remove repetition.*

Over the past several decades—even before the Americans with Disabilities Act (ADA), and more emphatically ever since—the idea of disability shifted from a medical signifier to an emblem of cultural identity. People will tell you, in various ways, "Don't say I have 'special needs' or am 'physically challenged.' Don't even call me a 'person with a disability.' I'm a *disabled* person"—with *disabled* first and foremost, imparting an unapologetic pride.

Pride in disability isn't new—there have been Disability Pride Parades at least since the early 1990s—but the language preference and the culture and identity shift it reflects *are* new. At least, to me. My generation of activists preferred "person first" language, which is why the law isn't called the Disabled Americans Act. Clunky and awkward as it sounds, the phrase "people with disabilities" became the standard. It emphasized our humanity, we thought.

But the new generation has pointed out the error in that kind of thinking—that putting *disabled* first is a badge of honor. In fact, it's become so widely accepted that it practically feels required. No hesitancy or shyness allowed.

As a lifelong disabled person, I'm ashamed to admit that I struggled a bit to embrace this concept.

My increasing weakness is not something I like, but if I think about it, I realize that that doesn't mean I'd prefer to be nondisabled. I like myself, I like my life, and I honestly can't imagine existing in any other way. I'm not ashamed of my disability. But am I *culturally* disabled? Do I want to proclaim my disability as a primary identity marker?

When I was growing up in the 1960s and '70s, my parents insisted I could be anything I wanted when I grew up. It wasn't true, of course, but this was a much better message than the unwittingly heartless prognosis of gloom and doom that some of my peers received. My mom and dad went to great pains to make sure my upbringing was as "normal"—or at least similar to my nondisabled brother's—as possible. As a result, I never knew other "handicapped kids," as we were called then.

It wasn't until I was in college that I heard about the disability rights movement. But at that point I had no interest in joining it. I figured I wasn't the activist type, but the truth is I didn't want to associate with other crips.

Something happened after graduation, though—or rather, didn't. I couldn't find a job. My prospects looked good on paper but not in person, apparently. In interview after interview, potential employers' jaws dropped when they met me face-to-face. Confronted with so much rejection, I began to feel kinship with the disability-rights brigade. Slogans such as "Build Access For ALL!" and "I can't even get to the BACK of the bus!" started ringing true for me. The righteous rage didn't seem so outlandish or radical anymore; on the contrary, these activists were modern-day visionaries! They understood aspects of my life that I'd never quite cottoned to myself. How could restaurants and stores get away with refusing me service, claiming that my presence might upset other customers? Why should I feel grateful if allowed the same courtesies as anyone else? Why must I harbor guilt about my limitations and requirements?

In memory, I was rarely confronted with outright rudeness. But attitudinal barriers (not to mention architectural ones) were everywhere. Inaccessibility and ableist bigotry—terms I was learning to get the hang of—truly did more harm than my muscle atrophy.

Over the next few years, I wrote letters to Congress and newspaper editors. I went to group meetings and protest demonstrations. Any chance I got, I gave "testimony" about how I'd faced discrimination. The July morning when the ADA was signed into law, I was glued to the live TV coverage. I couldn't believe our ideas had become reality. I was twenty-seven years old and had never felt more awestruck or validated.

Not long after, my wife and I had kids and got busy with the rest of our lives. I never landed a full-time job (until 2022), but I managed to eke out a meager income as a freelance writer. In time, many of my friends from the movement died. Advocacy fell behind me. I didn't exactly become complacent, but I knew that I had rights and if I had to assert them, I would. I enjoyed a degree of security in that knowledge. But I thought that perhaps disability activism had died out with my generation.

I was wrong.

Somehow, while I wasn't looking, a new generation had made incredible progress. They'd taken the rights my peers and predecessors fought for and made them their own in ways I'd never imagined. On social media, everyday disabled folks were posting selfies that plainly displayed their wheelchairs, crutches, facial deformities, tracheostomies, or a combination of these, posing at home, in busy marketplaces, at golden beachfront oases, in elegant urban settings, and on snowy mountaintops—laughing, kissing, dancing, shopping, eating and drinking, or just voguing. Hashtags such as #DisabledAndCute, #WheelsNoHeels, and #DisabledFashion expressed their blatant moxie. They'd achieved a degree of self-confidence that even their prophetic forebears hadn't dreamed possible.

How had this happened? It was as if, by confirming that we were in reality a discriminated-against class of citizens, a profound upswelling of expectations and norms had been set in motion. It had fired up the younger generation's courage even as it had, in drips and drabs, upended society.

Many events in disability history have happened since the ADA. Ironically, much of this post-ADA progress had to do with addressing the shortcomings of the movement I had known. We—my "cohort"—overlooked so many types of people. We scarcely acknowledged the contributions of nonwhite and queer or nonbinary disabled folks and the intersectional intolerances they face to this day. We were often dismissive of neurodiversity and other less visible conditions, prompting the rise of autistic self-advocacy networks. Still more pockets of disability that had been marginalized or erased from the broader narrative began laying claim to full inclusion and parity, such as those with emotional disabilities and chronic illnesses.

To comprehend how disabled Americans can make up more than 61 million souls, according to the Centers for Disease Control and Prevention (CDC), or roughly 26 percent of the adult population, you have to recognize that we include the half-million Americans who contract Lyme disease annually, 1.2 million Americans who are HIV-positive, 1.5 million Americans with lupus, and between 7 million and 23 million Covid long-haulers, among many others.

This broader, more diverse, and inclusive sense of who and what comprises the disability community does not blur boundaries. Rather, it only makes us a deeper, richer, fuller, and frankly all-the-more-compelling culture. The severity of my own disability certainly made me a full-fledged member of cripdom, but I've come to realize that my experiences are not necessarily typical for the group.

I've come to see that my disability is about more than myself. It's a connection to a deep, multilayered heritage. I am inextricably linked to an enduring community of all colors, shapes, sizes, castes, ethnicities, orientations, and capabilities. A community that not only contributes to society but has always done so, often despite impossible odds. Embracing disability as an ennobling marker of kinship is almost inevitable once you start appreciating the connection it gives you to this complex, tenacious crew. To put it another way, the more I know about my disabled peers and ancestors, the better I feel about being a member of the club.

So in this sense, yes, I *am* culturally disabled. It's part of my identity, something I feel deep in my bones. Being culturally disabled not only means I'm proud of the way I am, it also tells me I'm not alone.

Adapted from Disability Pride: Dispatches from a Post-ADA World *(Beacon Press, 2022).*

Afterword

WHERE ARE WE GOING FROM HERE?

Five Agents in Twenty-Five Years

WHAT I'VE LEARNED ABOUT NAVIGATING THESE RELATIONSHIPS

Reviewing all this stuff that I've said and published over the past three decades or so, I'm struck by two contradictory facts. First, the disability community has become more a part of the cultural and political landscape, with a greater presence in all aspects of society. Second, we nevertheless have to keep reminding the spokespeople and gatekeepers of our society that we're here, we're just like everybody else in many respects, we matter, and our rights and justice continue to be violated. Too many still live in peril.

So what's to be done?

I'm often asked about the next steps or stages of disability activism. A fair question, but one I'm not prepared or qualified to answer. It's honestly not for me to say. I can't speak for the disability community even if I wanted to. But I will go this far: We still don't have people in positions of power who identify as disabled—and some of those we do have aren't so great on disability issues (I'm looking at you, Texas governor Greg Abbott!). I sincerely hope that as more disabled folks enter all areas of society, more of them will move up into echelons that can help those who struggle below. But maybe that whole hierarchy scenario is wrong. Maybe what's really necessary to make the world better for more of my siblings in disability is a flat, egalitarian model where everyone counts the same in terms of resources and opportunities and everyone is judged worthy.

Perhaps a similar arc could be traced for my development. My disability awareness has broadened and deepened, just as the disability community's participation in society has expanded and diversified. But I'm still not the advocate I should be any more than my peeps have been able to be everything they should be in society. Even with my many advantages and privileges as an upper-middle-class, educated, straight white cisgender male, I still find myself having to explain to strangers that I'm not a child or a vegetable. Honestly, do I resemble a rutabaga? I should be used to this struggle by now. I've lived with it my whole life.

Alas, that's about the extent of my activism these days, other than doing the occasional interview or essay—advocating for myself and my needs. I don't do enough for others. I don't have energy for more.

Recently, in a dusty storage bin, my big brother unearthed some of our late mother's papers. She had a file marked "For Ben." It was not intended for me to see, I think, but it was about me. The folder was jam-packed with notes about all the advocacy she did for me growing up—from educational inclusion to funding for necessary expenses such as personal attendant help to accessible travel options, and on and on. All of this research occurred during the 1960s and '70s (she died in 1981), when the only tools at her disposal were pen, paper, typewriter, telephone, and the library. No internet, of course. In those days, what resources were there for disabled folks or their parents, other than doctors, medical charities, and "experts" who invariably recommended "compassionate" separation and isolation, with limited prospects (which my parents thankfully knew was an unacceptable course to follow)? Nowadays, we're more civilized and welcoming of disabled kids, right?

In theory, maybe. Parents of today's crip kids still have to struggle and hustle to get what they need. They battle with the school system's Individual Education Plans (IEPs), which lay out exactly which supports a disabled child might need in school. It's often a push-pull confrontation between parents and administrators, I'm told. Even then, what happens when the kid graduates? Is there a reasonable expectation of a good life beyond school? There are more resources today than when I was a kid, to be sure. But more resources don't necessarily equal better resources. Still, if they're lucky, disabled kids do grow up with an expertise in managing the challenges of their lives. No one else can tell them what's right for them. They know. They've had a lifetime of learning, of lived experience. And those who've become disabled later in life almost inevitably develop this skill, too. It comes with the territory.

The following piece about my literary adventures was drafted for a writers' magazine, but the advice about finding and keeping literary agents might also apply to other areas of life, the give-and-take and patience and advocacy required to accomplish what you feel you want and deserve.

It never got published. Until now.

When I was in my twenties, I heard two conflicting messages about literary agents.

1. Don't fall for the first one who accepts your work. Interview them as job applicants. Check references.
2. The author-agent relationship is a lot like marriage. Each one works differently.

No doubt both contain a degree of truth. But twenty-five-plus years and five agents later, I've learned a good deal more besides.

Don't get starry-eyed. Way back at the beginning, I boldly phoned a big-name agency in New York and asked to speak to one of its leading lights (I'm omitting names and changing a few identifying details to preserve anonymity).

Big agencies don't have much time for newcomers, I learned. The screener politely heard my pitch before turning me down. Before letting her go, I asked for a referral. A stupid idea, it turned out. Everyone she referred me to asked why, if my project had merit, didn't she take it on herself?

I kept in touch with her, though, since she was associated with a famous agent. One day she said she was quitting to launch her own independent agency—and would take me on.

Alas, if there's a moral to this chapter of my life it's this: Don't let fantasies of fame and fortune, of hobnobbing with literary luminaries, cloud your common sense. She did get me one good magazine assignment, but we never managed to get any book offers. She ended up leaving the business, but we've remained in touch.

Too much pampering can be harmful. Next, I turned to an old chum of my father's, who had just started agenting. He was kind and enthusiastic, eagerly coaching me in how to rev up narrative drive and use evocative details. He was a nurturer, which I needed at that point.

But when publishers' rejections started coming in, he fell silent. I would call and call for news. Finally he admitted he was waiting for better news before getting in touch. He didn't want to disappoint me.

I didn't want coddling. I could take rejection, but it seemed he couldn't.

It wasn't long before he retired from the business. We have since reestablished our friendship, and I'm forever grateful for the early editorial advice.

Most agents have a niche. Around this time, it occurred to me that my manuscript—an autobiographical novel—might be the problem. So I wrote another, using a different style (or so I told myself).

When a friend referred me to her agent, another independent who had a solid track record, I jumped at the chance. Never mind that his specialty was business books.

In desperation, I willfully ignored the awkward fit between the agent's interests and mine. I made all the revisions he asked for, then waited patiently.

He tried, I'm sure. But he had no connections in or reputation for fiction. I hoped for a miracle, but we were a mismatch.

Be realistic about what you have to offer. At this point, I was so frustrated that I opted to scrap fiction altogether. I had already published articles in trade magazines and a few op-ed essays in newspapers. Maybe nonfiction was my true métier.

I was in my forties, able to take a frank look at certain events in my past. Once I had about thirty pages, I composed a killer pitch letter and emailed dozens of agents. The response was good. One suggested I read a few memoirs and then try a rewrite. Which I did, but she rejected me—I mean *it*—in the end.

I believe agents truly mean well. I was just too green, too untested, for a busy agent to spend much time on.

Be patient, but take charge. In the end, my new sample pages proved good enough to land an agent who was looking to expand. He schooled me in writing a proper proposal, for which I'll always be thankful.

Unfortunately, he quickly tapped out his roster of contacts. But he never gave up. Even when I began emailing publishers myself (remember that strong pitch letter?), asking, "May I direct my agent to send you the proposal?"

You'd be surprised how well this works! My agent dutifully submitted my proposal anywhere I asked.

My relentless, indefatigable networking finally led to a publishing agreement. My loyal agent only had to negotiate the terms.

The relationship is about friendship, yes. But it's a business partnership, too. That first book gave me a platform which I hoped would make a second book deal easier. But when I came up with an idea, my agent was doubtful.

I discussed it with friends, one of whom happened to be a literary agent. I'd hesitated going to her before, because I worried she'd feel obligated. But when she asked, I obliged her with what I'd drafted.

Her reaction was so gung ho I offered her the job. I should've given my previous agent a chance to reconsider, but we made peace afterward.

My new agent quickly found a publisher for the second book. [And two more after that, and counting.] But I know her limits. It's up to me to initiate conversations. And she doesn't do magazines, newspapers, or publicity. That's okay. I've learned to have realistic expectations.

What's more, no matter how good the agent, they will never champion your cause better than you yourself can. Ultimately, it's up to you to keep producing good ideas.

The Dignity of Risk

Over the years, I confess, I've frankly been more motivated by the compulsion to become a great writer, however you define that, than to become a great advocate. At the beginning, I fantasized about being a novelist. I wrote several short stories in high school and college. None of them concerned disability. Call me closeted. But after graduating from college, while jobless, I had plenty of time to explore my creative impulses. So instead of short stories, I drafted a full-length novel. It revolved around a young man with a disability like mine. I recall one publisher who rejected it saying it beggared belief that someone like me could live the life I have or be with a love interest like the one I wrote about, who was based on my wife. "But it's true!" I said, or wish I'd said. This publisher's reaction, I see now, came from ableist assumptions and prejudice.

My next two attempts at novel writing had nothing to do with disability, in case that was the problem, the reason I wasn't yet rich and famous. It didn't help. They never got published either.

My novel-drafting days ended in the early 2000s. That's when I got busier doing financial journalism, where I did find opportunities. Somewhere along the line, I also discovered that memoirs and essays could be just as engrossing to read—and write—as fiction. That's how I started doing books that I could sell to publishers.

No doubt it helped, too, that cultural awareness of and interest in disabled people was growing. Indeed, my bookshelf today is full of eye-opening disability books—most if not all of which are nonfiction. Publishers have realized there is a market for disability perspectives, though they haven't yet embraced much realistic fiction with disability themes. Or at least not if they're written by disabled authors. There's plenty of made-up stuff about disabled characters written by nondisabled writers that just doesn't ring true for many of us. A few examples: Mark Haddon's The Curious Incident of the Dog in the Night-Time, *Jojo Moyes's* Me Before You, *Stephen Spotswood's Lillian Pentecost series, and Talia Hibbert's* Get a Life, Chloe Brown. *Whatever the merits of these works, they imagine disabilities from a nondisabled perspective.*

I never gave up the dream of writing fiction. A couple years ago, I tried writing a story that was basically a true account of a chapter in my life that I can only partly remember. I wasn't trying to be journalistic but to capture the mood and feeling of being a boy in a wheelchair before disability rights in a New York City that was on the brink of collapse. I fictionalized most of the details, but the tale is essentially accurate to the time and place. It portrays a piece of my disabled life that I'd never fully captured before in print: the budding of a kind of adolescent autonomy.

The star of the yarn is my first electric wheelchair, which I named Sleuth after the Hardy Boys' speedboat. I imagined Sleuth would take me on numerous adventures.

And in a way, it did. Motorized wheelchairs were still pretty rickety and primitive in those days. They weren't as rugged or powerful as the minitanks that you see everywhere today. I could only go so far and so fast, but those limitations didn't matter. I had never before been able to transport myself on my own, and Sleuth allowed me to envision, to believe in, a better, richer existence.

The pioneers of the independent-living movement understood the power of self-propelled mobility when they formed the Rolling Quads in Berkeley, California, in 1969—an activist group of disabled college students in motorized wheelchairs who went around destroying curbs so they could be ramped. That's just one example of how the quest for disability fairness and inclusion isn't just about legislation. For many of us, it's about technology, medicine, and services that allow us to live our lives the way that, say, automobiles and airplanes allow the nondisabled world to function and fashion new possibilities. They are the necessary tools, the building blocks, for a fully accessible society.

But for me, the freedom and mighty potential of autolocomotion came at a cost. Going places on my own meant a loss of safety, of protection. So I titled my fiction tribute after a fitting old concept I'd learned from a veteran activist and pal: the dignity of risk.

All of us who take that risk are better off for it.

In the early 1970s, not long after my family moved to the West Side, I got my first motorized wheelchair.

It felt like a luxury, no longer having to be pushed or carried all the time because of my genetic abnormality (I won't say *defect!*). The first thing I did with my new power was try to run over Elliot, my big brother. He's not disabled. I had no real reason to feel aggressive toward him, or maybe I sort of did. All my life—almost ten years—he'd teased me a lot and been able to do things I couldn't. Anyway, all I knew at the time was that for a short while I could scare him. The tables were turned.

For years afterward, the walls bore the gouges and scratch marks of that glorious moment, before I learned to drive better and he learned how to turn off my chair.

I could not take my new vehicle to school. In those days, electric wheelchairs were cumbersome and heavy. My school had stairs out front. Every morning, Dad would bump me up the steps in my lightweight manual wheelchair. In the afternoon, Mom would bump me down. Once at home, though, she'd carry me to my new electro-powered wheels, and I'd zoom around the apartment. Sleuth, I called the new chair. After the Hardy Boys' speedboat.

I don't remember when exactly I learned about the basement. Our building was one of those big old structures with multiple lobbies and elevator banks. The basement was the one part that connected all of them. What I do remember is that one boring Saturday afternoon Mom was looking for a package that hadn't been delivered. She yelled over the phone at someone, then told me she was going down to "the package room." I looked up from the superhero comic I was drawing. I loved drawing muscular arms and light beams that shot out of outstretched hands. "There's a package room?"

"In the basement. Where the mail is sorted. You know."

I asked if I could tag along. In Sleuth.

At the end of a dark corridor in the vast, foul-smelling subterranean maze was a brightly lit bustling office full of men in janitorial uniforms. In one corner was a wide door that swung open now and then to reveal a ramp that appeared to lead up to the street. Too steep for Sleuth, I surmised. But tempting.

Mom was talking to someone behind a desk. He was big and soft-spoken and looked like he was in charge. Behind him, a lot of other men were conversing in rapid Spanish and laughing. Farther back, behind the men, I spied a bulletin board covered in pinups of girls in bikinis. Maybe nude, some of them. It was a good thing Mom didn't notice. I tried to pretend I didn't either.

All that was before Dad moved out. Before Mom's part-time job became a full-time job. From then on, Elliot and I would only see Dad on alternate weekends and holidays. They called it a "trial separation," but the way Mom said those two words gave me the impression she felt *she* was the one on trial. I was famous for adapting—one of the advantages, you might say, of being disabled—but even I had to admit the disruption was sad. Still, on some level I thought I understood. It was about independence, autonomy. Wasn't it?

Naturally, there were some adjustments to make. For one, Dad had been responsible for getting me dressed and to school every morning. Mom took over for a while, then started interviewing hired helpers. Not nurses exactly, because I wasn't sick and didn't need medical care. Attendants, Mom said. But she did expect them to go to the market sometimes, too, or make dinner. Their main job, at least to me, was helping get me up and out in the morning and ready for bed at night. I was not thrilled. When they weren't around, Elliot and I would cruelly make fun of their accents.

We went through several of these helpers—two went "back home," one got married and moved away, and one disappeared with some money and some of Mom's jewelry. Eventually, after a year or two, Mom declared I was getting too big for women helpers. She hired a guy on break from medical school, an immigrant from Trinidad named Kevin who was the first paid helper I liked. He didn't act like a child minder. He asked me what I needed and how I wanted it done. I got to direct my own handling. ("When you wash my face, try not to get my hair wet so it won't frizz" was one of my special requests, which he followed.) Even better, he enjoyed playing chess. So, that summer, while Elliot went off to a sleepaway camp in the woods of New Hampshire, I practiced my chess skills with Kevin. (I had tried "adaptive" sleepaway camp for disabled kids once. After about three days I'd called home and begged to be rescued. "I don't belong here," I cried, fed up with making Naugahyde keychain-purses and pencil cups out of coffee cans.)

I spent the long summer days watching TV, drawing my own comics, and playing chess with Kevin. Between games, we got to know each other. We talked about everything from religion to politics to sports. We argued about baseball. I liked Yankees third baseman Jerry Kenney, but Kevin said Mets pitcher Tug McGraw was better all-around. I decided he was probably right.

"How fast can that thing go?" was the first thing Josh said, even before he stepped into the apartment. Josh was a new friend from school, and he'd never seen my power chair before. It was a humid day, and he stood in long khaki shorts and a red-and-yellow striped T-shirt. His hands were shaking. He leaned toward me, made like he was going to touch Sleuth. "Ten, fifteen miles an hour or something?" he asked.

More like three, I thought, but it was better to demonstrate, plus I wanted to move away from his grabby fingers. With the small joystick under my palm, I drove Sleuth around the entryway of our apartment, forward and backward, making tight circles, tires squeaking on the black-and-white linoleum that looked like a giant chessboard.

I stopped circling. I had an idea.

I bid Josh to come all the way in (not that he needed any encouragement) and led him to the kitchen table, where I told Kevin we were "going downstairs." He was the only adult around. The only other person at all. I'd never before left the apartment without an adult. Usually I had to be pushed in my wheelchair, but not with Sleuth.

Kevin barely looked up from his sports magazine. Then, without a word, he started to get up, but I said it was okay. I didn't need his help. Which he accepted.

In the next moment, Josh and I were back out the door. He seemed gung ho for the expedition. "Push the elevator button," I urged him. When it opened, I said hello to the elevator man, then, "Basement, please. We're checking on a lost package." That last part, a lie, really wasn't necessary. A polite "handicapped" kid can get away with murder.

"Go! Go!" Josh practically screamed once we were alone in the basement. "Race me!"

I darted through the fluorescent-buzzing expanse at maximum speed. Josh could definitely run faster, but that didn't matter to either of us. We both laughed until I began to feel silly and stopped moving. We weren't alone anymore. There was a laundry room, noisy with washers and dryers and the idle conversation of people working there, mostly brown-skinned women. I saw an open passage to my left, away from the laundry room, and rolled in. The lights were off, but as my eyes adjusted I began to make out a fenced-off storage area stuffed with orphaned furniture, bikes, boxes, and assorted claptrap covered in sheets and plastic drop cloths. A previously undiscovered treasure trove, full of shadows and mystery.

"Josh?" I called.

There was no answer. Then: "A roach! I see a roach!"

Josh was with me, somewhere. I wasn't sure where, plus I couldn't get down on my knees to look at a roach, and wouldn't really want to, so I took his word for it.

"*So* humongous," he went on. "Like a rat!"

If I was supposed to say or do something to confirm his discovery, I was at a loss as to what it was. I liked Josh because he didn't seem the least bit interested in taking care of me. But was I supposed to be taking care of *him*? I wondered if, for Josh, being with me made him feel like less of a loner. Or less of a loser. I drove deeper into the mazelike darkness, confident Josh wasn't far away. Around the next turn there was light—an opening to the main corridor. I rocketed out, slaloming around invisible flagpoles as my motorized wheels whirred. I came to a giant door marked BOILER ROOM and backed away. I didn't know what a boiler room was, but it sounded important, like the engine room of the USS *Enterprise*.

"Hey, young man. You got a license for that thing?"

It was Carlos, our maintenance man—tall, solid, imposing in his beige uniform and soiled black work boots and heavy-lidded laser eyes.

I smiled. Carlos's hands were suddenly on my chair, holding me still. I didn't like that. He was trying to push me, which really didn't work since my motors were engaged. Finally he released me, and I turned Sleuth a smidge to make sure I was free to leave. He winked, smoothed his uniform front, mock saluted, and walked on. I wasn't really afraid. My parents had funny misgivings about the building workers. Don't be too trusting. Never rude, but not careless either. It sounded snobby to me. Besides, I was learning to like things a little rough-and-tumble.

Josh (where had he been?) was suddenly by my side and asking if I was hungry. Which, of course, meant *he* was hungry. Or bored. A lot of my friends were like that, indirect or unclear or shy or something, but I tried not to be. Mom constantly drilled into me, *Ask plainly for what you want and need. Don't expect people to be mind readers.* Other kids didn't seem to know that. Other kids didn't have the benefit of being in a wheelchair. When you're in a wheelchair, you have to learn to speak up or else you'll never get anything.

On the way back to the elevator, we passed a wide incline I hadn't noticed before. A sign over a wide doorway said LOADING DOCK. The basement was full of mysteries.

To me, it was a ramp that was calling out.

"Watch this," I said, maneuvering Sleuth up the slope. Its motors groaned and its drive belts squealed as I ascended, which made the detour feel more daring. I got to the top, a flat place, where I paused. I was starting to tremble and sweat, frightened that my clammy fingers would slip off Sleuth's joystick. Honestly, it was a sort of thrilling new fear, taking a risk that my parents wouldn't like if they saw me doing it. I turned my chair around. Was Josh even looking? One hard swallow, and I was off again. Racing downhill, sailing faster than ever. Josh was standing at the bottom, staring. I was headed directly for him. I cut a sharp right to avoid running him down. He leaped out of the way.

"Scared you?" I said.

Josh didn't answer.

The next time I saw Josh was a lazy August afternoon. He came over to play, so I asked him if he liked chess. He shook his head. "Board games are called that because they're boring," he said. "Let's go out."

It had barely been two months since I'd seen Josh, but he seemed different somehow. Older. His reddish-brown curls danced on his shoulders as he bounced up and down in Chuck Taylor All Stars. I mostly noticed his black T-shirt with a giant red tongue and lips on the front. Was he cool or weird?

"Okay, Danno," I said. "There's a strange disturbance downstairs." I was thinking he wanted to return to the basement. I was wrong.

Waiting for the elevator, Josh suddenly became talkative. "Let's go *out* out," he said. "I need fresh air. We can check out the girls in their skimpy summer clothes, and I wanna buy smokes."

That was all I heard. I looked at him. We were a mismatched pair, him in fraying cutoffs and rude T-shirt and me in long jeans and button-down oxford cloth shirt. I hated exposing my string-bean arms and legs. Besides, all my TV heroes wore long sleeves and long pants. I wasn't sure if Josh was serious about buying cigarettes. I didn't have any money and didn't smoke. But when the elevator came, I told the silent elevator man, "Lobby, please," instead of "Basement, please." I suppose it was what Mom would call momentum or inertia that was driving me.

I'd never taken Sleuth outside before, not since the day we brought her home. When the elevator opened again, I felt a refreshing breeze. The lobby door was open, and soft-yellow sunlight was streaming in. I wasn't sure I could manage going outside without an adult. Almost fourteen, I still never went anywhere unsupervised. On we went, Josh hanging close to my chair. The air outside felt sticky and gritty, exhaust fumes everywhere, but as a city kid I pretended not to notice. Welcome to Shitty City. I craved a chocolate Italian ice from one of those guys in Riverside Park, though of course I didn't have any money.

Josh broke away from me and was bounding toward Broadway. I tried to keep up.

We rounded the corner of Broadway, passed a store sign that read, *Please check your guns and knives at the door.* I knew it from my morning walks to school with Kevin. Ditto the custom Cadillac "pimp mobiles" that were always parked in front of nice-looking buildings of limestone and red brick. A few blocks over was the chess club that was rumored to have gambling in a back room. Maybe today I'd be brave enough to go inside, though I doubted Josh would want to. I felt a *bumpety-bump* as I rolled over a manhole cover. Sometimes I liked to pretend they were land mines like in the old war movies. Dad had told me that land mines could be buried for years, undetected until they blew someone to bits. *Boom!* But honestly, this particular steamy afternoon what I was mostly worried about was what I would do at the crosswalk. There were no curb cuts then. Could I roll myself down, off the sidewalk, or would I have to find the courage to ask Josh for help? And how would I get back up on the other side? I just might be able to bump down without tipping over or toppling Sleuth's giant acid-filled batteries. Sweat began running down my nose as the moment of truth arrived.

All my life up to that point, and ever after, I refused to let my disability stop me from anything. There is nothing to fear but fear itself! (Mom had told me that.) So I kept my eyes focused downward, watching for potholes and cracks in the pavement, and plotted my course. I would roll down backward, very slowly and very carefully, then drive Sleuth around the median that cut through the avenue. That way, I could skip the extra curbs, not to mention the old folks who were always sitting on the benches feeding the pigeons.

As I rolled down and spun around, a gust of gritty wind hit my eyes, and I could barely see.

"Let me give you a hand," someone close by said.

It was a woman I didn't know. I should've been grateful. I ignored her. All my life I'd heard, *Don't talk to strangers*. People I didn't know and didn't want to know were always approaching me, asking nosy questions, wanting to give me things or pray over me. As my eyes cleared, I muttered, "No thank you" and went around the median as planned, holding my breath. I almost got all the way to the other side before the light turned red. I had to stop in the street. For a moment. Cars whooshed around me. I felt someone pushing me, shoving my chair forward and shoving *me* off-balance. Trying to be helpful, I guess. I wasn't able to explain, to say no. Somehow I managed to right my hand on Sleuth's joystick control. The light turned again. I got to the other side, veering around a divot in the asphalt, and Sleuth magnificently mounted the curb with a *Ka-thump!* before a rush of cars barreled passed.

The "helpful" woman asked if I was okay now. As she patted me on the shoulder, my eyes jumped down the front of her Day-Glo orange peasant dress. I told her I was fine, thanks. She told me to be careful and went on her way.

"Who *was* that?" Josh asked, reappearing beside me. I didn't really expect him to applaud my triumph in street crossing, but he could have been more concerned for my welfare. "Was she in love with you or something?"

"People are weird around me sometimes," was all I said.

I didn't know where we were going, and I wasn't sure Josh did either, but on we went toward Amsterdam Avenue, squeezing through piles of trash that overflowed onto the sidewalk. I held my breath against the stink as a matter of habit. At the next corner, Josh stopped in front of a small store. A bodega. Cigarettes, candy, and Coke were advertised on the outside. He didn't go in, though. Didn't buy "smokes." Instead, as I watched, he reached into his raggedy jeans pocket and pulled out a Magic Marker and scribbled something on the wall, beside the ads for Coke and candy. Something unreadable. There was already graffiti there, as there was everywhere. But I'd never seen anyone write it. He offered me the marker, and I said no. I must've looked shocked. "Just tagging, man," he said. "Nobody cares."

Maybe he was right. Maybe nobody cared. My world was opening up in weird ways.

We were near Columbus Avenue when I heard a crowd. There was often loud singing from the Mission Bethel on the next block. But this was different. Then I saw a police barricade. Again, not exactly unusual or unfamiliar. What was curious to me was the crush of people. Onlookers.

For the first time in my life I was free to take a closer look myself, instead of being hustled away by whoever was pushing me in my old wheelchair. From my earliest memories, whenever someone said I shouldn't do something, a defiant streak burned like lightning inside me. I'd always accomplished things people said were impossible for me. Like going to regular schools instead of special ed. Like having plenty of friends. These were supposed to be unthinkable for a boy like me. Plus, I had skills and talents. I had opinions. I wasn't just some disabled kid. I swerved Sleuth to get a better look. I heard Josh hollering my name. Josh *was* like a lot of other kids. He gave in to emotions and impulses in ways I never had the luxury of doing.

As his host, I felt a responsibility. So I turned around and maneuvered Sleuth back the way we had come. This time, Josh followed *me*.

I never told my parents about this adventure. The street crossing. The graffiti. The police barricade. The crowd. To me it *was* an adventure. To them it might have seemed too dangerous. I told Kevin.

"Look at this," he said the next day, showing me his copy of the afternoon *Post*.

There was a front-page article about a shoot-out at a Columbus Avenue bar. Four or five men had entered and ordered everyone to lie on the floor and empty their pockets, the paper said. They collected watches and purses and rings and neck chains. They pistol-whipped one person before the police arrived. Then the robbers came out shooting. "So many shots were fired," said the commissioner, "that we lost count. Bullets ricocheted . . . putting pedestrians at danger." Three men had been arrested so far, and two officers were in critical condition at Roosevelt Hospital, a place I knew well from a bout of pneumonia the previous fall. The leader of the gang was a "radical militant political activist," the paper said, and one of the FBI's Most Wanted.

He was in custody at the Manhattan House of Detention for Men, which the paper said was called The Tombs.

Was this what I had almost witnessed?

As soon as I was dressed and in Sleuth, I wanted to go and assist the detectives. I wasn't sure how, but they should know that I might've been there, on the scene. Hadn't seen anything useful, as far as I could tell, but maybe I could help. I wanted to, to be involved. To prove I could face whatever dangers there were. This felt like my due, my reward for venturing outside, so close to the action.

"What, you're Mannix now?" Kevin said.

No, but I was brave. I was tough. I had endured things my parents and most other people I knew had not. I'd had my first surgery at age three. When I was seven, I had such bad pneumonia I had to be hooked up to a ventilator for weeks. At ten I had to wear a back brace that pinched and chafed. I still had the scars, even though I wore a lighter cloth brace now. I'd lived in hospital wards with kids who had full-body skin grafts because of fourth-degree burns and where every night I awoke to other children screaming and crying for their mommies. I was intimately familiar with danger and tragedy and risk. I wouldn't crumble.

"I stay away from cops," said Kevin. "They might think I'm part of the gang."

Frustrated, I sat at home and drew a comic book about the events of that afternoon, the robbery and shoot-out, all the gory details from the newspaper. I was stuck picturing what everything must've looked like from the inside, imagining being on the spot in the fray. My fantasies seemed more real than real life sometimes, visualizing the flow of life outside my apartment and school. From then on, I no longer drew comics about flying or invisibility or other superhero stuff. Instead, I tried to capture regular people's interactions, people who could go anywhere at any time. With Sleuth, I'd begun to believe I could have that kind of life, that kind of mobility.

By the time school started up again, the headlines about the holdup had dwindled. I never saw Josh again either. From mutual friends, I heard he went to live with his mother in the suburbs. Kevin stayed on with me for another year, sadly never managing to return to medical school. Mom and I went to his wedding, before he moved back to the islands. In our final weeks together, though, before I graduated from high school, we played chess whenever we could. In one of those matches, I thought I had him beat when I seized his queen. "Don't rush," he said calmly. "You have to concentrate."

In the end, he won that game. Whether his queen sacrifice was a shrewd tactic or I'd become careless in my overconfidence, I cannot say. "Rematch?" I asked, and he set up the pieces for a new game.

Confessions of a Reluctant Spokesperson for the Disability-Rights Community

Thinking back over the years, one necessary component of my life journey, and maybe everyone's, is figuring out not just what you want but who you are—your authentic self. I believe this is essential to "finding your voice" as a writer and, more importantly, to feeling comfortable in your own skin. And believe me, it's not as easy as it may sound.

For instance, I never saw myself as an activist. I was too much of a bridge-builder, a diplomat (and maybe too cowardly) for that. Similarly, I never imagined myself as a writer of personal essays and memoirs. I wanted to be artsy, witty, smart, clever, perhaps deep, but never sentimental or emotional or inspiring. I wanted my writing and the actions of my life to make a good impression, maybe one that was different from what I imagined my atrophied, skinny-limbed physique gave. I wanted to look cool, to sound cool. But cool has many definitions, doesn't it? In any case, fate had something else in mind.

The following, too, was a submission that never got published.

I never wanted to represent a cause, but when people look to you as a kind of poster child, what else can you do but smile and carry the flag?

It started with a letter from a famous writer I admired, whom I met when he was giving a reading. It was his reaction to my first attempted novel, some twenty-five years ago. I don't have to see it to quote it, because I have this part memorized: "Intelligent, funny, and stylishly written. A very pleasant read and, it seems to me, a publishable manuscript."

Yet, alas, that manuscript never got published.

I milked this newfound connection for all it (and he) was worth, but novel writing was not to be.

In the meantime, however, nonfiction writing had become my profession. I really didn't think it was my calling, but my apprenticeship in fiction came in handy when I started crafting my memoir about growing up with a disability. I'd learned how to address readers from the heart, I felt. I'd learned that if parts of the writing don't hurt you deeply—don't actually make your pulse quicken or bring tears to your eyes—you're probably not doing it right.

When I was younger, I thought that if I wrote about something as personal as my disability, I had to embellish it with a sort of authorial gloss. That's partly why I felt I had to write fiction. Later, I saw that the truth is stronger. When you speak with honesty, you might not feel hip or cool, but you will in fact command attention.

Still, I wasn't comfortable with becoming a kind of "voice of disability." My story was just mine; other disabled people have their own stories. But I also knew that whatever I had accomplished wasn't truly due to my own skills or pluckiness. That's a cliché, the overachieving person who turns adversity into a strength through sheer grit and stubbornness. No thanks. I didn't want to tell that sort of story. It had been told before, too many times.

So I decided to couch my life journey in the context of the disability-rights movement. Though I didn't know it at the time, I had benefited greatly from activists in Berkeley and New York and Washington, D.C., and elsewhere. Without their efforts, I might not have been able to go to college, let alone fashion a more-or-less independent life. So I attempted to tell twin stories—mine and the movement's.

After that, it was the usual long slog of rejections and false starts. In time, though, I landed a book deal. I really didn't care that the advance was minuscule. The book came out, and I promoted the hell out of it.

But what to do for a second act? Once you've written about your whole life, what else is there to say? What was I to do next with this "voice" I had fashioned?

The answer came from an appreciative reader who tracked me down online (not hard to do, honestly). She wanted to know more about my marriage. "All marriages take work," she said. "I think for many of us it's tough to imagine adding a disability into the mix."

I didn't want to write about my marriage. I was living it every day and had no distance. But, as before, I came to see that she had a point. There are a lot of misconceptions about romantic unions like mine. Perhaps I should set the record straight.

Again, though, I wasn't happy focusing on my particular experiences as any kind of indicator of anything larger. So I decided instead to interview a variety of other couples and interweave their stories with my own. The more I told people about this idea, the better it sounded.

The final hurdle to my second book was more practical. I wanted to do justice to the disability community, but I also wanted to write a good book. If it was too political, it might turn readers off. If I was too namby-pamby, I would be betraying my community.

I carefully constructed an outline and sample chapters. Any doubts I had about tone or content would become part of the narrative, a discussion within the book itself. What I came up with may have presented more questions than answers, but I felt it was sincere and accurate.

This time the publisher's advance was more than quadruple the first one's.

I've kept going in this vein, trying to fashion books that are true to my heart but also accurate and fair toward the disability community, my community. I'm not sure if I'm an activist or merely a reporter who is writing about activists. But these dogged activists—thinkers, visionaries, warriors—have taught me so much, I believe I owe it to them and to others to share what I've learned.

ACKNOWLEDGMENTS

A book like this owes so much to so many people. First and foremost, I'm eternally grateful for you, the readers, without whom there wouldn't be much point in my writing. Second, I'm beholden to the broad and diverse disability community, which has taught me so much. Third, I'm indebted to the myriad editors at the publications, networks, blogs, websites, and podcasts that have housed my words over the years. Fourth, this book would not have been possible without the enthusiastic support of Lynn York and discerning eye of Robin Miura at Blair, or the indefatigable loyalty of my longtime agent and pal Jennifer Lyons. Finally, I would not have been possible without my family—especially ML and our two kids. Thank you, thank you, thank you. Love you guys now and forever.

www.ingramcontent.com/pod-product-compliance
Lightning Source LLC
Jackson TN
JSHW022005310525
84538JS00001B/1

* 9 7 8 1 9 5 8 8 8 8 5 2 0 *